BEST FACT CRIME

—*Mystery Writers of America*

". . . a splendid big book. . . . a model of murder-study, in research and in writing; and it gives back to us our most beloved murderess."

—Anthony Boucher
The New York Times Book Review

"The story of Lizzie Borden and the murders of her father and stepmother has become an odd if minor cultural phenomenon. . . . That in the proper hands it can still make an arresting story that generates its own tensions (even though we know how it comes out) can be seen from this retelling of the case by Victoria Lincoln. . . . It is a tribute to her handling of the story that she can give us the facts without destroying the mystery."

—Thomas Lask
The New York Times

"The result does much more than provide a wholly convincing solution. Her remarkable portrait of a mill town and its people makes us see the passions of classic tragedy—love and hate—expressing themselves, in New England's Indian summer, as passionate greed and equally passionate propriety."

—*The New Yorker*

A PRIVATE DISGRACE
LIZZIE BORDEN
BY DAYLIGHT

VICTORIA LINCOLN

INTERNATIONAL POLYGONICS, LTD.
NEW YORK CITY

A PRIVATE DISGRACE

Copyright© 1967 by Victoria Lincoln

Cover: Copyright© 1986 by International Polygonics, Ltd.

Library of Congress Card Catalog No. 86-80380
ISBN 0-930330-35-8

Printed and manufactured in the United States of America
First IPL printing June 1986.
10 9 8 7 6 5 4 3 2

To ARTHUR FIELDS, *with my gratitude and admiration*

Acknowledgments

———————

I AM indebted to many people for their help with this book, too many to thank individually.

The superb newspaper room of the Library of Congress considerably reduced the need to seek out far-flung newspaper morgues, and the Anglo-American Law Library in Washington, D.C., was also indispensable.

I have long observed that doctors and lawyers tend to shy away from acknowledgments from writers, so I shall allow myself to thank only three. My old friend, Dr. Jerome D. Frank, director of the Phipps Clinic for mental disorders at the Johns Hopkins Hospital, was the first to point out to me the genetic bond between epilepsy and migraine and to guide me to the reading that I found most valuable. Dr. Louis Lasagna, Professor of Pharmacological Medicine at the Johns Hopkins, gave me permission to quote him on the possible effects of Lizzie's sedation before the inquest (since the drugs and dosages were on the court record). I am also indebted to Edward Kelley, Executive Assistant to the Chief Justice of the Commonwealth of Massachusetts. Mr. Kelley, a man able to blend great brilliance and energy with unfailing quiet, thoughtfulness, and patience, not only allowed me to read the trial transcript in his busy office but set me right on a legal point which I had misunderstood, thereby correcting my first unfair judgment of the Attorney-General's conduct at the time of the case.

As for the clerks of court to whom I am particularly indebted, I should especially like to thank two. Mrs. Estella Margarido, Head Clerk of the Superior Court of Bristol County in Taunton, Massachusetts, finally unraveled for me the mystery of the missing trial transcript in the High Court of New Bedford; out of sheer kindness she made phone calls and wrote letters in my behalf, and eventually forwarded Assistant Attorney-General James J. Kelleher's explanation concerning the missing volume. I also received much help and encouragement from Miss Martha Pellisier at the Second District Court in Fall River, from which the inquest and preliminary investigation had been so promptly removed; we showed ourselves true daughters of little Fall River by promptly placing each other (she is a kinswoman of our long-admired Mayor Kay).

I also had help from my friend, the late Constance Winslow, past head of the Fall River Historical Society, and from my friend Mrs. Ellis Gifford, its present head. My thanks to my friend Hyalie Gray for introducing me to John McGinn, long-suffering present-day owner of the Andrew Borden house on Second Street, and for charming him into letting yet one more with a "glint in the eye" go through his house—and to Mr. McGinn for kindly permitting himself to be so charmed.

I thank Mollie O'Meara of Butte, Montana, for her story of the latter end of Bridget Sullivan. I am also very grateful to Mr. Fox, of the State Library in Boston—indeed, most grateful —for it was he who told me where I might find a carbon of the missing trial transcript. And I should like to thank my husband, not only for his long patience with a working wife but also for the frequency with which he said, "How can you document that? How do you *know?*"

I could present a long and altogether worthless bibliography. To those who want to do research, I can say that Edmund Pearson's edition of the trial, with its brilliant introductory essay is wholly honest, though sometimes, to my mind, misguided, and that Edwin H. Porter's privately printed *Fall River Tragedy* is invaluable. Arthur Phillips' *History of Fall River* (also privately printed) is, to say the least, suggestive. I cannot honestly recommend any other books on the case as informative, though most of them are entertaining. The only full and un-biased local newspaper coverage is that of the Providence *Journal;* the best out-of-town coverage is, unsurprisingly, that of *The New York Times;* I also recommend that of the Balti-more *Sun.* Nor should one neglect the full coverage of Lizzie's inquest testimony run by the New Bedford *Standard-Times* on the day after the final jury was chosen. This, with the exception of Pearson's introductory essay, is all firsthand material and well worth your study.

London, England
June, 1967

VICTORIA LINCOLN

Contents

1. WHY LIZZIE TOOK AN AXE
17

2. WHY LIZZIE WAS SUSPECTED
101

3. WHY LIZZIE WAS ACCUSED: THE INQUEST
165

4. HOW LIZZIE BECAME A CAUSE
197

5. HOW LIZZIE'S CAUSE WAS WON
227

6. LISBETH OF MAPLECROFT: AN EPILOGUE
297

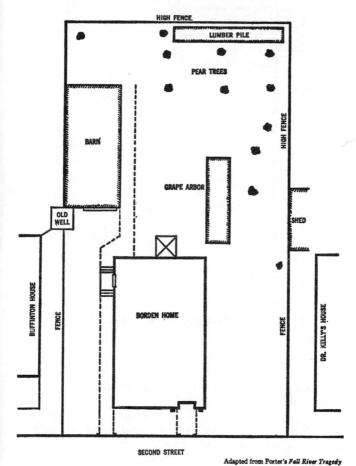

HIGH FENCE

LUMBER PILE

PEAR TREES

HIGH FENCE

BARN

GRAPE ARBOR

OLD WELL

SHED

BUFFINTON HOUSE

FENCE

BORDEN HOME

FENCE

DR. KELLY'S HOUSE

SECOND STREET

Adapted from Porter's *Fall River Tragedy*

PLAN OF BORDEN HOUSE AND YARD

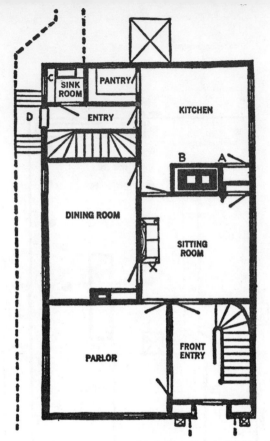

Adapted from Porter's *Fall River Tragedy*

GROUND FLOOR, BORDEN HOUSE

Mr. Borden's head rested on sofa arm by door—see X—as he took his nap.

A. Lizzie stood here, in angle of coal-closet door, as she burned the dress she had placed on the closet shelf some hours before.

B. Stove in which she burned it.

C. Where Emma was washing the dishes when Lizzie began to burn the dress.

Note that upstairs guest room (5, next floor plan) can be reached **from** kitchen entry (D) only by way of the kitchen and sitting **room.** Shelves at left side of sink room and two sides of pantry; **sitting-room** closet also filled with shelves. Extremely small broom **closet** facing stairs at right side of front door is not indicated on **this** floor plan.

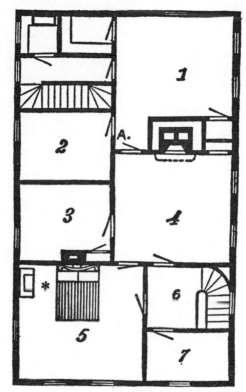

Adapted from Porter's *Fall River Tragedy*

SECOND FLOOR, BORDEN HOUSE

1. Mr. and Mrs. Borden's room. 2. Mrs. Borden's dressing room.
3. Emma's room. 4. Lizzie's room. 5. Guest room, in which Mrs.
Borden was killed. 6. Landing at head of stairs. 7. Dress closet.

Asterisk (*) marks Mrs. Borden's body, between the bed and the
bureau.

A. The door that was kept locked and fastened on both sides
from the time of the robbery until the murders, thus making
it impossible to get from 5 to 1 without going down the
front stairs, through the sitting room and kitchen, and up
the back stairs.

BOOK ONE

Why Lizzie Took an Axe

→→→ 1 ←←←

LIZZIE BORDEN is an American legend: the lady with the axe. The Greeks had Clytemnestra; we have Lizzie. Lizzie is also a perennially fascinating *cause célèbre:* she is the sane, civilized woman accused of a madman's crime—mid-morning slaughter in a tiny house where she was not even alone with her victim parents; they kept a maid. The driving motive behind this bloody—and indiscreet—violence is most commonly given as a cool desire to inherit their considerable fortune.

The case has always held its honest students spellbound, because the factual *evidence* of her sole opportunity and her guilt is so overwhelming, yet the bare *idea* of her guilt is so humanly incredible, so absurd. Ever since she was acquitted, Lizzie the legend, Lizzie the case, has fascinated writers; she has to be made plausible. There are two popular ways of doing this: either by laughing at her, transmuting her story into a protracted sick joke, or, more simply and tastefully, by proving that somebody else did it.

But I am writing about Lizzie from another angle. For to me, Lizzie is not a legend or a case; she is a woman I remember, a woman with whom I will always have a lot in common. When I say, "I knew Lizzie Borden," I do not merely mean, "I remember the face and the voice of the woman who lived at the other end of the block, in the house called Maplecroft, when I was young." I mean that Lizzie and I grew up in the same provincial mill town, that we belonged to the same stratum of its highly stratified society and were both creatures of an era that ended just as I reached my dancing days on the far side of World War One—the watershed.

We may fight our background, or come to uneasy terms with

19

it, or accept it without question, but it is always a large part of the complexity that we call *me*. There is a very real sense in which a man who grew up in an urban ghetto, say, or as one of the old English landed gentry, or as a cattleman in the Southwest understands even the least congenial member of the world that bred him better than he can understand the most congenial spirit that he may meet in the world outside.

Lizzie was of my parents' generation, but if she had been of mine we could never have been close friends. In mind and temperament we had next to nothing in common. But the background that I rejected and to which she remained loyal is still a stubborn feature in my own reality as it was in hers.

I want to show you the world that made us both. I want to show you Lizzie and her family. I want to try to tell you a story in which many long-familiar—and confusing—facts dovetail into an unfamiliar picture, a picture never guessed at by more than a small-town few, most of whom are now dead. While many books have been written about Lizzie, they were necessarily written without the benefit of certain key facts, and, which is far more important, they were not written out of first-hand knowledge of the world that made her. Little by little I have come to realize that only such first-hand knowledge can save any writing on the Borden case, however careful and honest, from being only another deceptively well-documented fiction.

This book is no plea for Lizzie. Like everyone, she had her good points, but I believe that she plotted one murder and committed two, and it's not a belief to laugh off or sentimentalize away. I don't even ask you to understand Lizzie, for in many ways she continues to baffle me: we come through on different wavelengths.

But I do intensely want you to see her not as a legend, a case, but as a real person—Miss Borden who lived up the street in the house called Maplecroft. Her crime, trial, and acquittal are fascinating, and I have some hitherto unused information about them all, but taken by themselves I would not find them worth writing about. Lizzie *is* worth it to me; Lizzie and Andrew and Abby and Emma, the family that I know not only from court records, not only from that always dubious source, in-group hearsay, but because I know the family from which my own father came—its code, its way of life, even its tensions—all so much a part of the world that was once old Fall River, "up on the hill."

But first I must try to tell you why Lizzie's story, so famous, is still so inaccurately known.

In the town where I was born and bred, there's a divinity that still doth hedge the richer Bordens; before the presses could roll everyone had heard the news by word of mouth that Andrew and Abby Borden had been slaughtered by bright mid-morning in their own home. It was unbelievable.

The little obit, buried deep under the screaming front pages in the death column, presented the facts with the proper Borden touch:

> Died, in her home at 92 Second St., Fall River, Mass., on Aug. 4, 1892, Abby D. Borden, second wife of Andrew Borden, age sixty-five; also died at eleven o'clock at the same time and place, Andrew J. Borden, age seventy.

Abby, by the way, had been Andrew's second wife for twenty-eight years, but nobody at all close to the family would have forgotten to mention her numerical order.

On December 2 of the same year, a Grand Jury charged that Lizzie Andrew Borden with a sharp instrument "feloniously and of malice aforethought did strike, cut, beat and bruise in and upon the head of . . . the late Abby Durfee Borden divers, to wit, twenty mortal wounds, of which the said Abby Durfee Borden then and there instantly died." The mortal wounds upon the head of Andrew, the charge continued, were only ten.

They were also weaker and more wavering. The folk song has it that Lizzie gave her mother forty whacks and her father forty-one; but this is not merely statistically inaccurate, it distorts the true heart of the matter, as any of us could have told you "up on the hill."

The song was obviously composed "down under the hill" by outsiders. But even up on the hill we children sang it when I was young, and our parents were tolerant and amused. They could afford to be by then, for Lizzie had been tried and acquitted.

She was tried out of town. When the jury returned its prompt verdict, the courtroom burst into cheers, and many wept. At home, up on the hill, old Fall River did not cheer or weep. Old Fall River breathed a faint sigh of relief, and did not thereafter discuss the case with outsiders.

Incredible though it sounds, this is still true, though an outsider bent on research might well come away believing that he had received inside information. It would be an easy error to fall into, for when the mills failed forty years ago, the social structure of the town changed; many now dare consider themselves *in* who were hopelessly *out* in the small world that made Lizzie Borden.

An outsider might also find it a little hard to understand why we, who protected Lizzie by our silence, were also so quick to ostracize her once the trial was safely over.

Our archetypal pattern was set by Mr. Jennings, Lizzie's Fall River lawyer. After the trial he broke off legal and personal relations with Lizzie and her sister, but he also sequestered what his ever faithful young assistant, Mr. Phillips, was to describe in print fifty-four years later as "the mass of documents" bearing on the case. He took them home and hid them along with his pocket memorandum book of the period and other memorabilia of the trial, and thereafter refused to have the whole unpleasantness so much as mentioned in his presence.

The cache, incidentally, went into an old tin hip-bath and was covered by an awning. His daughter still keeps the container and its contents safe from the world's eyes. We did not know about the hip-bath when I was young, but we respected Mr. Jennings and his silence. Our respect was not lessened by our belief that his extreme reticence sprang from a purely personal anxiety. We knew—or thought we knew—that he had become involved in the buying-off of a key witness. But we were convinced that the deal had been essentially the Borden sisters' doing, not his, and in any event it had cleared Lizzie—and, by extension, the rest of us—in the eyes of the world. Though Mr.

Jennings had a more specific reason for his secretiveness than we had for ours, we were pretty well in the same boat.

For it was ourselves we protected, not Lizzie. She was the skeleton in our cupboard, the black sheep in our family, a disgrace, but a private disgrace. I left Fall River in the year Lizzie died, which was also the year the mills failed and the year I married. I have been free of Fall River for a long time. Yet we never wholly outgrow our origins, and throughout the preparation of this book I have been haunted by a ludicrous, irrational sense of guilt. Somewhere in my marrow I am shocked to discover that I am the sort of person who would *talk to outsiders* about Lizzie.

I was born an insider. My family had lived in Bristol county for three hundred years, marrying neighbors. My great-grandfather, grandfather, and father manufactured the textile machinery for the mills that were the *raison d'être* of Lizzie's little world. And it is essential to *Lizzie's* story that *I* had to come of Yankee stock with mill money to be able to understand either the Borden murders or why and how they became a mystery.

Lizzie, the secretive Mr. Jennings who set our tone, and many of the witnesses at the trial were my neighbors. My parents, of course, knew Lizzie and her circle. Lizzie's own parents, strictly speaking, had no friends, except for Abby's half sister and Andrew's brother-in-law by his first marriage, but my grandfather sat with Andrew on many of the same mill boards and they were both presidents of local banks, a circumstance that has enabled me to uncover the precipitating motive of the crime. I myself was a close friend of Lizzie's sole friend of her later years, Miss Helen Leighton, a gentle spinster from Boston, who "knew" that Lizzie was innocent because of their shared passion for animals and Lizzie's gift for endearing herself to her servants.

I left Fall River knowing what all these people knew, what they surmised, and what they dreamed up; and the years added false memories of my own. There was a lot to be sorted out, when I finally came around to it.

Yet from the start I was spared some waste effort. For old

Fall River, the inner circle, never had any truck with either of those two legendary Lizzies who have popped up alternately throughout the years to delight the reading public with "new" light on the story.

One of these Lizzies was conceived in the womb of the Second District Court of Fall River at the time of the preliminary investigation and came to birth at the final trial. She was a simple, upright, warm-hearted girl, a victim lamb offered by corrupt police to the sacrificial knives of a power-hungry D.A. and a weak-kneed Attorney-General. The whole country once fell in love with her, and when she was acquitted *The New York Times* hymned her in a long editorial.

The other Lizzie was born down under the hill, among shop owners whom Andrew Borden had mulcted and tenement dwellers whom he had evicted. Their Lizzie, a cut from the same nasty bolt of goods, had killed her miser-father and his wife because of an uncomplicated desire to inherit their considerable fortune. This second Lizzie—a heart of ice joined to a surprisingly impulsive hand—began to flourish in the wider world shortly after the trial. Few women can have set out on the royal road to riches more abruptly or with such abandon, but, after all, we love legends not because they are likely and commonplace but because they are singular.

Both of these legendary Lizzies continue to spring up like fresh-mown dandelions, however often devotees of the one mow the other down.

Up on the hill, we never gave either of them a thought. We had no doubt that she did it. We also had no doubt that though Lizzie loved money fully as much as old Andrew ever did, she had loved him even more.

We wasted little time wondering how anyone, even Lizzie, could nurse for five years a smoldering, mounting, murderous hate for anyone as dismally uninteresting as Abby Borden, and plot for two weeks her death by prussic acid.

We did, however, attach grave importance to Lizzie's "peculiar spells."

They had to be mentioned in whispers, since such "spells" were said to "run in families." Lizzie, as we saw it, had taken out one of her spells on the hated Abby and had been swept on by its sheer momentum to kill her father, too.

We were closer to the truth than the rest of the world, I have discovered, though the facts were more complex than we knew and, so far as the death of Andrew went, nearer to the stuff of tragedy.

Here, for the first time, I will attempt to clarify the nature of those "peculiar spells," to demonstrate that in fact they were seizures of epilepsy, epilepsy of the temporal lobe, a strange disease whose symptoms (as I have recently learned and as I will try, in time, to show you) explain more than one mysterious crime in the Borden house on Second Street. Lizzie's affliction has never been openly mentioned before. I did not diagnose it; I put the available hard evidence—two sets of police records, the hitherto disregarded evidence of a defense witness, and certain relevant facts dug out by the prosecution—into the hands of a top-ranking psychiatrist at the Johns Hopkins Hospital and let him draw his own conclusions.

Lizzie's other documented attacks were not violent. Nor were those we knew of by hearsay, except for the ludicrous, persistent myths that we heard from outsiders and laughingly discounted, myths such as that of her shooting a horse in a fit of sudden rage because it had thrown her. (She couldn't ride, and the nearest the family ever came to weaponry was her father's habit of keeping a heavy knobbed stick under his bed at night.)

Calmly—and correctly—old Fall River assumed that she would never do anything *quite* so peculiar again. Why should she? Abby was dead, and nobody else got her stirred up to the same dangerous degree. There was no doubt of that, for Lizzie was thumpingly forthright. She was famous for it, even in a society that tended to distrust tact as a weakness perilously close to dishonesty.

Of course, even the most honestly intended scraps of hearsay get garbled, and memories go askew. I found out once and for all how important it was to check everything I *thought* I knew against documentary evidence—court transcripts and the written word of contemporaries who had been on the scene—when I went back to Fall River to freshen the landscape in my memory.

I went back. And I could not believe my own eyes. For years, in perfect good faith, I had dined out on my vivid memories of having once been Lizzie Borden's next-door neighbor. I was wrong. Lizzie had lived at the near end of the next block.

But the house she bought with her inheritance looked just as I had remembered it. And photographs assure me that her eyes, too, were as I remember them, though in some pictures they show as darker than they really were, because their pupils were so distended. The eyes themselves were huge and protruding, the irises an almost colorless ice-blue. They were strangely expressionless. I have heard many speak of them as dead eyes, but the eyes of the dead are dull; Lizzie's had the shine of beach pebbles newly bared by the outgoing tide.

For the rest, she was tall, stocky, jowly, dressy, and unremarkable.

When I was small, I was shy with other children but quick to make friends with grown-ups; yet I never got far with Lizzie. Occasionally I tried to talk to her while she was out filling her bird-feeding station and feeding the squirrels, but she never quite seemed to see or hear me. It damped conversation.

In school, I began to make friends of my own age, and observed with interest that one was supposed to shudder and giggle when Miss Borden's name was mentioned. I asked Mother why.

"Well, dear, she was very unkind to her father and mother."

→» 2 «←

We children took a pleasurable excitement from the knowledge that we had a neighborhood parricide. A few years back I was amazed to read in a book that Lizzie gave cookies to the "toddlers," among them "Victoria Endicott Lincoln." The "toddlers" would as soon have taken cookies from Lucrezia Borgia.

Still, the statement showed research. My middle name *is* Endicott, and so far as I know the fact has only been made available to the public in one other book, a book that I have found wonderfully helpful, the privately printed, three-volume *History of Fall River*, by the late Arthur Phillips, Mr. Jennings' one-time assistant.

Fortunately for history, by the time Mr. Phillips finally burst into print with his lifework he had forgotten—if he had ever fully grasped it—a hard fact of life at which his senior in the firm never blinked: if you want a thing disbelieved, it is far better to keep your trap shut and let it be forgotten than to mention it and deny it. I discovered the hidden wealth in Mr. Phillips' book with surprise. I had been given a copy of it twenty years before and had not bothered to read it.

On the other hand, like most of Fall River, I had always wanted to read Edwin H. Porter's *The Fall River Tragedy*. However, Lizzie bought off the printer, a local, and had the books destroyed before they hit the shops. There was no cheaper way to handle it, for the work was not actionable; it expressed no opinions and gave no damaging information that had not already appeared in out-of-town newspapers. I may be wrong, but I think that Lizzie acted on the advice of Mr. Jennings, and that it was about the last advice he ever gave her.

The book is made up of Porter's day-to-day coverage of the case from the moment the murders were discovered until Lizzie was acquitted. Porter handled it for the only newspaper in town that did not belong to Andrew's chief pallbearer, Mr. Almy, and his pallbearer's friend and partner, Mr. Milne. The Reading Room copy in the Library of Congress seems to have vanished, but they have another in the Anglo-American Law Library. There is also one at the State House in Boston and one in the possession of the Fall River Historical Society. I wish there were more, for I should like to recommend it; it has the very smell and texture of the first world I can remember. Aside from Mr. Phillips' work, it has been my only hard-cover source, so far as the crime itself goes. (I owe one vivid glimpse of Hosea Knowlton, the District Attorney, to a conversation that the late Edmund Pearson, Knowlton's friend, once had with the Boston lawyer John W. Cummings; Cummings had been called in as consultant at a crucial moment of the trial. I am also in Pearson's debt for his long and meticulous study of Knowlton's correspondence. And Pearson's scholarly edition of the trial,[1] despite its sometimes ill-judged deletions, is a useful desk-book which has saved me much note-taking.)

Mr. Jennings had reason not to want Mr. Porter's book lying about in the awful durability of hard covers. It contained just enough of Lizzie's inquest testimony to make one want to read more, and from that testimony one can learn just what specific fact the Bordens' maid, Bridget, was paid not to tell. Mr. Jennings need not have worried. What must have looked so obvious to him was hidden in a sea of sand, for the full inquest is too smotheringly dull for any uninitiated eye to bother with it. Furthermore, no possessor of the initiated eye would have made him trouble. The whole town liked and respected Andrew Jennings.

In large part, this is why I did not ask to see the hip-bath. I remembered him, and I knew that he himself would not have shown it to me. Such delicacy cost me little, since I was also fairly sure that it would be off bounds for me as it had been for the late Joseph Welch, who was shown the container but politely waved away from the contents. In fact, I know of only one writer who ever had the privilege, and he was one with a preconceived plan for a book that would clear Lizzie, accuse the maid, and so by extension scotch any rumors of a pay-off. I do not think that Mr. Jennings, that overconscientious soul, would have liked the idea; but since he had refused to discuss the case with his own family, his equally conscientious daughter had no reason to doubt that the plan was ethically unexceptionable by her late father's rigid standards.

However, after the jury was locked up, Lizzie's uncut testimony, that sea of sand, was published in full by the New Bedford *Standard-Times,* a public service which received neither thanks nor attention. And the preliminary investigation (which also contained a transcript of that testimony) was covered by forty out-of-town newspapers, not only with remarkable fullness

[1] Edmund Pearson, ed., *Trial of Lizzie Borden.* Famous American Trials Series. Garden City, N.Y.: Doubleday, Doran & Company, Inc., 1937.

but, as I discovered by comparing reports one against the other, with a stenographic accuracy downright awesome to our degenerate age of tape recorders. These two court records were, I supposed, what Mr. Phillips meant by "the mass of documents." But I had to check up.

I learned at the Second District Court that of all the documents mentioned in the docket from the court's founding in the early nineteenth century to the present day, only two are missing from the files—the inquest on Abby and Andrew Borden and the preliminary investigation into their murders. There is no chance that they are simply mislaid; Fall River has a proprietary interest in the case as well as a burning curiosity. More than one hopeful, protracted, and incredibly dusty search has only proved that gone is gone.

But a Grand Jury trial, I thought, would be harder to make off with. Though that, too, contained the official legal dynamite, Lizzie's inquest testimony, I fully expected to find it in the Superior Court in Taunton, the county seat. A Grand Jury trial is, of course, secret, but it would no longer be classified matter, since Lizzie, her defenders, and her accusers are long since dead.

I expected to find it, but I didn't. By a legal custom of which I was ignorant, no stenographic record of that process was ever made.

However, the only new evidence given the Grand Jury favored the prosecution and was given again at the final trial. Jurymen later leaked that much to the press. And the final trial, of course, would still be safe at the High Court in New Bedford, since it was ruled that the inquest testimony might not be presented there.

I was thankful. The trial ran to two thousand pages of typescript, and many cuts were made in the published edition to fit it into one oversized volume. I had often noticed that reporters working nearer to home covered important passages which the editor of the published edition, no local and working forty years too late, deleted as insignificant. It stood to reason that the reporters, too, had made similar errors in judgment as the long trial dragged on.

I was eager to read it all through. I was also overconfident. I had reckoned with sequesterings, but not with souvenir hunters. In 1960, I discovered, the Assistant Attorney-General, James Kelleher, on finding that the ponderous Volume I was missing, had sent off Volume II to the State Library for safekeeping.

It was better than nothing. I went to Boston, to the State House. Several librarians remembered *receiving* Volume II. So far as I know, the archives are still being searched in stubborn, undying hope.

I was sunk. Carbons were far from routinely made in the nineties, and if one existed, where was it?

A gentleman at the State House, one of the many who were wonderfully helpful to me in my wild-goose chase, found out and called me up. A complete carbon was in the private library of the Chief Justice of the Commonwealth. His administrative assistant, Edward Kelley, gave me prompt permission to read it —in his busy office and safe under his eye.

My first hour's reading turned up an interesting sidelight on the techniques of those who defended, and still defend Lizzie the victim lamb. A recent popular book has accused the editor of deleting a crucial word, *Monday*—which in the context would have been a splash of whitewash—from the evidence of a witness. The word does not appear in the transcript, though the margin bears the recognizable pencil markings of Lizzie's champion.

This was an amusing but a minor discovery. The actual transcript was all and more than I had dared to hope. I read avidly, learning with equal delight how often my wildest guesses had been dead right and how often I had been dead wrong on some point of which I had felt sure. I knew that this would cost long rewriting, but the excitement outbalanced that. I read on, visualizing one remembered face, hearing one remembered voice after another. At last I heaved a great sigh, like a glutton halfway through a stupendous feast, and said, "I'm ready for the next volume."

I met blank looks. The *next* volume? I had the whole thing there, a thousand pages long.

I laid my finger on the foot of the last page: "End of Vol. I."

But there was no Vol. II. I had read half the trial, correcting my own misconceptions, seeing old facts take on new meanings at almost every step of the way—and the second half was gone. It was gone, and the first half had taught me that the second half was essential to any honest job.

If I had found none of the trial record, I could have written a book from the available material and believed that it was sound. Alas, I had now lost that innocence. I had to face up to it: I had read that incredible amount of newsprint, I had done those preliminary reams of note-taking for nothing. A good hunk of my life had gone down the drain.

It was less than a fortnight later that the letter came from Edward Kelley, may he be forever blessed.

Dear Miss Lincoln:

Rejoice with me—the sheep that was lost is found! Volume Two of Lizzie Borden is here. You may examine it at your convenience.

It was found, and I could write the story that I had thought about for the better part of a lifetime, and researched on and off for six years and then intensively for one more. Pearson's editorial judgment—shrewd, but an outsider's—had worked better on the well-organized case for the Commonwealth than on the rambling defense. I do not blame him; on the surface, everything he cut sounds trivial. But what he cut from Volume II was substantiation I needed on two key issues; and as a bonus it gave me more than one fresh, valuable insight into my cast of characters. It was, indeed, worth much rejoicing.

⇒⟫ 3 ⟪⇐

The Lizzie Borden case has been called an insoluble mystery, a mystery that hangs upon a missing weapon, a missing blood-stained dress, and a young lady's impeccable character.

A magician's patter made the weapon disappear in the High

Court of New Bedford; I am only one of many to have expressed awe at that feat of legal legerdemain. In the same court a state detective explained the mystery of the missing dress; to my own amazement, I *am* the first to point this out. But Lizzie's character is a human mystery, and real. To understand it at all—and to her last day it was baffling—we must first understand the town that made her, made her and held her as its lonely captive until the end.

Fall River owes its name and its existence to the Quequechan, a wild stream that rises in twin lakes on a high plateau at the city's eastern border and dashes, broken by waterfalls, through the city's heart. It was waterpower before the age of steam, and it brought the first mills there. Oddly enough, nobody who lives in Fall River has ever set eye on it. I grew up beside it, and I could not tell you just where it pours its secret excitement into the waters of Narragansett Bay at the city's western edge. Like a lot of things in the town where I grew up, it was built over and has run underground for a long time.

On the other hand, everyone in Fall River knows where "the hill" is and what it stands for. It is not really a hill, but a steep drop from high land to the waterfront at the northern part of the town, and to live "up on the hill" became in Lizzie's girlhood what it still remains, the goal of Fall River ambition. It had not been so in her father's youth, and she moved there only after his death.

In Fall River we did not say "downtown"; we said "downstreet" in the village habit of a past not as remote as some of us liked to think. Lizzie's grandfather sold fish in the village center of a township numbering less than thirteen hundred souls. Her father died in a mill town, pop. 47,883. He was just under seventy, and the town had nearly doubled in size since his fiftieth birthday.

He started out as a small-town undertaker. In those boom years he branched out, as slum landlord, as owner of downstreet commercial property, as investor in those mills whose thumping looms beat out such plenitude of cotton cloth and hard cash. Andrew Borden ended up not an undertaker but a bank president, a director of mills, and worth three hundred thousand dollars plus real estate that pulled his actual assets up to half a million.

He belonged up on the hill, for he was a Borden and the social structure of the town at that time was what you might call a limited plutocracy. That is, an old Yankee name was neutral without money; but lacking an old Yankee name you couldn't buy in.

At the time of his death there were one hundred and seventy-five heads of families named Borden in the city directory, occupying every place in the hierarchy. In my youth, our chauffeur was a Borden and so were the greatest swells in town; their cars and notepaper bore the Borden crest which, by charming coincidence, is a lion, rampant, bearing a battle-axe, proper.

Andrew did not live up on the hill; he lived on Second Street, the shabby wrong-end continuation of proper Rock Street. It was an address that Lizzie must have found a social handicap from her high-school days onward.

The newly rich society, like the newly rich man, cares for status symbols; a hierarchic demarcation of neighborhoods is still strong in Fall River. In Andrew's heyday, the coming of steam, which shifted the mills from the stream-bank to the waterfront, also shifted the residential areas according to social rank. The sense that one must not live west of Rock Street or south of Franklin Street was so strong that many of the finest old mansions now on Rock, some built of wood, some hewn from blocks of native granite, were moved bodily at vast expense when Second Street became, as it was when Andrew moved there, a place just beyond the pale of propriety.

The one relic of past glory on Second Street during Andrew's last twenty years was "the old Mayor Buffinton residence"; it was roomy, and rich with gingerbread work, but t was shorn of its grounds by later, meaner building, mostly two-decker, two-family houses, many of which converted their first floors to small, unprosperous shops. The house Andrew bought was a gaunt little two-decker built in what had once been Mayor Buffinton's side-yard. A small cottage, which backed onto that noisy business, a stone-yard, pushed close to this unpromising dwelling on the other side. But the house had a back lot deep enough to accommodate to the left a small stable—"the barn," as the Bordens called it—and a disused privy tucked behind it and the back fence, and to the right a woodpile, a grape arbor, and two or three pear trees.

Both the scale of this house, so much smaller than its floor-plan indicates, and the floor-plan itself will be important in our story. If you follow me as I describe it now, I hope it will make a picture that will later help you to understand not only the murders, but an earlier, minor crime that took place in it.

When Andrew bought it, it was made up of two little identical tenement railroad flats, one above the other. It had no space to be wasted on hallways; the rooms simply opened into one another. As a consequence of this, the room that became the Bordens' sitting room and the bedroom above it (which was first Emma's and later Lizzie's) each had five doors and remarkably little wall space, even for rooms of such modest size.

The flats as originally planned each had two middle-sized rooms, two tiny rooms, and a kitchen. Over the front entry, at the head of the stairs, there was also a walk-in dress closet which had a window; nowadays it holds a baby's crib. And at the top of a second flight of stairs at the back of the house, there were two half-finished bedrooms under the high-pitched roof, both opening into the unfinished attic space at the front.

It was not a lay-out planned for privacy or for secrecy. For example, it was impossible to get from the back door to the front stairs unobserved by anyone who happened to be on the first floor unless he also happened to be sitting shut off (and hard of hearing) in the never-used front parlor.

Andrew remodeled the house by making the upstairs kitchen into a bedroom and knocking the two tiny downstairs bedrooms (each, like those above them, not much larger than the dress closet) into a narrow dining room. An attic water tank had once serviced the second-floor kitchen, but Andrew considered running water on each floor a luxury; after his remodeling, the faucets in the house were two, for cold water only: one in a tiny sink-room off the rear side-entry, at inconvenient remove from the kitchen, and one in the cellar washroom. There was also a water closet in the cellar, and in the stable a faucet under the steps to the hayloft, for watering the horse. The house was a bargain for many reasons, one being that unlike the other houses on the street it was not connected with the gas-main. Throughout his lifetime Andrew continued to light it with kerosene, and he frequently sat in the dark to save kerosene; he also kept old newspapers for sanitary purpose in the w.c. It all came out in the trial.

He moved to Second Street when Lizzie was fourteen. At least it was a step up from the slum cottage on Ferry Street that had been his fishmonger-father's home before the days of steam.

Since Lizzie was by nature a spender, caring vastly for prestige and display, it is easy to see how the legend arose of the miser's daughter hacking her way to wealth, particularly since she moved up on the hill with such tactless promptness after the murders. Perhaps it was inevitable anyway, since Andrew Borden was himself a legend at the time of his death.

When he was an undertaker, people used to enjoy saying that he cut the feet off the corpses so that he could cram them into undersized coffins that he got cheap. To his last days, he collected his rents in person, trusting nobody else to do it for him. The defense, seeking possible enemies, turned up numerous stories of overprompt evictions and of his habit of raising the rent if he suspected that a tenant was prospering.

He was never known to give a penny to charity. He did once buy a pew in the First Congregational Church, but he did it to spite Central Congregational, of which he was (for less than five years) a technical if inactive parishioner; an influential member of the congregation at Central had raised the assessment on some of his real estate.

He was six feet two, and gaunt; his eyes were small, dull, and black, his voice and his skin were dry, and his lipless mouth turned down at the corners. My grandfather, a gentle soul with no malice in him, assured me that Andrew's pictures, grim as they were, did the reality less than justice. He was, in hard fact, almost too good to be true.

His clothes never varied with the season; he dressed the part of a man of substance as he had first conceived it as a rising young undertaker, always wearing a black string tie and a knee-length, double-breasted Prince Albert when he appeared in public. He wore it downstreet in the record heat on the August morning of his death.

The news of that death ran around downstreet like wildfire, and the commonest reaction to the news was, "Well, somebody did a good job." I always had attributed that line to hearsay; I have now found it in the printed words of a firm believer in Lizzie's innocence, who was downstreet that day.

Lizzie's mother died when she was two. Her name was Sarah Morse; when Lizzie's ancestry was studied for evidence of possible hereditary insanity, none was discovered, merely the fact that Sarah suffered from severe migraines and seizures of apparently unmotivated rage. Many felt that living with Andrew explained both. They married when Andrew was twenty-three. After five years they had a daughter, Emma; after another five, a daughter, Alice, who did not live; after a third five, Lizzie. It was not a typical pre-Civil-War family.

Two years after Sarah's death, Andrew married a thirty-eight-year-old spinster who had herself been a stepchild. Emma called her by her first name, Abby; Lizzie called her Mother, but when she wanted actual mothering the four-year-old child ran to her fourteen-year-old sister, who encouraged her continuing dependence. Before the family moved from Ferry Street, Abby had become a compulsive eater who lived virtually alone. She had one friend, her sister, who kindly asked her over to dinner once in every three or four months.

Emma was a narrow person with few interests; she was unacquisitive and unambitious, but what she had, she hoarded. Unlike Lizzie, who was lazy as sin, she always helped around the house. Her honesty, like her sister's, was proverbial, and after the murders a loyal friend of Lizzie's quaintly told a reporter that she would be far less surprised to learn that Lizzie had killed someone than that she had lied about it afterwards.

At the time of the murders, Emma was forty-two. She was smallish, dowdy, and plain as an old shoe. Her few friends always seemed to find something flattering in her friendship, as when we gain the confidence of a wild animal; for Emma, despite her

36

rigidities, was timid, and genuinely desired nothing so much as to be overlooked.

Lizzie was also shy, but she feared nothing so much as to be overlooked. The source of her hatred for Abby may well be summed up in Emma's words at the trial: "We never felt that she was much interested in us."

Lizzie longed for a place in the sun. But she was obsessed with her self-image, and her longing for popularity was self-defeating; she was always suing for favor, wounding without intent, or withdrawing into her shell. Like many who are both timid and competitive, she could be a charming, kindly benefactor, but she never learned the art of being a friendly equal.

Still, she was rich and a Borden. In high school she was accepted on the wistful outer edge of the inner circle. But when she graduated, and high-school rings were being exchanged, it was on her father's little finger that she put her own, asking him to wear it always. It was on his hand when he died.

Her hair was naturally curly; however, until it turned the mousy brown I remember in her later years it was red, and in her day red hair was considered ugly, a misfortune to be pitied. Her hands were large, but nicely formed and elegantly white. Her shoulders were rather broad, and no severity of whalebone and lacing could hide the fact that her waist was thick; so was her lower jaw. She learned early never to turn her profile to the camera. Her complexion was unfortunate: coarse and sallow, it flushed to a mottled crimson in moments of excitement. But her huge, protruding pale eyes photographed surprisingly well, and she had a passion for having her picture taken by professionals, even after the murders when her face had gone round and jowly.

In public, she dressed well, in clothes that were not only expensive but the last word in fashion. Her clothes were in startling contrast to her house, with its outmoded loud flowered carpets, cheap ornate U. S. Grant furniture, and horsehair upholstery, described by the newspapers as being all "of a style that was commonly seen forty years ago."

However, there was an upright piano in the parlor which was only twenty years old; all young ladies were supposed to "play."

But Lizzie never mastered it. Good works were her natural way to social recognition.

The good works were not pure self-seeking sham: *de haut en bas* Lizzie was always kind. I am sure that Miss Leighton, the sole friend of her later years, was not being simply sentimental-blind when she would tell of the mutual warmth between Lizzie and her household staff. Servants offer no threat to the self-image.

It was five years before the murders—at the time, in fact, when Lizzie fell out once and for all with her stepmother—that she joined Central Congregational Church, *the* church, socially speaking. She got her father to join, too. As we shall see in a moment, he was quite anxious, right then, to please her. I used to think that it was purely because of the place she had made for herself in that old red-brick bulwark of Fall River society that she would not leave it when her father did for the new First Congregational, a splendor of Prince Valiant Gothic a few blocks farther north on Rock Street. The written evidence now convinces me that I was wrong. The fatherly admiration of old Mr. Buck, the minister, the motherly admiration of Mrs. Holmes, a full-sailed lady ennobled alike by her purse and her piety, meant much to Lizzie there; and Mary Brigham, the one childhood friend whom she had not rather outgrown socially, was a parishioner.

At Central, Lizzie was Secretary-Treasurer of Christian Endeavor; she was active in the Ladies' Fruit and Flower Mission and the W.C.T.U. A year before the murders, she also joined the board of the Good Samaritan Charity Hospital, on which Mrs. Holmes already sat. She was good at sums and wrote a neat, bland, unfeatured hand; she did much dogwork for her charities, and her purse was open to them, a purse that in his final years her father kept well filled. And while in her own house she would not lift a finger outside her own room, she loved to help cook and serve the Church's yearly Christmas dinner for the newsboys.

But one task at Central she did not do well. Mr. Buck was also City Missionary, which in that town of Catholic labor meant that he had lean pickings. He rounded up a little Sunday-school class of Chinese laundrymen's children, and Lizzie taught it.

After the murders, a reporter from the Providence *Journal* interviewed the Sunday school superintendent, who found it unthinkable that one of Lizzie's "sensitive nature" should be suspected of a crime of violence. Asked for an example of her sensitivity, he cited her "disproportionate excitement" at being unable to maintain class discipline.

This has never been quoted before, but it is important. Lizzie, in fact, could never cope with rebuff, even from a child.

Emma was less sensitive in this regard. But she, too, once made a stand against her father. She was not a churchgoer, and willingly dropped Central; but she simply would not drop the Harringtons.

Mrs. Harrington was Andrew's sister. Her husband, Hiram, was a loud, powerfully built man who began as a blacksmith and ended up owning a large smithy—which, translated from an era of horse-drawn vehicles, places him as a garage owner specializing in repairs.

They had both been good to the girls when their mother died, though Hiram and Andrew, the loud extrovert and the total introvert, could never get along. When the final row between the two men came, Lizzie, who had refused to leave Central Congregational at her father's wish, dropped the Harringtons at once; Emma went right on seeing them.

Hiram Harrington, who did not stand high on the Fall River social scale, gave all this his own interpretation. As he said in a nasty interview after the murders, "Lizzie is a Congregationalist, moving in the best social circles." He was unjust; he had never liked Lizzie much, nor she him.

Because of her rigid personal loyalties, Emma always saw Abby as the usurper. To Lizzie, Abby was the rival; this was her feeling when she put her ring on Andrew's little finger, and it grew stronger as she got older and kindly hostesses found it harder to find "escorts" to fetch her to mixed parties. Nor is it likely that Abby, a lonely, self-pitying glutton in her sixties, did much to win the girls over.

Yet until five years before the murders, the atmosphere of the Borden home was only moderately unpleasant. Then Andrew made a mistake. It was a graver mistake than any but a silent few have ever realized. Furthermore, it introduces Uncle John, a key character in the mystery, who until this day has been written off as the relative who just happened to drop in on the night before the murders. (And how anybody could have studied Lizzie's inquest testimony and still believed *that* is one of the great secondary mysteries of the case.)

Abby's sister Mrs. Whitehead had not married well. She owned and lived in one side of a little double house, the other half of which belonged to her mother, Mrs. Gray. Mrs. Gray wanted to sell, but she could find no buyer unless the whole house went up for sale. Mrs. Whitehead's half would bring in only fifteen hundred dollars, for which she would find it hard to find another livable home.

The half-house, Andrew knew, could be profitably rented. His impulse was to buy it and put it in his wife's name, since it is not prudent to have impoverished in-laws feel too directly in your debt; it can raise further hopes. On the other hand, the girls disliked Mrs. Whitehead almost as much as they disliked Abby. They might raise a fuss.

He talked the matter over with his first wife's brother, John Morse, who was back on a short visit from Iowa, where he now lived. Morse, a tight-lipped, tight-fisted old chap and something of an eccentric, always stood oddly high in Andrew's estimation, perhaps just because he was so tight-lipped and close-fisted. It appears to have been at Morse's suggestion that Andrew decided simply to go ahead with the deal and not tell the girls.

However, Mrs. Whitehead told somebody, who told somebody else, and the cat was out of the bag. The fifteen-hundred-dollar half-house was, in fact, the only property Mrs. Borden had in her own name; to the day of her death she could not so much as write a small check. The girls, however, never forgave her for this treachery; she had, they felt, connived with Uncle John to get Andrew to "go behind their backs." Lizzie talked about this widely all over town; I have never heard it reported that she blamed Andrew for anything but weakness under pressuring. Abby was the villain, abetted by the uncle from "out West," whom Lizzie had previously rather liked because of their mutual fondness for horses. (She could drive, though she could not ride; and the horse is a dumb animal.)

In any other household, it would have been a tempest in a teapot, soon over. Andrew had the old Ferry Street cottage, which was worth three thousand dollars, made into a double house, and gave one-half to each daughter with no stipulation as to how they should spend their rents. Emma, Lizzie, and Abby now each owned a half-house assessed at fifteen hundred dollars, all fair and square, and one might have expected Abby's treachery to be forgiven.

In any other household; but the Borden household was different. Lizzie never called Abby Mother again; she both addressed her and spoke of her as Mrs. Borden. And she and Emma ate with their parents only when they could not avoid it. Usually the maid kept things hot and produced a second serving.

They did not, however, indulge in that popular Yankee form of the family feud known as *not speaking*. As Emma said at the inquest. "We always *spoke*."

They spoke; they did not talk. It was an absurd and unhealthy situation, and not one of them knew how to laugh it off, how to snap out of it. It was particularly bad for Lizzie; she was given to obsessive, self-righteous brooding.

It would have been bad even if she had not suffered from temporal epilepsy.

➡ 4 ⬅

Obviously a firm diagnosis of epilepsy of the temporal lobe can be made only by running an electroencephalogram. John Hughlings Jackson was making the pioneer studies of this strange disease during Lizzie's lifetime. His studies are still valuable, but he would have been unable to prove that any single, individual case on his books was actually epileptoid, caused by sudden electrical discharge from the gray matter, and not neurotic or simply faked. He lacked the equipment. His diagnoses, which provided the cornerstone for our understanding of temporal epilepsy, were founded upon odd incidents that occurred in his patients' lives with predictable, almost clocklike regularity. In other words, while an emotional factor was sometimes present, the somatic factor was stronger.

I came to this conclusion about Lizzie's ailment, let me state at once, as someone who has a strong scientific bias, combined with a healthy skepticism, for the murder of Abby Borden clearly was no impulse of an irrational moment. I did not arrive at my conclusion with any preconceptions—far from it; when first I began my research on Lizzie and the case, I knew nothing about temporal epilepsy. I did know about her celebrated "spells," however, and I did have a thorough familiarity with the court and police records. I was fully aware of the many supposed inconsistencies in her behavior, and I was plagued by many questions—unanswered and apparently unanswerable questions. No, I did not seek this "diagnosis," but when through lucky chance I happened to stumble across it, all at once the jumbled pieces fell into place, and at last I could make sense out of the events that culminated in Lizzie's taking up the axe. Even then I continued to doubt; the scientific bias is not easily thrown off. I did extensive reading, I consulted with authorities, and ended up convinced:

Lizzie Borden did not kill her parents *because* she had an ambulatory seizure of temporal epilepsy. But all evidence indicates that she killed her stepmother *during* one.

Epilepsy is both a common and a little-known disease. This is not surprising, for it was still considered diabolic possession a scant two hundred years ago; it was "the illness that is spat upon" and it is still the illness to which we react like primitives. There is small wonder that the epilept always wants to call it something else.

Migraine, its first cousin and genetic associate, is respectable. People even boast of their "sick headaches." They do not boast of epilepsy. Hence, you may be as surprised as I was to learn that Dr. Samuel Livingston, the chief authority on the disease at the Johns Hopkins Hospital, sets the current rate of incidence at about one in fifty. Until recently, when the computer joined forces with the encephalogram, tabulating many previously undiagnosed cases, the supposed rate was much lower, about one in two hundred. It is as unlikely that you have never been closely associated with an epilept as that you have never known a diabetic.

The rate of incidence is less surprising than it looks at first glance. The *grand mal,* or convulsive epilepsy—the showy form —is only one form of the disease. There are many reasons why an epilept can pass through life with his secret known only to his doctor and to his family. The *petit mal,* for example, may show only in small bodily jerks or less than minute-long blankings out, the face going unresponsive in a way that passes for flickers of absentmindedness. One form of epilepsy—Lizzie's mother, as we will see, may possibly have suffered from it along with her migraines—is often written off as "a hairtrigger temper." Furthermore, many epilepsies, minor or severe, attack only the sleeper; they are seen only by the sufferer's family. Many come only at the menstrual period. And while in some patients there may be a number of attacks each day, in others they come as infrequently as once in every three or four years. You can now see why the epilept finds it easy as well as desirable to enter the world's largest secret society.

Epilepsy is no respecter of persons. The genius, the feebleminded, the neurotic, the emotionally sound may all suffer sudden periodic abnormal electrical discharges from the gray matter. And so may the criminal.

Psychomotor epilepsy—epilepsy of the temporal lobe, that is —shows only one obvious, and strange, symptom. During a seizure, there are periods of automatic action which the patient in some cases forgets completely and in others remembers only dimly, through a "brownout." To name two simple examples from actual case histories: a man comes to and wonders why in the world he is digging a deep hole in his back yard; another finds himself strolling along a street in an unfamiliar part of town, eating a bag of doughnuts.

In some patients, the period of automatism is marked by fumbling, confusion, lack of response. In other patients it is altogether different. A man has reported feeling the familiar aura of the onset as he set out down a famous and tricky ski slope; when he came to himself on the frozen lake far below, he saw by his ski tracks that he had made the descent by an extravagantly showy path over rough terrain which he would have avoided, when properly conscious, simply because it was too difficult for him. As a case history, this is not exceptional.

Nor is another case history cited by Dr. William Lennox, author of the exhaustive and authoritative work *Epilepsy and Related Disorders*,[1] though I find it amusing. A young man "woke" in his office, knowing that he must have just passed through an attack. He discovered how remarkable it had been when, a few days later, his salary was raised. The boss, faced with his firm and lucid demand that he increase the pay or lose his services, had been most favorably impressed.

We should forget neither of these case histories as we come to consider the death of Abby Borden.

This necessarily abbreviated account, stripped of technical language, represents a distillation of many hours of careful reading. Once sheer luck had pointed me in this new direction I found it exciting reading. Many troublesome questions suddenly seemed to be resolved, but my scientific bias was still unsatisfied. It remained for me to test out each of the many inconsistencies, the numerous examples of Lizzie's "odd behavior," to see whether a "diagnosis" of temporal epilepsy did indeed provide that missing single rationale that, once and for all, would resolve the mysteries plaguing the Borden story.

First and foremost, why in the world would anyone commit murder by broad daylight in mid-morning—a time when it was least likely to go undetected?

Popular Fall River opinion attributed the murder of Abby Borden to the circumstance that "poor Lizzie was always sort of crazy." An overwhelming weight of evidence convinced me that this idea was wrong. I did not, and do not, feel that a plea

---

[1] Boston: Little, Brown, and Company, 1960.

of temporary insanity would have been justified, even if it could have been entered, for in Lizzie's day there was no plea of "temporary insanity." You were sane or "crazy," and it didn't take a psychiatrist to tell the difference; a good look and a few minutes' talk made the distinction plain to anyone.

No, I could not entertain a plea of temporary insanity, because of two facts that cannot be blinked at: I *knew* that on the day *before* the murders Abby betrayed a panic fear of being murdered—by poison. I *knew* that Lizzie, on the day before the murders, was trying in vain to buy some prussic acid.

Now, murder in epileptoid seizure is a medical rarity. Lennox, who studied many thousands of cases, has found only two such instances (three, if you count Hercules, who according to legend slew his children in an epileptic rage). As in hypnosis, the victim resists anything he would refuse to do while in full possession of his senses.

But Lizzie was, in fact, planning to murder Abby.

The Borden murders have long been considered insoluble because of two irreconcilable factors. When you read Lizzie's promptly sequestered inquest testimony, which the jury was not permitted to see, you will observe that it offers a choice of only two conclusions: either Lizzie committed the murders, or Bridget committed them *with Lizzie's full knowledge and consent.* Now, while well-brought-up and moderately intelligent young ladies may sometimes poison, they simply do not commit their murders with a hatchet, by bright mid-morning, with the maid at home, or coax the maid to do them, either.

The direct means, the hatchet, would not have occurred to Lizzie in full, waking possession of her faculties; for she did not want to get caught. It was *too* direct.

It was so direct that it made nonsense of the whole idea of an icily plotted murder for gain. It was so forthright, so downright masculine, that a carefully selected jury of nice old men could barely give serious thought to the possibility that a well-brought-up young lady could have been the murderer—though they would have thought hard about that acceptable, *womanly* prussic acid.

But dreams *are* often surprisingly direct; and Lizzie's form of epilepsy can be said to resemble a kind of daytime sleepwalking.

The duration of an attack of temporal epilepsy, like its incidence, varies widely from patient to patient, though in any given patient both incidence and duration can be predicted. Hearsay evidence as to the frequency and length of Lizzie's "spells" is in accord with previously unnoted evidence in the court documents,[2] and tidily parallels many medical case histories. Apparently her seizures came only during the menstrual period, and then only three or four times a year. They were of brief duration, an hour or so at most. Lizzie was going through a menstrual period on the morning of the murders: this is a matter of court records.

The preliminary aura of an attack also differs from patient to patient. A phrase that Lizzie used to Alice Russell on the night before the murders accurately describes one that is quite common: "This feeling as if something was hanging over me that I cannot shake off."

Just before the murders, Lizzie had spent a frustrating fortnight shopping about for poison. An amateur, she did not know enough to ask for arsenic, which in those days was freely sold over the counter. She kept asking for prussic acid, which is so highly volatile and dangerous that even then a responsible druggist would not sell it without a prescription.

When we come to the murders, I will detail a number of physiological circumstances that—quite aside from her state of tension—might have precipitated a seizure that morning.

In point of fact, the suspicion that Lizzie's "peculiar spells" might have some serious bearing on the murders was so prevalent in Fall River that any Fall Riverite writing in her defense would feel compelled to deny them. In his privately printed *History of Fall River*, the invaluable Arthur Phillips, who never knew what to leave unmentioned, touched on the subject thus:

> Although the police found a small spot of blood on the back of one of her skirts, evidencing not only her then physical condition but the fact they had carefully examined the cloth-

2 For example, Mrs. Raymond's testimony about the detective's call three months before the murders. Trial Transcript, Vol. 2.

ing that she was wearing when the murder was committed ... there was *no* evidence that she was ever hysterical or abnormal during these periods. *There are no abnormalities in the Borden family.* ... If Miss Borden's mind showed any lack of balance in her later years it should not be weighed as evidence of her former condition.

Why, fifty years after the trial, did poor Mr. Phillips take it upon himself *to deny in print something that had never been affirmed in print?* Nobody who moved in his circles would have found that a hard question to answer.

In the speech of Mr. Phillips' generation, "abnormal" was the polite word for insane, or as we now say, "mentally ill." By *later years* he refers, I think, to 1897 and 1904. By the time my friend Miss Leighton knew her, Lizzie had passed the menopause. The "peculiar spells" had ceased.

Incidentally, if there were no abnormalities in that tribe of 175 heads of families plus their children, they made some kind of a record for the old Yankee families in those parts. At least we know that the other side of the family was not so unusual. Quite the opposite. As a matter of fact, it is much to our point that Lizzie's mother, Sarah Morse, had suffered from migraine and from fits of free-floating rage of a kind which can now frequently be eliminated with dilantin or allied drugs.

These facts about Sarah were discovered, oddly enough, by the *prosecution,* in its attempts to find evidence to support the accepted belief that families with "crazy" people in them often had children with "criminal tendencies." Ironically, the prosecution also *shelved* them; mere sick headaches and bad temper were considered irrelevant.

Migraine, as we now know, is a genetic associate of epilepsy; and a physician looks for either one or the other in the family history of any epileptic patient. This genetic factor means next to nothing taken in isolation; few sufferers from either migraine or epilepsy have epileptic children. On the other hand, few epileptics who have neither brain tumors nor head injuries can show a family record without either migraine or some form of epilepsy.

47

But Lizzie's record showed not only a familiar inheritance but another familiar symptom. Quite aside from the odd incidents of which I know only by hearsay, Lizzie twice got herself into the police records—once a year before the murders and again five years later—in connection with rather senseless thefts.

Pointless, meaningless theft is a familiar symptom in the ambulatory episodes of temporal epilepsy.

This is a part of her story that those who wish to prove Lizzie innocent always suppress, while those who think her guilty seem to regard it as a good joke, part of the macabre legend. But to someone who is not thinking about a legend but about the woman who used to live up the street from the corner of French and High, it has always needed as much explanation as the unthinkable hatchet. For the theft itself was baffling enough to one who knew of Lizzie's ample checking accounts; but it was totally bewildering—until now—that a girl who valued the world's good opinion, and above all her father's, would commit a petty crime in such a way as to insure her father's detecting it almost at once.

Until I realized that the story could have come straight out of a medical casebook—wholly typical, wholly unsurprising—the circumstances surrounding the daylight robbery of the Borden house caused me no end of trouble. For I knew how intensely Lizzie always wanted to be approved of—by everyone, but most of all by her father. What happened that morning was simply out of character.

⇒ 5 ⇐

Andrew Borden would have called Lizzie's neurotic obsession "getting all strung up" and the epilepsy "peculiar spells," but he was fully aware of the importance of keeping Lizzie happy. This, being Andrew, he tried to do with the only source of happiness he understood: money. From the time of his mistake about the Whitehead house until his death, Andrew played Zeus to Lizzie's Danaë in a golden shower.

Her wardrobe became lavish; her purse was full. Her weekly pin money was still no more than the maid's weekly wages, but she had rents, dividends, and surprise gifts. Andrew did not protest when her checking accounts were always so much bigger than her savings; when she casually sold off stocks at far below their market value he put up with it without a murmur. He loved Lizzie, but it surely took more than love to pull Andrew Borden so far out of character. He may only have been trying to buy a little household peace, but that, too, is out of character for one so notoriously stubborn. While he would have been the last to admit it even to himself, it does look as if he had begun to fear for Lizzie's mental equilibrium.

Three years of this simple therapy did not help. A trip abroad in those days was both a rare event and a highly recommended cure for "nerves." Andrew let Lizzie make the Grand Tour with a group of young ladies, the richest girls in town.

She shared a cabin with Miss Anna Borden, whom I remember well. On the homeward voyage, night after night Lizzie talked with a heavy, frightening intensity of the hated stepmother and the dreaded home to which she was returning. (Miss Anna shrank from publicity and she was kind; she went through severe conflict before that memory drove her to offer herself as a witness for the prosecution.)

Lizzie was not happier or calmer when she came home. After some months Emma, who also knew the importance of keeping Lizzie happy, suggested that they exchange rooms.

There were, you recall, three decent-sized bedrooms in the house. One was the guest room at the front, one was Emma's, and one her parents'; they all opened into one another, though the guest room and Emma's room could both be entered from the landing at the head of the front stairs, and their parents' room from the top of the back stairs. The other two rooms were the size of the big clothes closet beside the guest room. One, which could only be entered through Emma's room, had been given to Lizzie when they moved there in her childhood; it had a single north window. Its mate opening off their parents' room —the pair had once duplicated the two little downstairs rooms which were now knocked together into a narrow dining room

—could similarly only be entered from the back bedroom. It was used chiefly as a linen closet, but it also held Andrew's safe and desk, and a small bureau in which Mrs. Borden kept her trinkets and underwear. The household spoke of it as "Mrs. Borden's room," though she neither sat nor slept there.

Emma's room was sunny, with two windows to the south; but five doors and two windows in a modest-sized room leave little wall space. A heavy secretary-desk with a bookcase top stood against the locked door to the guest room, and the washstand stood cater-cornered with a portiere hung before it. Besides the bed and bureau the room somehow managed to hold a little sofa, or as Lizzie called it, a "lounge." It was indeed an improvement over the cubbyhole, which Emma took over.

Shortly after Lizzie moved into it, the Borden house was robbed.

It was summer. Andrew had driven to Swansea, where he had a farmhouse. He had ceased to use it as a summer home when war was declared in the household and the girls began to vacation separately, but a Swede now ran the place for him, keeping poultry and raising vegetables. (On occasion, Andrew went downstreet carrying a little wicker basket of eggs, solemn in his long black Prince Albert, and peddled them to his business associates. To Andrew, money was money; he could reverence a nickel as much as a thousand dollars. He sold those eggs like an altar boy following the priest with a little tray to prevent a crumb of the Host from falling to the ground.)

On the day of the robbery, Abby, who so rarely went out, went with him. They left behind a house locked, as always, with paranoid thoroughness.

The cellar windows—the only windows of the house that were lower than seven feet from ground to sill—were barred; the cellar door was bolted on the inside; the side and front doors had two locks and a bolt apiece, though when someone was in the kitchen, the door to the back entry was occasionally only secured by a hooked screen-door. The neighbors' houses pushed so close on either side that you could speak from one to the next without raising your voice; and while the back lot was deeper, it was secured by a six-foot board fence with barbed wire at the top and bottom.

Even left empty, it was not, as you see, an easy house to rob in broad daylight. Nor was it left empty. Emma, Lizzie, and the Irish maid, Bridget Sullivan, were inside.

They were not the discoverers of the robbery; Andrew and Abby themselves discovered it upon their return. The thief had moved like a ghost—a well-informed ghost, for he had gone directly to "Mrs. Borden's room" and ransacked it. He had made off with her gold watch and chain and her very modest supply of jewelry; he had also broken into one drawer of the small desk and stolen the money Mr. Borden kept in it— between thirty and forty dollars in gold and eighty dollars in greenbacks—and a book of horse-car tickets.

Mr. Borden sent for the police.

Miss Lizzie Borden was overexcited. She talked incessantly, taking the police to the cellar to show them how she had found the door unbolted and a large nail stuck in the keyhole, which they put down in their records as "an eight or ten penny nail."

Considering the general preference for a skeleton key, this in itself was strange. It was even stranger that in a flimsily built small house, not one of the three women had heard a sound.

Mr. Borden requested at once that the theft should not be reported to the papers. Three times in the next two weeks he asked that the investigation be dropped. He said, "You will never catch the real thief."

He was quite right. That crime, like the later crime, was never solved.

In that day and part of the world, the Irish maid was the automatic suspect in cases of theft, like the Negro in the South. Bridget was not discharged.

Mrs. Borden locked and bolted the door that led from her bedroom into Lizzie's; Lizzie fastened the hook on her own side of the door. Abby and Andrew also took to locking their other door, which led onto the back stairs, when they left the bedroom. But Andrew saw to it that the key was thereafter laid out in plain sight on the sitting room mantelpiece.

Students of the crime often speak of Andrew's odd quirk of

locking his room from the maid and then leaving the key out under her nose. This no longer seems puzzling to me. The gesture, as I see it, was strictly in character. Andrew was never much for talking.

Besides, some situations don't bear talking about. The key, used and laid out in Bridget's sight, said enough to Lizzie.

You can see why the daylight robbery, that modest prototype of the second crime committed in that house under like conditions by a similar ghostly hand, is always so meagerly or incorrectly reported by those who wish to prove Lizzie innocent. The murder of a father by his youngest daughter is a notion we may reject in horror or seize upon with macabre delight; but it is not one that we think about dispassionately. Petty theft, on the other hand, is only too easy to consider from an objective point of view.

It says much about Bridget's longstanding fondness for Lizzie that no word of the theft leaked out until Lizzie herself first told of it on the evening before the murders. (Many years later, Bridget told her friend Minnie Green about that fondness, in self-exoneration for her one silence that was bought.) Bridget had not seen Lizzie's bank books, but she daily saw the mean penny-pinching that went on in the house. I, who was brought up by Bridgets and Delias and Bridies, know how readily she could have decided that Lizzie had no more than helped herself to a bit of what should have been hers by rights, the poor creature, and thereafter held her peace.

Lizzie gave varying reasons for the secrecy. She told the D.A. that her father had demanded the subsequent year's silence so as not to hamper the efforts of the detectives.

It is clear enough that Andrew did want it kept secret. So far as we know, it was the first time that one of Lizzie's "peculiar spells" had involved a theft; he could well have been confused when he first called in the police. Lizzie, with all her real—and terrible—faults, was baldly honest, and she also cared vastly for the world's good opinion. It must have looked impossible—a theft committed under the noses of two people who knew that the thief could have entered the back of the house unseen by no other way than through Lizzie's bedroom, or reached that bedroom unseen by any way but the front door, which had unquestionably been locked.

However, since Andrew knew Lizzie better than a subsequent jury knew her, he was the first to see that an apparent impossibility was no impossibility.

He could accept, as that jury could not, the heavy evidence that sole opportunity for a crime belonged to those who were inside a locked house when it was committed there.

⋙ 6 ⋘

The robbery took place just a year before the murders.

The amnesia covering an attack of temporal or psychomotor epilepsy is sometimes total, sometimes partial, a "brownout"; but the patient, recovering, always knows that he has just passed through a seizure. It is frightening knowledge, even if he understands his disease. To Lizzie, who would regard that attack as having briefly "gone crazy," the terror must have been great. People who "went crazy" were "put away." Lizzie may not have tried to deceive her family but herself when shortly thereafter she took to locking the hall door of her room whenever she left it, even to go downstairs for a few minutes.[1]

Her reaction seems to have been much like that of Andrew, who loved her. She shut off her mind and denied that it had happened; he shut off his and denied o himself that she was fully responsible for that act of spite against her stepmother. But, of course, the spite was real; the dream state had only acted out, with appalling directness, a waking state.

Apparently Abby alone had the sense to be frightened *and* to let herself know it. But nobody ever paid any attention to Abby.

At the time the thing happened, Uncle John had just moved

[1] Trial.

back East for good. Andrew should have considered Uncle John a bird of ill omen. The girls, suspecting his hand in the unforgiven matter of the Whitehead house, were on the chilliest terms with him. Indeed, whenever he dropped by to spend the night, Lizzie left the house or hid in her room and refused to see him.[2] Andrew chose to ignore this. Perhaps he was getting fed up with Lizzie's behavior, or had begun to wonder if a firm hand is not sometimes more stabilizing than overindulgence. Certainly he liked John Morse.

Two men, on the surface, could not have appeared less congenial. Andrew, so tall, somber, meticulously neat in his unvarying Prince Albert, made Uncle John look by contrast like a heap of last week's wash. Uncle John was bearded, always untidy, with permanently bloodshot eyes; he could have been taken for a tramp.

He was, in hard fact, quite well fixed. He had done well in the West. Andrew not only liked him, but admired his acumen; we know from Mr. Phillips that they made a number of joint investments.

Yet another bond between them may have been Uncle John's real aversion, as strong as Andrew's, to spending money. Throughout the year before the murders, Uncle John boarded with a friend, Isaac Hastings, in South Dartmouth, a village southwest of Fall River. He kept the horses that, even back in Massachusetts, he continued to buy, breed, and sell, over in Westport, a fair drive away; a group of horse traders were established there and gave them pasturage. It was an inconvenient arrangement based on thrift. Before the year was out, he and Andrew had thought up a better way for them to be thrifty together.

Incredibly, it was, in effect, the Whitehead house business all over again. One can only assume that Andrew was too single-minded to have much intelligence to spare outside the field of finance.

Andrew was fond of the Swansea place and did not want to sell it off. However, it did not pay for itself, the Swede's wages

[2] Trial.

54

were an item, and for five years (since the start of the cold war, that is, when the girls stopped vacationing with the family) it had only been used for very short stays. Morse liked Swansea. He had an unmarried niece, his sister's daughter, who would be willing to housekeep for him if he lived there; he would have pasturage for his horses; he still enjoyed farming in a small way; and he enjoyed Andrew's society. Andrew would always be welcome to visit Swansea when he felt like it. Since a note dropped off at the post office would bring Morse from over the river to pick him up, Andrew would even be freed from the expense of keeping his own horse any more, for he lived within easy walking distance of all the other places to which he ever cared to go.

Thus far, it made excellent sense; we need not wonder that he promptly sold the horse at the first good offer.

The fantastic element enters with Andrew's hitherto undisclosed decision to put the farm in Abby's name before Morse moved in. Small wonder it has remained undiscovered all these years. Why he would have done a thing like that twice, God only knows. But he did. It got out through a leak in banking circles. My grandfather thought that this explained how people first got the idea that just before the murders Andrew Borden was about to make a will. He assured me that this was a false idea; for Mr. Jennings, Andrew's lawyer, had denied it, and Mr. Jennings invariably told the truth or simply kept quiet. No, Andrew Borden wasn't planning to make a will at all— just to put the Swansea place in Abby's name.

For a long time, I only saw these facts as substantiation of the familiar inner-circle belief that the murders had no money motive, but only occurred because "poor Lizzie was sort of crazy." This was one bit of hearsay that I did *not* expect to find substantiated and enriched; I was wrong.

It was known in some quarters two weeks before the murders that Morse expected to move over to Swansea; it was known at the National Union Bank shortly before the murders that the farm was about to be put in Abby's name.

We do not know when Lizzie got wind of it. It may have been back in March, when the horse was sold. At my own guess, it was not until two months later, but in March, at least, Lizzie upset Mrs. Gifford.

Mrs. Gifford had a small establishment on Franklin Street where she made ladies' cloaks and suits. She was a Quaker, and gentle. (My doctor, a family connection of hers, charmed me as a child with that soft-spoken "thee," which he used with me as if I were a child of his own.) In the course of a fitting, she spoke of Abby as "Mother." Lizzie became excited.

"Don't call her that to me. She is a mean, good-for-nothing old thing!"

"Oh, Lizzie, you don't mean that."

"Yes. I don't have much to do with her. I stay in my room most of the time."

Mrs. Gifford tried to laugh the disproportionate reaction away: "You come down to meals, don't you?"

"Yes, but we don't eat with *them* if we can help it."

This was, of course, nothing new. But Mrs. Gifford stepped out of character, like Anna Borden, by offering to testify at the trial. She was given to understatement and I assume that there was more emotional force in the brief passage just quoted than the printed words convey.

In May, a minor incident took place that must have disturbed Lizzie at a fairly deep level, for she was passionately fond of birds and animals. She kept pigeons in the barn loft, and after the horse was sold boys twice broke into the barn to steal a few. Andrew decided to put temptation out of their way, which he did by decapitating them *with a hatchet*. Where property or infringement of his *rights* was concerned, Andrew did not think widely, or think twice.

Strangely enough, I have never seen this mentioned by anyone who has written on the case. The protracted unimaginative cruelty of that bedroom key, daily used and plunked down on the mantelpiece, is mentioned; it is mentioned as one of Andrew's inexplicable little eccentricities, though never as a too-often-repeated wordless word to Lizzie. But the slaughter of Lizzie's pigeons doesn't rate a line.

The tragedy of it is, nobody ever doubted that Andrew loved Lizzie. Only, he had no imagination, and he was obsessed with his property, large and small—though one of the richest men in town he saw nothing funny about peddling his spare eggs downstreet in that little wicker basket. He had no imagination, and Lizzie, who could not bear to be ignored, must have suffered not only for the pigeons but also for herself—he had killed them without even stopping to think how she would feel.

But Lizzie was a jealous woman, and a jealous woman unimaginatively wounded does not say, "He can't love anyone"; she says, "He loves her, not me."

Lizzie was jealous. Like Andrew, she loved possessions, but when Andrew had quickly given her half a house exactly equivalent to the one that had been his secret gift to her rival, it undid nothing. A woman who opens the bill that should have been sent to the office and learns of the bracelet her husband gave to some girl is not put at ease by the prompt gift of another bracelet, even of one more expensive. Yet, alas for women, she can be reassured by the right, sensitive, percipient, imaginative lie. Andrew could offer Lizzie no such reassurance; he used gestures, not words—a key on the mantelpiece, a gift of money. It is sometimes hard to interpret silent gestures.

And he killed her pigeons.

I freely admit that Lizzie's love for Andrew, like most love, was probably ambivalent, laced with hate. But I am a woman, and at one time or another I have suffered from jealousy. I know that, in Lizzie's place, I would have hated Andrew *briefly* over the death of those pigeons, but hated innocent Abby abidingly. In sum: "He did not think how I felt. It is her fault. She has stolen his love."

It was at this time that Mrs. Raymond the dressmaker came to the house for her two-week spring visit. Among other things, she made Lizzie the pair of two-piece housedresses that figured largely in the trial, a Bedford cord (which was a sort of soft cotton pique) of light blue figured in navy, and a pink-and-white-striped gingham. Lizzie alternated them as they got soiled until the day of the murders; in small-town Yankee fashion, she kept the numerous fine dresses of which she was so proud for public appearances only. Even her two housedresses, however, were stylishly made; the pink-and-white had an elegantly shirred front, and both had half-trains, the blue one flounced with a ruffle. These matching blouse-and-skirt sets, incidentally, were confusingly called *wrappers*. (I mention this because the edited trial can conjure up a false picture of Lizzie in a dressing gown.)

Uncle John, whose visits Lizzie always found most unwelcome and disturbing, was also at the house during this time; at the trial he mentioned having had to sleep in the attic since the guest room was being used by the dressmaker.

The dressmaker was a star witness for the defense, such an amusingly obliging star witness that a serious-minded editor deleted her testimony from the published trial, and all who have since written in Lizzie's defense find it wise to treat it very lightly and scantily indeed. Yet, when I got that despaired-of Volume II in my hands, I found that Mrs. Raymond had something thought-provoking to say; the best coached female tongue will occasionally run away with itself.

Her bit of information came late in the trial. A weary and discouraged prosecution showed no interest in it, and it has never been mentioned since. But it is interesting.

Lizzie's "peculiar spells," as I have mentioned, were reported to have come about three or four times a year, at the menstrual period. The slight irregularity, it was said, seemed to depend on whether or not she had "got worked up." This, I have been told by a specialist, is medically sound. Uncle John's visits were upsetting. The bloody death of her pigeons was unthinkably upsetting (Lizzie's almost pathological love for birds and animals is one of the best known facts about her; she left a large part of her inheritance to the Animal Rescue League "because they have so few to care for them").

The pigeons died; Uncle John dropped in; and toward the end of her stay, the dressmaker mentioned casually, Bartholomew Shaw, head detective of the city police, came to see Miss Lizzie Borden and talked to her for a long time in private. "I don't know what they talked about." [8]

None of us will ever know. Shaw was not asked to testify.

[8] Trial, Vol. II, Mrs. Raymond.

The defense quickly diverted Mrs. Raymond from the subject, and the prosecution did not bother to cross-question her at all, the rest of her testimony being so patently what it was, a rehearsed piece.

Yet, it is interesting. Detective Shaw's call came just three months before the murders—the normal lapse of time between one "peculiar spell" and the next.

Arrangements for the transfer of the Swansea farm hung fire. We can only imagine what was going on in the Borden house. In early July, a group of Lizzie's friends, "the girls," rented Dr. Handy's cottage in Marion, at the head of Cape Cod not far from New Bedford, for a protracted holiday. Lizzie was unwilling to leave home and go with them.

Two weeks before the murders, Uncle John drove his niece —the proposed housekeeper—over to Swansea to look the place over; she had not seen it before. This little fact, which I learned from the Providence *Journal,* has never been mentioned in print elsewhere, since its relevance to the crime was unknown. It was briefly interesting to a reporter only because Uncle John lied about it and was caught out. (I do not wonder that he lied about it. If it had come out that the farm was going to be put in *Abby's* name, people who had known of Uncle John's expectations concerning the place might well have decided that Andrew had changed his mind at the last minute and thus precipitated a quarrel—or a murder.)

Two weeks before the murders, Emma was planning to go for a visit to her friends the Brownells in Fairhaven, across the bay from New Bedford. She did not like the idea of leaving her sister at home, and talked about it to her bosom friend and neighbor, Miss Alice Russell.

Two weeks before the murders, Andrew bought back the Ferry Street house from the girls for five thousand dollars— two thousand above its assessed value—thus giving them, in effect, a soothing gift of a thousand dollars apiece. Lizzie put two thousand in her checking account and five hundred in savings (the defense had the statement read at the trial) and said that perhaps she *would* go to Marion after all, traveling with Emma as far as New Bedford, the parting of the ways.

But Lizzie did not go to Marion when she left Emma. She spent the rest of that day, the next, and the night that followed it, in a small boardinghouse on Madison Street. A painstaking D.A. found satisfactory evidence that during that time she made more than one unsuccessful attempt to buy prussic acid. Having failed, she went to Marion for part of a day, but she was restless and abstracted and left by mid-afternoon to go back to her room on Second Street.

Andrew was secretive as a clam; he never mentioned his family or his private business to anyone. In the terrific heat wave that began just *two days before* the murders, the treasurer of one of the mills asked if he weren't going over to Swansea to get out of the heat. Andrew suddenly and strangely opened up. He said that there was a lot of trouble going on in his house and he couldn't talk about Swansea until it was settled.

At once he clammed up again and left.

The incident was so out of character that the man who witnessed it (I think he was my courtesy "Uncle" Ben Read, though I may be mistaken) talked about it. After the crime, a police detective called upon him, and he bore it out, requesting that if possible his name should not be used. Reporters recognized the detective and questioned him after his call. It was a slender story; the prosecution did not think it worthwhile to subpoena the treasurer. I myself should not have given it a second thought as I read of it in the Providence *Journal* if it had not been precipitated by a casual mention of the Swansea place—two days before Andrew died.

On the other hand, everyone who knows anything about the Borden case knows how Abby betrayed her state of mind on the day before she died. One can scarcely doubt that she was as wretched in her own way as Lizzie was over Andrew's stubborn notion.

⇒⇒⇒ 7 ⇐⇐⇐

Abby was wretched, she was frightened, and she knew that poison is the woman's way to murder.

Infectious gastrointestinal complaints were not recognized in Abby's lifetime; whether a family fell sick in unison or one after the other, it was always "something you ate." And in the days of the old wooden ice chest, few actually did get through the hot months without a mild case of food poisoning. It was called "summer complaint." The classic suspect was left-over fish, a suspicion, of course, well earned.

On the Tuesday after Andrew had blabbed downstreet about "a lot of trouble in the house," he came home to dine on yesterday's warmed-over fish. He and his wife retched all night; Bridget and Lizzie began to feel queasy the next day. "Wednesday, the day we was all sick," Bridget called it in court; she herself was still vomiting on Thursday morning. It sounds to our modern ears as if the family had just picked up a virus.

Abby's point of view did not include this possibility. It included left-over fish and a stepdaughter who hated her, who had robbed her, and who stuck to her room in all that heat, like a watchful bird of prey, while her friends were at the seashore. It included left-over fish, a stepdaughter who had not called her Mother since her husband had put a small piece of property in her name five years before, and the husband who was planning to repeat that offense with the farm that was not merely *property* but a place the girls loved for its childhood memories.

Mrs. Borden never gave the warmed-over fish a thought. As soon as she could get dressed in the morning, she rushed across the street (they had no telephone) to tell Dr. Bowen that she and her husband had been poisoned.

Andrew was furious. As she left the house to tell the doctor

God knows what, he shouted after her, "Well, my money shan't pay for it."

There were three doctors in the immediate neighborhood, but two were Catholics and did not count. Dr. Kelly and Dr. Chagnon, the nonexistents, lived respectively in the cotttage that hugged the south side of the Borden house, and the house at the back, behind the high fence with its barbed wire at the top and bottom. Dr. Bowen lived in a double house directly across the street. The other half belonged to a family named Miller, not considered social equals, though their hired girl was a friend of the Bordens' Bridget.

Dr. Bowen did not have one of the better practices in town. Why, I do not know, for his photographs indicate a devastating bedside presence; though well on in middle age, he was over-handsome and excessively dressy. I never met him, and I always heard him referred to as "that old Bowen" in tones that somehow wiped him out of existence.

He had watched Lizzie grow up, and he liked her much the best of the family. I mean just that, and no more; I am not spicing parricide with a pinch of adultery. I doubt that Dr. Bowen knew of her "spells." The family did not think of them as a medical problem, and he saw the family only professionally. (In court he boasted that he "knew the Bordens socially" but admitted that he and his wife did not pay calls.)

Mrs. Borden was not a fool. She wanted desperately to be taken in earnest. But it was obvious that if she told her story straight, Dr. Bowen would have no doubts as to which of the two, she or Lizzie, was going crazy. Intelligently, she told him that her husband had received an anonymous note threatening poison.

Dr. Bowen examined her, questioned her, learned of the left-over fish, laughed, and offered to go across the street and have a look at the others. Mr. Borden met him at the door and drove him off with surprising fury—as if he had been meddling in private business.

Had Mrs. Borden simply felt hate in the air? When Hosea Knowlton, the District Attorney, first entered that house, his eye fell on a book lying on one of the small draped tables in the sitting room. A reader, as the Bordens were not, he picked it up idly. It was a book of household hints; its spine was broken and it fell open at a section on poisons, in fact at an article on prussic acid. Prussic acid works instantaneously and smells like almonds. Lizzie, as we shall see presently, was in no state of mind to cover her tracks just then. Possibly Mrs. Borden, at her daily dusting, had also noticed that her book of household hints had a broken spine.

In any event, she was afraid; and Andrew was angry with her. In all likelihood, she assured him she had not mentioned Lizzie to Dr. Bowen but made up a story about an anonymous threat. If she did, and if Lizzie overheard her, she knew that Abby had provided her with an alibi.

But I doubt that Lizzie was thinking clearly that day. In moments of excitement she often did not. Eight- or ten-penny nails, for example, are not commonly used by burglars to pick locks. Nor does one with her wits about her go straight out and try to buy prussic acid at the nearest neighborhood drugstore.

Perhaps, on being once more refused at a drugstore, it occurred to Lizzie that she had been indiscreet. At least, that day she did something most unusual; she came down to dinner with her parents, not after them. She was wearing her blue Bedford cord, and so far as Bridget could see the atmosphere at the table was wholly agreeable.

However, nobody ate much, though Andrew and Abby had restored themselves with castor oil and a proprietary herb tea. The main dish was warmed over mutton and mutton soup.

This mutton, which figured largely in the trial, had first appeared at the Borden table on Saturday. (This is the gospel according to Arthur Phillips. The elder Bordens had been brought up as Sabbatarians and gave their maid all Sunday off.) On Sunday, the mutton had been the staple of the day's three meals. On Monday, there was mutton for breakfast, fish for dinner, and mutton for supper. On Tuesday, there was pork steak for breakfast and warmed-over fish for dinner; supper is not in the court record. The mutton had now come back, to be the main dish of Andrew's and Abby's last three meals on earth.

The dinner of their last day had also been planned; it was to have been mutton and mutton soup.

Lizzie went back to her room directly after dinner. Bridget cleared up and retired to her attic; the family complaint was gaining on her. Andrew and Abby were alone downstairs when Uncle John arrived. As usual when he only planned to spend the night, he brought no luggage, not so much as a nightshirt or a clean collar.

They let him in, and Fate dotted the last *i* and crossed the last *t*. Andrew had twenty-two hours to live, Abby twenty; John Morse, by a narrow brush, would escape death on the gallows.

The moment is worth a snapshot before Abby waddles off to the kitchen to heat up the mutton soup again and slice some more mutton.

They stand in the ugly little sitting room with its noisy-flowered, worn, outdated carpet, its furnishings that reflect the taste and purse of a pre-Civil-War undertaker who has not yet prospered; nothing has been reupholstered, for horsehair holds up. The five doors, and the clutter of non-functional tables, each with its crocheted doily, make the tiny space seem even smaller. A meaningless mantel juts from one wall; the chimney space beneath it is bricked up and papered over, and the hole that once accommodated the pipe from a Franklin stove has a fancy cover of embossed and gilded tin with a dim landscape painted on its center. The keys to the bedroom and "Mrs. Borden's room" lie in their usual place.

Andrew's predestined deathbed, a sofa so short that it can accommodate only his lounging body—when he rests on it his long legs sprawl onto the floor—is still so large for its cramped setting that it must stand with one arm set flush with the door into the dining room.

Here they are, two men with something neatly planned, and a frightened woman. Click the lens. Here is Morse, a man of property who could pass for a tramp. Here is Andrew, a man of property who looks it, even though as always upon entering the house he has exchanged his long Prince Albert for the short house-coat that he calls his "dressing gown." (One or the other of these garments, turn and turn about, is always ready for his exits and entrances, hung neatly on a hat rack at the door.) He is tall, gaunt, and even in dishabille, meticulously tidy. And here is Abby, like an underdone suet pudding wrapped in shabby calico—five feet; over two hundred pounds; white with a night's vomiting, a dosing of castor oil, a dosing of mutton soup, and her unabated, clutching fear of poison. The day is hot; the calico is damp and crumpled with the sweat of her eighty excess pounds of fat, and her pale face shines with it.

Look at the picture and put it aside. It is a picture whose meaning has been guessed up to now only by a few Fall River bankers, all long since dead.

The first of several *idées fixes* upon which all study of the Borden case has foundered is the unquestioned belief that Uncle John's visit at the time of the murders was pure coincidence. He merely happened in, and that was that.

This is accepted without question, despite the wild and mutually contradictory lies that Lizzie told about that visit at the inquest, that inquest at which she told no *gratuitous* lies in any other connection, but, rather, amply bore out her own reputation for dismal, plodding honesty. She could only lie from grim necessity. But her evidence, so calm and well controlled at the start, fell abruptly into panic and chaos at the bare mention of Uncle John. Her terrified lies about this visit, following her anxious attempt to conceal the fact that he had paid a visit five years before (when the Whitehead house affair, the prototype of the Swansea place affair, occurred) are lies that stand out from their drab context like a red flag. She showed a similar lack of control at only one other point, when she tried to give the impression that Bridget knew nothing about a damning circumstance of which she might have told, but did not—to her eventual reward.

Why has nobody ever studied these panic lies? For two reasons, I think. In the first place, Uncle John—for reasons that we shall soon understand better—was as anxious as Lizzie that his easily misunderstood connection with the trouble at the Bordens' house over the Swansea place should never be known. Like Lizzie, like Emma, he was a bad liar; he almost spoiled a perfect alibi by telling a reporter on the Providence *Journal* a clumsy lie in this connection, though once his immediate danger was past, his silence about Swansea became lifelong and absolute.

But there is a second, simpler, and more strongly operative reason for ignoring Lizzie's testimony on Uncle John. Uncle John *did* have a perfect alibi for the death of Andrew. Not for Abby, who died around nine in the morning; but for Andrew, who died somewhere in the neighborhood of quarter to eleven. The prosecution lost interest in him. They had no reason to go to the right people and ask the right questions, and they never got wind of the precipitating motive, the Swansea place, or his connection with it; it stayed off the court record. And nobody ever studied Lizzie's inquest testimony for its *human qualities,* observing *how* and *why* she lied; her lies were too colorless, too dismally drab to seem worth it.

I am sure that Uncle John did not merely happen in. But why, specifically, was he there at the house just then? How did he get into our snapshot?

≫ 8 ≪

The transfer of the Swansea place to Abby's name was to have taken place on the next morning—Thursday—at the National Union Bank. Andrew, as it was discovered at the time of the inquest, kept his papers in his own safe at home; he and Abby would bring the deed along with them when they came.

Or so my grandfather believed—a bank president, as Andrew was. As I said before, he thought of it as a minor matter; he did not realize that it was Andrew's fatal repetition of his mistake about the Whitehead house. When he told me about it, he had no notion that he was giving me new evidence, nor did I guess the importance of what I was learning. That was in 1923, and I had no thought I'd be writing about Lizzie some day. But that it *is* new evidence I can no longer doubt. Once this seemingly irrelevant fact is known, too many other seemingly irrelevant facts fall into a coherent pattern, bearing out my view of the precipitating motive and explaining why August 4, 1892, was the day on which five years of cold, brooding hate finally exploded into murder.

The more I have studied the evidence, the more I realize that this proposed transfer was the precipitating motive for the crime.

Now, let us think again about that snapshot just laid aside.

We know about the household situation, so tense that a casual mention of the Swansea place had the clamlike Andrew blabbing about the "trouble at the house" downstreet on Tuesday morning, so tense that Abby, on Wednesday morning, disregarded the hot-weather, warmed-over fish that she had eaten and rushed to tell the doctor that she had been poisoned—first *threatened* with poison, and then poisoned in fact. Why was Uncle John in the picture? I never knew him, but I know his breed well. Old Yankees of his type admire spunk, on occasion, but even more they admire a sensible caution. As I have often heard them say: "It's one thing to stick up for yourself and another to stick your neck out." I am sure that Uncle John would have kept his always unwelcome nose out of the house at such a tricky time if he had not been, somehow, indispensable to a plan for getting the transfer made without Lizzie's knowledge.

That there was a plan, and one that Uncle John was terrified would be discovered and misunderstood, he himself will give us repeated evidence. But what was the plan?

I believe that John Morse had come that Wednesday to spend the night only because Andrew faced a particular problem.

The problem was, in essence, Abby's fat; if she had weighed thirty or forty pounds less, Andrew Borden might well have died in his bed.

At the inquest, Lizzie claimed that Abby waddled almost daily to market. In truth, Emma marketed, and when she was away Bridget could be trusted to choose a joint that would last a nice long time. At the trial, the defense tried to make it appear that Abby went to church with Lizzie; all it managed was to bring out that Abby had not *left* Central when her husband did: which would have been, for Abby, an imperceptible gesture.

Abby hardly ever went out, yet they had to get her to the bank without Lizzie's knowledge. On Friday afternoon, twelve days before, it had looked briefly as if things might arrange themselves without the need for careful plotting. Lizzie set out for Marion, and Andrew expected a fortnight of unobserved freedom. But even if Andrew had snapped into prompt action then and planned to make the transfer at the bank by Monday morning at the latest, he would still have been too late; by Sunday evening, Lizzie had come back. Since then she had sat in her room, day after day, watchful as a hawk at a rabbit warren. And if Abby went out, Lizzie would know where she had gone and why.

If Andrew had not been so cautious, a simple solution to the problem was at hand, and one that would not have involved Uncle John.

Andrew could have left the house in the morning and taken the documents to the bank. Abby could have said that she had a notion to spend the day with Mrs. Whitehead, crossed the street to the livery stable next door but one to Dr. Bowen's, hired a hack, met Andrew, and then gone on to Mrs. Whitehead's, where Lizzie would have found her if she had decided to go and check up.

He was cautious. And Abby did not take such notions out of the blue. Mrs. Whitehead sometimes dropped in on her, but she went to Mrs. Whitehead's house only rarely and in response to invitations sent some time in advance. Unless some *urgent* summons from Mrs. Whitehead, or what appeared to be one, was actually delivered, Lizzie would smell something wrong.

But who could bring it? Messengers talk, and so do hack

drivers. One wrong word, and the whole thing would get around as fast as had news about the Whitehead house.

John Morse would not talk. But John Morse could hardly come to the front door, hand Abby a note, and drive her away himself. On the other hand, if he hired some man from out of town, South Dartmouth, say, or Westport, to take a rig unfamiliar to Fall River and one of John's horses and hand in the note under John's direction, that hired man would afterward find nobody in his town interested enough in the Borden's doings to listen to his tale and pass it on.

Whether or not Andrew arrived at this particular solution to his problem you can decide as the evidence unfolds. Here we need only note that while Uncle John was rich in horses and known to be an outdoors man who preferred suprisingly long drives to a ride in the "steam cars," he arrived at the Borden house that Wednesday on foot.

After the murders he told reporters—out of a clear sky, since he was not asked—that he had come to Fall River on the New Bedford train, thus underlining it that, for once, he did not stable a horse. He did not mention, nor was he asked, how he got over to Swansea that afternoon and back by suppertime. At that time the Swansea farm could not be reached by public conveyance. It lay ten miles as the crow flies from the far end of Slade's Ferry Bridge on a winding country road laid out to avoid salt marshes and seek bridge-spots over the estuaries. And Slade's Ferry Bridge itself was a sizable hike away.

It was too far to walk, and Uncle John did not use the livery stable that was just one house down from Dr. Bowen's. He had to drive; nobody has ever wondered what carriage he drove.

Two things, at least, we do know. Uncle John did not put up a horse and carriage, as was his custom, in the back-yard stable that the Bordens called the barn. And a strange horse and buggy stood just one house up from the Borden's from a time attested as being somewhere between nine and nine thirty until just before Andrew came back from downstreet to die.

If I am anywhere near the truth in this conjecture about Andrew's plan, we have sidestepped a major false question on which the study of the Borden case has always been hung up; the second of those *idées fixes* that have always blocked our view becomes transparent.

The classic statement of the question goes as follows: on the next morning, the murder morning, around nine, was a note delivered asking Abby to come at once to the bedside of a sick friend, name unknown? Or was it *not?* Such a note was never found. Wide advertising for the name of either its sender or the messenger who fetched it brought no result, though five hundred dollars was offered as bait, a tempting sum in those days, to a messenger boy. The story of its having been delivered came only from Lizzie; and Abby—though the defense labored mightily to obscure the fact—was notoriously friendless and housebound.

This note quickly became and has remained the second stoutest red herring in the Borden case, the first being the question of which dress Lizzie wore on the murder day.

The evidence that no such note ever came is impressive. Because her size made it so taxing for her to get about, Abby only went out by carriage, three or four times a year and on occasions always planned well in advance, to dine with her sister, Mrs. Whitehead. If she received an emergency call to waddle forth on an errand of mercy to any other house than Mrs. Whitehead's, it was a historic moment—and Mrs. Whitehead had not sent for her.

But there is also impressive evidence that the note did come. In the first place, a young man was seen going to the front door at nine; it was briefly opened to him, but he did not go in. In the second place, Dr. Bowen tried to read the scraps of a torn-up note, refused to show them to the police, and burned them in the kitchen stove a little over an hour after the murders were discovered. This second bit of evidence is stressed neither by Lizzie's defenders nor her accusers; both sides, for reasons that will become only too plain, find it inconvenient.

Yet something else, which I see as far stronger evidence that the note did come, has never before been mentioned. Nobody can *study* Lizzie's inquest testimony without being struck by something odd: she *manipulates* fact, but she cannot *invent* it. If no note came, it is the only *specific object* that she mentions that was not later proved to have actual, physical existence. Either a note came, or she told one solitary lie totally out of keeping with all the rest, totally out of keeping with her own style.

It has never before been suggested that a note *did* come for Abby but that its contents were not quite what Lizzie reported.

Let us think of one more factor. Lizzie had, as you will see almost at once, two lengthy chances to overhear Abby and Andrew and Uncle John down there in the sitting room. If she overheard this plan (whether or not Abby lived long enough to explain about "a note from Mrs. Whitehead"), it *would* have been perfectly in keeping with her plodding style as a liar to transpose "Mrs. Whitehead's" sudden illness to the illness of an anonymous "somebody."

According to Uncle John's testimony at the trial, he talked to Andrew and Abby from dinner until about three, in the sitting room. Its window, open in the heat, was directly beneath Lizzie's; the little, cramped house was anything but soundproof, and old Yankee voices carry. Lizzie said later that their voices "annoyed" her. If those three touched at all on either the current situation or the next day's plans—and they were not the type for small talk—that word *annoyed* is probably worthy to rank with my mother's *very unkind*.

Uncle John left; he went over to Swansea, and then to supper with relatives on Weybosset Street, thus avoiding another go at the mutton and mutton soup.

That evening, before he came back, Lizzie slipped out of the house for the second time that day. She paid a call on Emma's friend Alice Russell. The call has been laughingly compared to Cassandra's foretelling of the fall of the House of Atreus. Well, Fall River was once called Troy, we learned in school, but to me the words that Alice Russell would eventually quote in court sound almost like the suicide's veiled call for help. Or, more accurately, they sounded not like Cassandra, but Clytem-

nestra compulsively talking. Murder, like suicide, must be frightening in the prospect; and Lizzie was determined to poison
Abby. One feels that she is not only providing herself with an
alibi; she is also saying, "See through me; stop me."

Lizzie's first words as she burst in on Alice were, "I am afraid
someone will do something. I don't know but what someone
will do something." And then, abruptly, "I have taken your advice and written to Marion that I will come."

Miss Russell said that she was glad. She urged Lizzie to have
a good time.

"Well, I don't know. I feel depressed. I feel as if something
was hanging over me that I can't shake off."

She told of how she had not been able to join in "when the
girls were laughing and talking" on her brief call in Marion
after she left New Bedford. She began to tell of the family illness; the bread they had bought from the baker might have
been poisoned. Miss Russell pointed out that in that case they
would certainly have heard of others who had been taken sick.
Lizzie suggested that perhaps someone was putting poison in
the can they left out each night for their milk.

It was nonsense, but Miss Russell tried to reason with her
and reassure her. The farmer would see anyone who tried to put
anything in the milk at the farm, and since it was delivered after
dawn, nobody would dare tamper with it on their steps.

But Lizzie went on about how dreadfully sick they had been;
Mrs. Borden had thought they were poisoned and had gone to
Dr. Bowen.

Miss Russell remained reassuring, unimpressed. Lizzie tried
harder.

"Father has had so much trouble. I don't know, I feel afraid
sometimes that Father has got an enemy."

She had overheard him talking to a possible enemy. Her
father had said to him, "I don't care to let my property for such
business"; and the man sneered, "I shouldn't think *you* would
care what you let your property for."

And she had seen a man run around the house one night.
And the barn had been broken into twice.

She was getting nowhere fast. Miss Russell only soothingly

reminded her that the barn had been broken into by children who were after the pigeons.

Lizzie took a deep breath and really let her have it. "Well, *they* have broken into the house in broad daylight, with Emma and Maggie and me all there!"

(Maggie was Lizzie's pet name for Bridget, who liked it and called her Lizzie, often forgetting the Miss.)

Miss Russell, after all, was Emma's closest friend. She only said, flatly, *"I* never heard of that before."

"Father forbade our telling of it."

She did not say why she had obeyed him so long, only to tell of it now, but she described the robbery in detail. When she came to the nail in the keyhole, she added dubiously, "I don't know whether they used that to get in with, or what."

Miss Russell asked if the family had done anything about it.

Oh, yes, Lizzie told her; her father had got the police working on it at once, but they had never found anything out. He'd told them that they would catch the thief when he used the horse-car tickets, which were numbered.

Perhaps Andrew had felt it advisable to mention at home the fact that the tickets were numbered; for Lizzie ended her story abruptly: "As if anybody would use those tickets!"

Miss Russell's response to the story of the robbery seems to have left something wanting. It is not to be wondered at, for the recounted circumstances surely seemed strange enough to have made Emma ignore any parental request not to whisper the story to her best friend—if it had really happened.

Lizzie shifted back again to her father's enemies, to poison, to his rudeness that morning to Dr. Bowen ("I was so mortified!"), and again to enemies, vague, lurking, *they:*

"I feel as if I wanted to sleep with my eyes half-open—with one eye open all the time—for fear they will burn the house down over us."

Someone will do something: on that same note she got up and went home. It was nine o'clock.

Uncle John had come back before her. He and her parents were sitting together in the dark. Andrew had not lit the lamps. They ignored Lizzie's coming in and she ignored their pres-

73

ence. She bolted the front door for the night and went up to bed.

Her call on Alice, you observe, had in one way been very like Abby's call on Dr. Bowen. They both wanted to be taken seriously. Dr. Bowen would not have believed that Abby was in danger from Lizzie, so she told him a lie about an anonymous threatening letter. Alice might possibly be made to believe that Andrew had dangerous enemies, but not that Abby had.

For, outside her own house poor Abby Borden could scarcely have been said to exist.

Shortly after Lizzie came in, Abby, too, went to bed and left the men still sitting together in the dark.

Had she just uttered her last vain protests against Andrew's stubbornness? She was not acquisitive; her sole possession, the half-house, she had only wanted for her sister's sake. We may be sure that she did not want the farm. She only wanted peace and quiet in which to eat her way on through her living death.

We know that she was afraid. And she was not a practiced liar; she was not even a practiced talker. She could hardly have dared hope that when the note "from Mrs. Whitehead" came and she got ready to leave the house the next morning there would not, at bare least, be talk, words, perhaps even screaming words in front of Bridget. Lizzie was no fool. Surely she would guess what was afoot if a man handed in an unaddressed envelope saying that it was "a message for Mrs. Andrew Borden." Why had Lizzie refused to go to Marion? Why did she stay up there in her room watching? To make sure that Abby did *not* go out to the bank. She was already half-crazy with that brooding. She would not care *what* Bridget heard her say.

Such a prospect would have horrified Abby. Abby had a strong middle-class horror of what was called "talk" in the presence of the help. Bridget, through all those years of dishing up a second service for the sisters, had kept no illusions that all was sweetness and light in the Borden ménage, but I am sure that she spoke the truth when she said at the final trial that she "never knew *what* it was between them," and replied to searching questions about quarreling, "No, sir, never a word *in my presence*."

Yes, the thought of a scene in front of Bridget would have horrified Abby. And so, I think, she spelled out her own doom.

For one question about the Borden case that fascinates every insider has never occurred to the outsiders who have studied it so long: why was Bridget washing the windows when Abby was killed? It was a heat-record day, she was sick and throwing up; yet the fact is always explained by vague, false ideas about New England housekeeping, and vague, true generalizations about the unhappy lot of the nineteenth-century domestic.

I remember the housekeeping standards of southern New England: in the better run homes, they were more like those of the Old South than of the spic-and-span Middle West. And Abby, enclosed in fat and self-pity, was of the kind who make indifferent housekeepers in any part of the world. She was a singularly undemanding employer.

Bridget considered herself luckily situated, despite the trying atmosphere of the house. She did not get two half-days off starting after dinner, like all her friends; she got all of Sunday, and Thursday from just before dinner, yet her wages were high, four dollars a week, paid only to cooks. Her household chores were also light; besides the cooking she did only the wash and occasionally a little heavy cleaning. Abby and Emma did the dusting and sweeping; Lizzie made her own bed and in Emma's absence dusted her own room.

Bridget was genuinely devoted to lazy Lizzie, who called her Maggie and charmed her as she always charmed her servants; but she spoke with obvious sincerity when she said that "Mrs. Borden was a lovely lady to work for."

Yet she was sick, vomiting, and Abby sent her outdoors in the heat to the cumbersome, heavy job of washing the outside windows, beginning with those of the sitting room, which placed her at the furthest possible remove from the door to the kitchen entry, the door by which both deliveries and guests routinely came to that house, as we will observe when we study the murder day.

It was out of character for Abby as an employer. It was very much *in* character for the Abby who had a horror of unpleasant words before the help. It was the last nail in her coffin, poor woman. But it has gone unnoticed. Alive or dead, she was not the sort of person who attracts attention.

After she had gone to bed, Andrew and John still sat talking in the dark; the windows of the sitting room and of Lizzie's bedroom just over it were still open to the heavy night air. Lizzie, lying on her bed, must have heard almost every word.

＊ 9 ＊

August 4, 1892, was hot even at dawn; it became the hottest day in memory for all who lived in a town remarkable for its summer heat. "The hill," that steep slope to the northeast, cuts Fall River off from New England's cool wind from the open sea.

Our witnesses for the hours before the crime will be sixteen, fourteen outside the house and in it only Bridget and Uncle John. This makes a break with custom. Lizzie also described the morning at the inquest, in many versions that not only contradicted each other but also contradicted the testimony of Uncle John, Bridget, and all who came in directly after the murders. It has long been the convenient method to select from her testimony such statements as bear out the thesis of her guilt or her innocence, passing over her other statements in silence. We, as an innovation, will forego it, stick to those witnesses who bear each other out, and let her give her own separate version where she gave it, at the inquest.

Uncle John got up at six and sat in the sitting room waiting for the rest of the family.

Bridget came down fifteen minutes later. She still felt sick. She put out the pan for the iceman, brought in the milk, and latched the door again. She started the kindling in the stove and went down cellar for a hod of coal.

In another fifteen minutes, Mrs. Borden came down and gave her breakfast orders, adding a company touch for Uncle John:

besides their mutton, mutton broth, bananas, and cookies, they would have johnnycakes. (Many have read that menu and felt no need to look further for a precipitating motive.)

Mr. Borden came downstairs and emptied his slop pail on the grass outside: organic fertilizer. Before he joined his wife and Uncle John, he took a basket and carefully garnered the pears that had fallen from the trees in the night.

Around seven thirty, the family sat down to a rich and leisurely meal. As if Mrs. Borden had not yet noticed what a scorcher the day was rounding up to be, or that Bridget still felt sick, she said something about washing the windows. Bridget either only half-registered, or pretended not to hear. From Morse's evidence we cannot tell which.

When they had gone back to the sitting room, Bridget began to clear away, but she felt queasy and worked slowly. She tried to eat a little, in the misguided hope that it might settle her stomach, and puttered about.

Slightly before quarter to nine, Andrew let out Uncle John by the door to the kitchen entry. Bridget was in the sink room just beside it, drying the dishes. They stepped out into the yard and talked for a minute or two in lowered voices; she could not hear what they said. Then Andrew called out, "Come back to dinner, John."

He came back in, brushed his teeth at the kitchen sink, drew a basin of water for his washstand, and carried it up the back stairs, which debouched on the entry just across from the sink room. Bridget did not see him again before he left the house.

Perhaps Lizzie heard Andrew call out his farewell. As Bridget finished at the sink and came back into the kitchen, Mrs. Borden started her invariable morning rounds with a feather duster; Bridget heard her speak to Lizzie as she passed through the dining room, and Lizzie answer her "very civilly."

Lizzie came out into the kitchen. She, too, apparently felt sickish and not much like eating, but she said that she guessed she would have some coffee and cookies.

Bridget was always unable to remember on the stand what Lizzie was wearing that morning—nothing unusual, one would say, for a hot, sickish day of lying upstairs on her "lounge." But she remembered vividly what Lizzie had worn the day before—the two-piece, corded cotton "wrapper" of pale blue with a navy figure. (Men uninterested in women's dress, please note: the jury gave this insufficient thought.)

At that point Bridget gave up fighting her stomach and went outdoors to vomit for ten or fifteen minutes on the grass, where Mr. Borden had emptied his slops. The cellar w.c. was called on for minimal service in the Borden home.

When she came in she went to Mrs. Borden, to find out, perhaps, if she had heard her right at breakfast, or if the sounds of her long-protracted retching had not changed the morning's plans. If Bridget had hoped for a reprieve, she was in for an ugly surprise, and a surprise it almost certainly was, for it was not like Abby to send a girl who had just been vomiting to wash the windows on the hottest day that Fall River could remember.

Yet Abby did just that; and she sealed her doom. Whoever killed Abby Borden could not have done so if a strong young woman had been at some mercifully easy task indoors, within sight of the kitchen entry, of the cellar stairs, within hearing of the guest room where Abby's two-hundred-pound body shortly would go down with a crash. Or at least, the murder would not have gone undetected.

Mrs. Borden walked off toward the front of the house, flicking her feather duster. Bridget did not see her alive again.

Bridget went through the house shutting down the windows. Lizzie was not on the first floor. She collected her equipment, including a stepladder, for the windows were so long and lean that their top panes could not be reached even with the long-handled mop, which was kept out in the stable. The mop was inside the stable door, only a step or two from the back entry. As she came back with it, Bridget was startled to find Lizzie standing at the screen door—like an apparition, since Bridget had assumed that she was up in her room, from which she had not had time to get down. It has not occurred to her that Lizzie was in the cellar, whose steps, like the back stairs, opened on the entry.

As Bridget put it, she *"appeared* in the back entry and says, 'Maggie, are you going to wash the windows?' I says, 'Yes,' I said, 'you needn't lock the door, but you can lock it if you want. I can get the water in the barn.'" (Bridget believed that Lizzie did lock it, and went to the barn each time she needed more water for the washing and rinsing.)

But Bridget was in no hurry to begin. The girl who worked at Kelly's was out behind their cottage, and the two hung over the dividing fence and had a good long talk.

It was shortly before nine. Lizzie was alone in the house with Abby. All the supporting evidence—including Lizzie's own *first* version of the murder morning which she gave at the inquest (she gave three on this particular point)—indicates that Andrew left the house to go downstreet while Bridget was out vomiting in the back yard, not long after he had called out, "Come back to dinner, John."

At this point, while the girls chatted on over the fence in the rear side lot, people began to notice things.

A buggy with two men in it made a U-turn and stopped in front of the Kelly cottage.

Next, a witness observed that the buggy had one man in it. The witness gave him only a casual glance and did not recognize him—apparently he left the neighborhood almost at once, for he was not seen again.

At approximately the same time—"around nine"—another observer saw a young man go to the Bordens' front door and ring the bell. The door was opened and quickly slammed in his face —by Andrew, it has long been assumed, though this was reported by a neighbor on the same side of the street, not a vantage point for seeing *into* the Bordens' hall. (The assumption has rested on the fact that under normal conditions Andrew was the only likely door-slammer in the household.)

Then someone saw the wooden shutters to the guest room closed; several other neighbors noticed this, too, later in the morning, for they had never seen those shutters closed by day before.

Mark Chase, the proprietor of the livery stable, sat out front that whole morning, his chair in the shade of a tree. It was no day to make you feel like doing much. He first noticed the buggy when he settled himself there at half past nine. It was a good horse, and one that did not belong in the neighborhood; Chase noticed horses.[1]

At the same time Dr. Handy drove up the street on house calls. (He owned the seaside cottage where "the girls" were vacationing. Our useful Mr. Phillips stresses the fact that he was highly observant.) Dr. Handy saw a young man on the sidewalk before the Kelly cottage. He was well dressed, in a light suit, with a tie; Dr. Handy noticed him only because he walked so slowly, barely moving, as if he were waiting for someone and yet did not want to stand stock still, too obviously waiting.

Andrew was already downstreet, where he dropped in almost daily at the National Union Bank and the B.M.C. Durfee Safe Deposit and Trust Co. and otherwise kept busy collecting his rents in person, sitting on board-meetings, and practicing a little usury on the side. Regularly, he stayed downstreet until dinner-time and went back again in the afternoon.

This morning did not follow the usual pattern. Though he was well known to be no dawdler, he was first seen standing around *outside* the National Union Bank, as if—like the young man in the light suit—he were waiting for someone. But he did not go *into* that bank, or the B.M.C. Durfee Trust, or for that matter, to the Metacomet or to any bank except for two whose names a woman might have confused in her mind with *National Union*. He looked in, that is, only at the First *National* Bank and at the *Union* Savings Bank (where the Treasurer collared him briefly about a loan).

These three banks of similar name stood close together on Main Street, between four and five blocks from his house. A great search was eventually made for witnesses to his morning. While it has never been considered worth mentioning before, he was only seen for the next hour and a half hovering around between the bank at which he had been expected and the two with which Abby might have confused it.

(We cannot schedule Andrew's time downstreet very closely.

[1] At the trial he identified himself as "hostler"; he was overmodest, as we learn from Phillips' *History of Fall River*.

His was a more leisured era than ours. Few clocks agreed that day, and fewer consulted them. All the witnesses except the men at the police station who took down the first report of the murder gave themselves ten or fifteen minutes' leeway, to one side or the other.)

Abby did not turn up. She was not the type to linger long at the toilet table; it would have taken her only a few minutes to change from her dingy old white calico (the dress in which she was found) to proper street attire. And by carriage, the banks were not a three-minute slow drive from 92 Second Street.

As I see it, only a very stubborn man with a mind willfully closed to all uncomfortable possibilities would have waited around half so long within sight of the First National, National Union, and Union Trust. And only a man who beneath that stubbornness was deeply worried would suddenly have broken with custom and invited questions by going home an hour and a half too soon—for it lacked that much to dinner time.

Yet he seems to have hurried the rest of his short way home.

Usually Andrew stopped in at the post office each morning; that day he was not seen there, though there were many to remember if he had come.[2] It was not a small branch, but a main building in a sizable town and a local gathering place. The clerks at the windows, like half the city and surely most of those who had leisure to stand about there that morning, knew gaunt, towering old Borden, the rich miser, by sight.

Near his corner, Andrew passed a store that he rented out to a hatter named Clegg, one of the many Fall River Lancashire-men who came from the English Midlands to our mills.

On the Tuesday of that week, Mr. Clegg had called at Andrew's house to ask about renting a second store; but on Tuesday, as we learned from the mill treasurer quoted in the Providence *Journal*, Andrew had not been feeling like himself. He refused to talk business. He may have refused unpleasantly, thus forming the basis of Lizzie's story of the man to whom her father would not rent, that example of his "enemies" which she gave to Alice Russell. As I have said before, Lizzie's lies, even

[2] It is frequently stated that he did so, on the grounds that Lizzie said so three times; the rest of the court record is ignored.

the most absurd of them, invariably were founded on hard fact.

Mr. Clegg now sighted Andrew passing. He hurried out and caught him for a further word. Andrew stepped inside his door for a moment. Two of Clegg's countrymen, Mather and Short-sleeves by name, were doing a little carpentry in the front of the shop. As Andrew left, they had the pleasure of watching him exhibit his character as the town's living legend. A broken lock was lying on the floor, and Andrew stooped, salvaged it prudently, and dropped it into his pocket.

Remember this lock. It will eventually give us the same sort of satisfaction that it gave Mather and Shortsleeves. It showed them Andrew, and when we study the inquest it will show us Lizzie: the world's worst liar, struggling to use her crippled visual imagination. In the meantime, it deserves a word of its own, for upon it centers one of the more amusing *idées fixes* about the Borden case.

It has long been accepted without question that Andrew came home from downstreet on the morning of his death carrying in his hand a broken lock neatly rolled up in a foot-wide white mailing wrapper—or, as the summary for the defense simplified it for greater plausibility, and as it is more often stated, "wrapped in paper." This made a certain sense in court, for Andrew had been seen to pocket a lock, and a neighbor had mentioned passing him with an undescribed *something* in his hand wrapped in white paper.

Nobody but Lizzie would have been dull enough to hope that the broken lock, rolled, not folded, in a mailing wrapper, would be accepted for what Andrew brought home in his hand. Yet beyond asking Bridget to repeat her conflicting evidence, the prosecution had no legal means of casting doubt upon Lizzie's desperate substitution of a broken lock rolled in a mailing wrapper for a rolled-up deed upon the mantelpiece.

Not only the jury but the world has bought her singular contrivance ever since.

Bridget saw Andrew bring home a package shaped like a roll of documents: her statement has always been overlooked. A policeman saw a roll of documents in the kitchen stove: this has never been considered significant, since it was proved that Andrew Borden died intestate—and what would Lizzie have burned if not a will?

I believed it myself for years. I believed it until I began to study Lizzie's inquest testimony word for word in the light of my new understanding of the proposed transfer of the Swansea place, which let so many other scraps of seemingly pointless, irrelevant information show themselves for what they had always been—relevant parts of one coherent, sorry tale.

About midway through the past hour and a half, two ladies, one a former neighbor of the Bordens, had noticed a "young fellow" standing on the sidewalk. He was, when they saw him, leaning one elbow on a gatepost; his face was bent down, and he sheltered it from the merciless sun. Though the Second Street houses were built almost flush to the sidewalk, most of them had a fence that ran the full length of the lot, directly before the house as well as the side-yard. The ladies sighted the youth from the end of the block, but they believed that it was the Borden's front gate upon which he leaned. He stayed there the whole time that they were "admiring some pond lilies that a man had in a wagon."

It was on for half past ten—perhaps just before Andrew pocketed the lock—that Dr. Handy drove through the street again. The young man he had noticed before was still there, on the sidewalk near the Borden home. His face, Dr. Handy said, now appeared "agitated" and he "oscillated" in an undecided manner on one heel. Dr. Handy emphasized his physician's observation that the young man did not appear at all intoxicated, only perturbed. The buggy also stood in its place until around ten thirty or shortly before. At this point, Mark Chase, who had been watching it from his chair under the shady tree, went into the stable for a while. When he came back, it was gone; the young man was not seen again either.

As I have said, all the witnesses, including Clegg, Mather and Shortsleeves, tended to generalize about time; but the consensus indicates that the young man and the buggy disappeared only shortly before Andrew got home.

Until the early 1960's, Lizzie's defenders almost all claimed that this young man entered the house twice to dispatch Lizzie's parents, using the kitchen entry and passing her unnoticed the first time as she sat in the kitchen. His light suit and his person remained tidy and unbespattered throughout.

On his way back from downstreet, Andrew had met one other witness to the case, though he was too lost in thought to notice her as he hurried home after his delay by Mr. Clegg the hatter. Young Mrs. Kelly had passed him on her way to the dentist. Needless to say, no Kelly was personally acquainted with a Borden, but Mrs. Kelly always greeted her neighbor Mr. Borden when they met, and usually he responded. (I can still hear that return greeting of Andrew's class and generation: "How-do," unaccented, a perfect spondee.) This time, no how-do came. He was carrying something wrapped in white paper. Mrs. Kelly was not asked to describe its shape or appearance.

Andrew went around to the side as usual when he got home, but the screen-door was latched and nobody was in the kitchen. He came to the front door and put his key in the lock. It did not work. Bridget let him in.

⟫⟫ 10 ⟪⟪

Andrew had come home to die. Abby, as analysis of stomach contents showed, had been dead for at least an hour, more probably an hour and a half. Bridget had just finished the outside window-washing and come in. Lizzie had been in the house all morning. But what about Uncle John?

No witness in the neighborhood actually recognized John Morse from the moment Andrew called out "Come back to dinner, John," until John Morse did come back to dinner. And that return tells us something, I think, about *his* early morning.

John Morse came back to dinner with an absurdly perfect and overdetailed alibi for the death of Abby Borden, an alibi with only one flaw: the time element. For doctors cannot time a death to the exact minute. Abby might have died shortly after his perfect alibi began to account for his lapsed time away from the house or slightly before.

I do not find it surprising that outsiders, fascinated by the central character of the story, Lizzie, have wasted no time on wondering why Abby sent Bridget out to wash the windows; but I find it astounding that they have spent so little time at puzzling over why a man who ostensibly did not know that murder had been done should have made it so obvious that he expected to be accused of murder—the murder of Abby Borden —as to make himself immediately the prime suspect for both murders, a position he held until it was proved that he could not, at least, have murdered Andrew.

Clearly, one does not expect to be accused of murder unless one knows that murder has been done. Clearly, it strains coincidence to assume that on the same sunny August morning John Morse took a hatchet to Abby Borden and somebody else did the same to Andrew.

Yet there is, I think, an explanation. You will judge of its likelihood as you watch Uncle John through the next four days, after which he drops from the record. I want to suggest it here, for it concerns the household history *before* Andrew's death. Something that happened while Andrew was downstreet made Uncle John feel he had to have an alibi for the death of Abby, who died somewhere around nine.

John Morse shared Andrew's passion for thrift, but he was otherwise a far less rigid, more easy-going character, which almost by definition means that he was more realistic.

As he had sat in the dark with Andrew and Abby the night before, their tongues loosened by a comfortable awareness that Lizzie was out of the house, it seems to me that he may well have begun to wonder whether a tense family situation was not actually a dangerous situation, to wonder if Andrew's problem might not best be settled by forgetting the whole thing. Abby was afraid of being poisoned, murdered, and if he was not a fool, he knew why, whether or not names were named. He knew that she was afraid of Lizzie.[1]

If a note, ostensibly from Mrs. Whitehead, was to be Abby's excuse for leaving the house to join her husband at the National Union Bank, I think that Morse would have felt an uneasy urge to see that note delivered, to make sure that it had been taken from his driver by a fat old lady, or a maid, or at least by a casual and self-possessed young lady.

Let us assume that he did, that on leaving the house that morning he went to the livery where his horse and borrowed rig were stabled and told the young man that he would come along and show him where to wait. (This could explain the buggy with two men in it that made a U-turn, the same buggy that Mark Chase—a horse-conscious man—could not identify while it stood in the street empty until shortly before Andrew's homecoming.)

Let us assume that he warned the young man that Mrs. Borden might change her mind, but that he should give her plenty of time to come out, that he should *not* go back to the house himself, and that if it became clear that she *had* changed her mind, he should go right back to South Dartmouth and—as agreed—not mention the errand. (And, of course, be rewarded for his discretion.)

Let us also assume that the young man who had the door slammed in his face had just delivered the pretended "note from Mrs. Whitehead."

Uncle John waiting nearby, just cautiously out of sight of the door and the chattering maids at the rear of the narrow side-lot, would have been tense and vastly attentive to sights and sounds. Yes, I think we may safely assume that he was afraid of what Lizzie might know, and what Lizzie might do.

He was not alone in such fears.

Emma had clearly been worried about Lizzie; she had delayed her visit to Fairhaven until she believed that Lizzie would be going to Marion at the same time and leaving that bedroom where she watched and brooded day after day. She had confided

[1] It is amusing to note in the inquest and the trial that their fear of each other and unwillingness to name each other as suspects were mutual.

her worry to Alice, who for Emma's sake urged Lizzie to go and "have a good time."

Abby was afraid of Lizzie; she had run to Dr. Bowen babbling of poison.

Lizzie herself was afraid of Lizzie, and showed it in her call on Alice Russell.

Of the four who made up that delicate equilibrium in which the household had quivered ever since Lizzie first scented out the threat of new treachery over the Swansea place—Abby "getting him to go behind our backs" again—only Andrew, stubborn Andrew, with his one-track mind and the bit in his teeth, refused to be afraid of Lizzie.

John Morse was no fool; as we know from the pen of our Mr. Phillips, Andrew respected his judgment and acumen. John Morse was also far enough outside the family situation to see it in perspective. Furthermore, he knew from long acquaintance how totally Andrew could shut off his attention from inconvenient facts when he got stubborn; he knew how Andrew came as close to loving Lizzie, his baby, as he could ever get to love, and how little he liked to face up to her hate for Abby. Morse knew Abby; he knew that though she was depressive and a compulsive eater, she was no hysteric; if Abby feared sudden death as she did, intensely and terribly, she had some grounds for that fear. Morse knew Lizzie; he knew her obsession with Abby and her increasing instability. Lizzie had not been on speaking terms with him for a long time—but he knew.

The fuss and secrecy over the Swansea place was absurd and trivial, like the fuss and secrecy that had changed the whole domestic set-up from moderate unpleasantness to permanent cold war five years before. Absurd and trivial, it could still be the spark that would fall on the oil-soaked rags. I see no reason to doubt that Morse had a sensible man's fear that something might happen.

But, how did he know *what had* happened?

He came back to the house fearing trouble. He came back to see who would open the door and take in that note.

By elimination we know who did. Andrew—by Bridget's indirect evidence and by Lizzie's own *first* account at the inquest

—had left the house about ten minutes after John. Bridget was out in the back yard, hanging over the fence, talking. Abby was upstairs, finishing off her work in the guest room, where she was found dead on the floor, and where Lizzie once—and then never made the slip again—said that she saw her at nine. The young man could only have reported to Morse that a young lady had opened the door and slammed it shut on him.

But, as even John Morse knew, Lizzie would not have slammed that door so in the face of a young man carrying a message unless she was in a very strange state indeed. It was not her way; her servants, both male and female, were so loyal throughout her lifetime just because it was not her way with those who work for a living. Even *mildly* upset, Lizzie would have thanked a messenger nicely and stood in the doorway for a moment making a few vague, friendly remarks about the heat, or something of the sort.

Morse must have known it; his tense attention must have been directed toward the house. And a moment or so after that front door was slammed shut, the blinds of the guest-room window were also slammed shut.

The crash that Abby's two hundred pounds made as it hit the floor of that flimsy house—the windows were still open, both of them, behind their closed slatted blinds—would not have reached the ears of two girls chattering over the fence in a back lot on the edge of a busy stone-yard. It would not have caught the attention of a young man, listening for nothing and expecting nothing, out there on Second Street, a semiresidential area full of other noises. But I think that an anxious man who got out of a buggy and stood on the sidewalk might have heard it and interpreted it correctly. I think that he might have interpreted those unexpectedly closed blinds correctly and the ugly, soft thwacks of the axe on Abby's skull correctly: he himself had slaughtered hogs and cattle.

What would you have done in John Morse's place? I know what I should have done.

I should have known that people would think twice when they heard that the place I had expected to take over was instead going to be given to Abby. I should have realized that the horsetrader uncle from out west was a likelier suspect than a youngest daughter in a crime of violence.

At which point, I should have turned and walked quietly to the next corner, and made tracks for Weybosset Street, there to build up the most detailed and perfect alibi possible. Which, as we will see, is just what John Morse did.

As for the young man, he must have realized that he was involved in some kind of odd hanky-panky. I do not wonder that by the end of his long wait Dr. Handy saw that he had begun to look "agitated."

But let us return to Andrew, who has just got home.

⇛ 11 ⇚

Throughout the time Andrew had been away, Bridget had been washing windows with the long-handled mop and rinsing them by flinging up water by the dipperful. It was a long and clumsy job, which demanded many trips to the faucet in the stable. She had to mount her stepladder twice, to wash and rinse the top of each tall, high-placed window. Thus mounted, she could see into the house. Throughout the whole time she was working she saw nobody on the first floor, neither Lizzie nor Mrs. Borden.

It was getting close to half past ten when she finished and found that she did not need to knock for Lizzie to let her in; the screen door was unlatched. This was really odd, for she had been outside, nobody was downstairs, and Lizzie not only equaled but rather outstripped the general family paranoia in the matter of locking up.

The defense treasured this unlatched door. The mad maniac entered by it, dispatched Mrs. Borden silently and unobserved by Lizzie—who claimed to have spent the morning on the ground

89

floor—lurked in a tiny, narrow broom-closet at the right of the front door [1] (along with the mops and the dining-room-table extension boards) wedged upright in breathless, unventilated heat for at least an hour and a half, and probably two—until, with intuitive perfect timing, he emerged to finish off the half-done job.

The prosecution preferred to overlook this unlatched screen-door, strangely, it seems to me, for I know that if I had just committed a murder I should either give myself up to the police or make certain that some intruder had been able to get in. Yet, in Lizzie's place, I should have unlatched it with misgivings; for in the Borden house a door left unlatched with nobody downstairs was almost as striking as an eight- or ten-penny nail left in a lock.

Bridget, entering, found the first floor still vacant.

Abby, by the medical evidence, had probably been dead since shortly after nine, up on the guest-room floor; and Lizzie, in her adjoining bedroom, was readying for the street. She had, I believe, come to herself. She did not need to rush things, she could take her careful time, since Andrew would not be home until dinner time. Except in case of illness, he never was.

We shall eventually learn from Lizzie's own lips how she spent the morning. But here and now we should consider the probability that she had wakened, that day, in one of her brief seizures, that when she answered Abby "very civilly" and had her coffee and cookies and "appeared" from the cellarway so suddenly, startling Bridget, she was all the while sleepwalking, like that preternaturally skillful skier, or the young man who got the unexpected raise.

Her seizures were said to come three to four times a year at the menstrual period. She was menstruating, and it was just three months from the hatchet-death of the pigeons and Chief City Detective Bartholomew Shaw's unexplained call during which he had talked to her for a long time in private.

In connection with this particular morning, I find a few sen-

[1] Not shown on floor-plan; considered too small to get into, which Mr. Jennings later tried to disprove.

tences from Lennox's great book on epilepsy also worth giving a moment's thought.

"Epilepsy prefers to attack when the patient is off guard, sleeping, resting, idling." The robbery followed an afternoon nap; the first murder took place not long after she had got up in the morning.

"The explanation for the therapeutic activity of brain and muscle, namely the acidosis which accompanies it, has been explained before." Lizzie felt sick that morning. On Tuesday night she had not vomited, but if she failed to do so on Wednesday night, she was the only one of the four in the house who escaped the ailment; vomiting rids the stomach of hydrochloric acid, leaving the alkaline condition that predisposes to epileptic seizure.

But: "Mere acidosis associated with brain activity would not seem to be of exclusive importance because the kind of activity makes a difference. Mental concentration associated with *conflicting sentiments and suspense* seems to invite seizures." The concentration, the emotional conflict, the suspense, were certainly there.

Purpose and function can remain unaffected during such seizures; it is not surprising that neither Bridget nor Abby noticed anything strange about Lizzie's early-morning appearance. I think we can say that it is likely, in view of the five predisposing factors just considered, that the defense was quite right about the murder of Abby Borden, at least: a mad maniac *had* got into the house.

Bridget was set on getting through with her job as fast as she could. She took her stepladder to the front entry, but she left her bucket behind; she had only a basin of water and a rag with which to give the insides of the windows a lick and a promise.[2]

She had just started in when she heard Andrew's key fumbling in the front door, for she herself had latched the neglected side-door. She tried to open the door for him. By day it was kept closed only by a spring lock, but this time she found that the

[2] These details from the trial.

night lock and the bolt were fastened as well. As she worked at this frustrating triple barrier, she uttered a monosyllabic expletive. Questioned in court, she hesitated long before telling what she had said, and then gave it as, "Oh, pshaw!"

And upstairs, Lizzie laughed.

That short jerk of reflex laughter was enough to make Bridget realize that she had spoken loud enough to be overheard; perhaps—ah, God help us—even by Mr. Borden.

As Bridget told it: "She must have been in the entry or at the top of the stairs, I can't say which. Mr. Borden and I didn't say a word as he came in. I went back to my window-washing. He came into the sitting room and went into the dining room. He had a little parcel in his hand, same as a paper or a book."

The prosecution asked her to repeat those words, so that there might be no mistake. But the prosecution did not ask her to put it into English that a jury of Yankee farmers who kept no Irish help could understand: "He had something wrapped in his hand; it looked like a rolled-up newspaper or a magazine." (The "papers," like the "books" were thin by today's standards.) Bridget could not have given a better description of a roll of documents to one who understood her kitchen colloquialism. The defense, wisely, did not question her, but only mentioned casually in the final summary that Andrew came home with a broken lock wrapped in a piece of paper.

Abby by custom spent her mornings downstairs. Abby was not downstairs. Mr. Borden sat down in the dining room.

Lizzie came down the front stairs and joined him. She wore her hat and she was dressed for the street; though somewhat oddly on such an excessively hot day. For she wore—as she claimed, as the defense claimed, and as I quite believe—a heavy winter-party bengaline: India silk thick-woven over the stout linen cording commonly used as the warp in better grades of this material.[8] A curious latter-day defense of Lizzie states that "bengaline" is a word meaning "better than average cotton"; in fact, the word applies not to *fibre* but to *weave*. It is merely a heavy suiting-material.

[8] The cheaper grades used cotton cording; Lizzie always liked the best.

This was the dress that Lizzie claimed to have put on when she first got up in the morning. It was exhibited in court, immaculate. Medical experts had found on it not the faintest trace of blood. It was a dress that went well with the chic little hat that she now took off and laid upon the dining-room table, but it was an astounding dress to have chosen in which to lounge about the house through a record-breaking scorcher of a day.

It was astounding—and it is the one key to the Borden case that no male would ever notice.

For Lizzie had good reason for wearing that heavy dress as she came down the stairs to her father. Hot as the day was, she had good reason—though a woman's reason.

At the trial, the defense struggled to prove that the Bedford cord "wrapper," which Bridget, whose memory lapsed for the actual murder day, clearly remembered her as wearing the day *before,* could not have been worn even then. It had been, they claimed, so stained with brown paint at the very time it was made (in May when the house was painted) as to be useless.

It was for this reason, indeed, that Lizzie destroyed it in the kitchen stove three days after the murders: a fact that even the defense never tried to deny.

Men, only men, have studied the Borden case. They have never noticed that bengaline is a *ribbed* fabric, like Bedford cord. Or that both the "wrapper" and the India silk were cut alike, with separate matching blouse and trailing skirt. (Yes, half-trains were always filthy in one wearing, but the dirt was inside the hem and could be disregarded.) Most important of all, they have never noticed that the "wrapper" was pale blue printed wth a navy blue figure, and the elegant bengaline was navy with a woven figure of pale blue.

A woman, imagining these dresses described on the witness stand, would expect them to *sound* confusingly alike. A woman with a terrible reason to hide the blue "wrapper" might have been driven by desperation to put on a winter party dress in which to go out that hot day and establish her alibi simply because—like the dress her father and the maid would remember she had worn that morning—it also was two-piece, cut with a half-train, made of ribbed material, and figured pale and navy blue. And any woman who expected to hear a carefully detailed description of one dress, so like another in so many ways, given in court and considered by a jury, would have been, in the days of the all-male jury, an idiot.

For men, with sweeping indifference to such details, would boil the question of what she wore to its basic elements: "Did she dress in cotton that morning, for a hot day around the house, *or* did she, as she claimed, spend the morning alternately sitting by the hot coal range and bending above her ironing board in silk?"

To this hour, it has never been suggested that she might have changed her dress.

Do not be tempted to leap ahead and ask, "How did she hide a bloodstained housedress for three days?" This is a good question in its right place. But not here. Here and now I only want to suggest that a totally confusing question—the false either/or "Did Lizzie wear cotton or silk?" has been the chief stumbling block to thinking out the *modus operandi* of Abby Borden's murder. Just as another false either/or, "Did a note come, or no note come?" kept the few who might have come up with the right answer to the precipitating motive from asking themselves the right question: "What was *really* in the note that Lizzie said was from a sick friend?"

Lizzie changed for the street and put on her hat; she was ready to go out and establish her alibi. But her father came home too soon.

She had overestimated his patience, his well-known caution; they had kept him downstreet until only half past ten. He had come home. He would look for Abby, and find her; and he would know that she and Lizzie had been alone together in the house.

Lizzie loved her father. She loved him too much. Abby could not even write a small check, yet she had a half-house in her nominal possession, and because of it Lizzie had called her Mrs. Borden for five years. And for fifteen years Andrew had worn Lizzie's high-school ring on his little finger. He hated ornaments;

even his pocket watch was silver, not gold—but he wore that ring.

I have never thought that the defense overplayed Lizzie's devotion to Andrew, nor his to her; nobody who knew them ever doubted this. I do not think that Lizzie would have killed Andrew simply to save her own skin; though perhaps she could have saved it in no other way.

Perhaps, I say. It is conceivable that he never would have taken the witness stand against her—and not alone because he loved her. I think of our secretive huddling-together in the face of our private disgrace; of the protection that old Fall River gave her in its Republican establishment press, and even, I have been told, in its conversations until the trial was safely over. I think of Andrew, proud, secretive, rigid, and always somewhat scornful of the law. He had once refused to prosecute an embezzler whose full story, it was thought, would have inconvenienced his business dealings if told in court. Andrew was known to be a merciless creditor, and nobody believed that simple kindness had moved him to let the man make a token return and escape to New York. And I think that Lizzie, who often showed a lack of proportion in her moral and emotional judgments, might have remembered how, a year before, he had saved her from the police, and dared to hope that he would do it again.

But the Sunday school superintendent who spoke of Lizzie's "disproportionate excitement" when her class of Chinese laundrymen's children disregarded her avid—and rarely, rarely requited—desire for affection, for admiration, had touched on a pivotal point in her character. Everyone who knew her at all well spoke of it. Her need to be loved outstripped her ability to love. She found the faintest hint of rebuff, of disapproval, a torment, even when it came from people who were quite unimportant to her.

Andrew was not unimportant to her; he was the center of her world. Whether he decided to protect her or to let the law take its course, how could she bear to see him look at her, bear to see in his eyes that he knew she had killed Abby?

She had killed Abby, the hated rival; and he would know it.

For five years, no fine clothes, no bank accounts, not even a trip abroad had been enough to mute that jealous hate. Emma always blamed herself for Lizzie's hatred of Abby, but I think that she was only partially responsible; Emma, who had identified herself emotionally with her mother and at her death took over the mother's part, saw Abby as the usurper, yet even she could not understand Lizzie.

I do not understand Lizzie, but I understand why that gift of a half-house, Andrew's secret gift to Abby, was not smoothed over by the present of a half-house of equal value. Jealous hate is not stilled by bookkeeping methods: "Now you're all even Stephen."

Andrew had learned that much, the hard way, in the past five years. And for the last year, ever since Abby's trinkets were stolen and her possessions left a shambles in the ransacked room, the key had lain on the mantelpiece. Whether it lay there in silent rebuke or in loving warning, lie there it did. Yes, Andrew knew that Lizzie hated Abby.

He also knew that Abby was afraid Lizzie would poison her. And that very day he had given her cause to hate Abby even more: he had written the note. (And that Lizzie almost certainly knew he had done so is borne out by the inquest testimony; that strange testimony—in which she tells *no pointless, gratuitous* lies —is full of demonstrable lies and wild self-contradictions when she tries to make it clear that she *did not, could not,* have heard a word they said!)

Andrew knew Abby's fear, Lizzie's hate. If he had not come home then, perhaps Lizzie could have hoped he would persuade himself she was innocent (as Emma actually did for many years). But to have enabled him to do that, she should have been out of the house already and seen downstreet in the dress that so closely resembled the one he had briefly glimpsed that morning.

It was too late. He had come home and found her and knew that she had been in that little locked house alone with Abby all morning: the only opportunity rested with her, or with her and Bridget acting together.

He had come home too soon. He would know, he could not

avoid knowing. Her ring was on his finger, but his ring was on the third finger of Abby's left hand—and Lizzie had killed her.

Lizzie Borden was not an important or an endearing person. The whole Borden family and their milieu lacked, shall we say, dignity? The mutton soup and johnnycakes and the largely disregarded w.c. and the multitude of similar touches are intrinsic to their story. Yet it seems to me that this one brief moment takes Lizzie out of the ordinary crime story and into the realm of Aeschylus.

Lizzie had achieved nothing by killing her rival; she had only given her far more power than she had ever possessed alive. Perhaps some hate for Andrew, too, was mixed with that awful, defeated awareness of Abby's final victory. The more deeply we love, the more furiously we can, on occasion, hate the beloved. But I do not see hate, even jealous hate, as the motive for Lizzie's second murder.

I think that she could not bear to lose her father's love. She had to keep it unchanged; and now there was only one way that she could keep it unchanged.

We say that love has many faces (though more accurately we should say that in our English language love is a furry word, capable of many definitions). Yet, within one definition, I do not hesitate to say that Lizzie murdered her father out of her love for him.

Lizzie was on her way downstairs when Andrew came in. She followed him into the dining-room, where he had gone to be out of the way of the window-washing. She spoke to him, hesitated. She took off her hat and laid it on the dining-room table.

At the trial, Bridget ended the first part of our story: "They had some talk between them that I didn't understand, but I heard her say that Mrs. Borden had a note and had gone out. The next thing I remember, Mr. Borden took a key off the mantelpiece and went up the back stairs."

He did not find Abby lurking there, safely locked in the back of the house, as she might well have been if things had gone wrong. There was no point to going up the front stairs, to Lizzie's part of the house, to look for her; surely it was the last place she would have chosen to hide out if things had gone wrong.

Lizzie was apparently calm, self-possessed, dressed to go out. Yet obviously something *had* gone wrong, for Abby had not turned up at the bank. Lizzie must have overheard the plan and learned about the "note from Mrs. Whitehead." Abby had been afraid of just that and of how Lizzie would act. Yet Lizzie was calm and Abby was not hiding. But the carriage had been standing outside, waiting for her.

Andrew Borden must have been a deeply puzzled man.

Bridget's story goes on:

"When he came downstairs again, I was finished in the sitting room." (Bridget had obviously decided to give the never-used parlor a miss.) "I took my handbasin and stepladder into the dining room. Mr. Borden moved into the sitting room and sat in his rocker. Then Miss Lizzie took an ironing-board from the kitchen and put it on the table and commenced to iron.

"She said, 'Maggie, are you going out this afternoon?'

"I said, 'I don't know, I might and I might not, I don't feel very well.'

"She says, 'If you do, be sure and lock the door for Mrs. Borden has gone out on a sick call and I might go out, too.'

"Says I, 'Miss Lizzie, who is sick?'

" 'I don't know. She had a note this morning, it must be in town.'

"I finished my two windows; she went on ironing. Then I went in the kitchen, washed out my cloths and hung them beside the stove. Miss Lizzie came out there and said, 'There is a cheap sale of dress goods at Sargent's this afternoon at eight cents a yard.'

"And I said, 'I am going to have one.'

"Then I went upstairs to my room. . . . I laid down on the bed. I heard the City Hall bell ring and it was eleven o'clock. . . .

"The next thing was that Miss Lizzie hollered, 'Maggie, come down quick. Father's dead. Somebody came in and killed him.'

"This might be ten or fifteen minutes after the clock struck, so far as I can judge."

We will not understand in detail what happened that morning until we study the inquest—the only two official court copies of which were so promptly spirited away.

Let us only say here that a witness for the defense, an ice-cream man, saw Lizzie come back from the barn, where she claimed to have been just before she called Bridget downstairs.

There was running water in the barn and a vise and some heavy hammers; there was a fire in the coal stove. A hatchet-head can be broken from its handle and the handle burned. But thus far we are not concerned with the possible *modus operandi,* only with the murders *per se.*

As we have said, the Borden case has long been obscured by several false either/or questions. None of them is more confusing than the basic question: whether a sane, well-bred young lady did or did not one bright morning commit a murder for gain in her own home with a househould hatchet.

The time has come, I think, to try to put it another way: could an obsessively jealous young woman, a sufferer from temporal epilepsy, have killed her hated stepmother during a seizure, and her father to prevent his discovery of what she had done?

BOOK TWO

Why Lizzie Was Suspected

Fʀᴏᴍ the moment Lizzie called Bridget from down the attic to the time she finally settled herself in bed for the night, we have many witnesses to her day. Both at the preliminary investigation in Fall River and at the final trial in New Bedford ten months later, their accounts were remarkably full, consistent in themselves, and consistent with one another.

Except for one point: no two witnesses agreed on what Lizzie wore. Doubtless Phoebe Bowen spoke for them all when she brushed off a question at the preliminary investigation with an impatient, "I was not looking for fashions that day." Pressed further at that time she offered a dim and uncertain suggestion that it might have been a white skirt and a blue shirtwaist.

Before the final trial, certain rumors swept the town concerning her husband and a missing note, and Phoebe Bowen was eager to see Lizzie cleared. She offered herself as a witness for the defense and on the stand she vividly remembered the silk bengaline. She was a loyal wife.

It is amusing that the one person who claimed to remember the dress that Lizzie, in all probability, actually wore under the eyes of all those witnesses, believed herself to be lying.

The memories were consistent and detailed, so detailed that I must assure you in advance that I am not inventing as I write. If I quote, if I describe a look, act, or gesture, or even tell what someone was *thinking about,* I am always quoting a witness's memories or making a running digest of actual evidence given in court. One or two touches in this narrative are drawn from the reportage of the preliminary investigation, but most of it, almost all, in fact, comes from the complete trial transcript, that two-thousand-page revelation, my chief source for all such details in this book, and my only source for the words that people speak.

The witnesses for this day supplement one another, and fortunately their memories also overlap, thus making it possible to follow the time-sequence. This enables us to watch Lizzie's changing reactions and to study the gradual development of her alibi.

Bridget had not noticed what time she went up to her room. She lay down. After a while, she heard the City Hall clock strike eleven, and then, "ten or fifteen minutes later" she heard Lizzie "holler." She had not taken off her shoes. At Lizzie's outcry she rushed down the back stairs. Lizzie stood in the entry by the screen-door. Her face was pale.

Bridget started toward the front of the house, where she had last seen Andrew, but Lizzie stopped her: "Oh, Maggie, don't go in. I have got to have a doctor, quick. Go over, I have got to have a doctor."

Bridget rushed across the street. Dr. Bowen was out. Mrs. Bowen promised to send him as soon as she could. Bridget ran back to Lizzie. She had not moved since Bridget left her.

"Miss Lizzie, where were you?"

Lizzie gave her first answer to the question that would be so incessantly repeated: "I was out in the back yard and I heard a groan and came in, and the screen-door was wide open. Go and get Miss Russell. I can't be alone in the house."

She would be alone with Bridget gone on an errand of several blocks, she was not alone with Bridget there, and for all she knew the murderer was still in the house. But Bridget did not ask why Lizzie did not want her there, or a neighbor, or even one of her own friends—Mary Brigham, say, or Mrs. Holmes— but Emma's friend Miss Russell. She got the hat and shawl without which no Irish girl of her time felt decent in the streets. Neither the heat nor the awful situation could alter her built-in reflex, strong as Andrew's when he had garnered the broken lock. Then she hurried off to Borden Street where Miss Russell —who was shabby genteel, though remarkably well-known and well-loved in that money-conscious town—lived in the little cottage by the baker's shop. Bridget, who shopped there for Mrs. Borden, knew the house.

As Lizzie leaned on the wall by the screen-door, she faced the Churchills' old mansion. The Borden's lot had once been part of its side yard, and its kitchen windows were only a pebble-toss away.

Mrs. Churchill, on her way back from market, had just seen Bridget rush to the doctor's house and back again. She was just Emma's age and Emma's friend; the two dropped in on each other often. Now, she thought that somebody at the Bordens' must have been taken suddenly sick. When she had put down her marketing she peered curiously out of the kitchen window. Even through the two screens between them she could see that Lizzie, at the door, was as pale as death.

She spoke to her: "Lizzie, what is the matter?"

"Oh, Mrs. Churchill, do come over. Someone has killed Father."

Mrs. Churchill came to her at once, by way of their two side gates. Lizzie was no longer standing; she had slumped to the bottom step of the back stairs and sat there, her face white and empty. Mrs. Churchill bent down, laying a hand on her arm.[1]

"Oh, Lizzie!" Lizzie did not answer. "Where is your father, Lizzie?"

"In the sitting room."

"Where were you when it happened?"

"I went to the barn to get a piece of iron. Then I heard a distressing noise."

(Not the yard, now; it would take only a few seconds to realize that in such a crowded, busy neighborhood one might have been seen coming back from the barn.)

"Where is your mother?"

"I don't know. She had a note to go and see somebody who is sick, but I don't know but what she is killed, too, for I thought I heard her come in."

She broke off. Mrs. Churchill had not seen Bridget go out

[1] Trial, as for all such details.

again; she assumed that if Abby, too, had been killed Bridget would by now have discovered the body. But before Mrs. Churchill could reassure her, Lizzie fell into a long, confused rambling, a sort of muted hysteria: they had enemies, their milk was poisoned, Dr. Bowen was out. . . .

Mrs. Churchill said: "Lizzie, shall I go and try to get a doctor?"

Lizzie nodded. Addie Churchill ran to the livery stable and gasped out her request that they send off for a physician. (Sensibly, they telephoned the police instead, reporting "some kind of a stabbing row" at 92 Second Street.) She did not think of Dr. Kelly, next door; even in my own childhood the Irish were still at the bottom of the heap. But her hired man, Tom, was out front washing the carriage, and she sent him running for Dr. Changnon; at such a moment, a French Canadian was better than nothing. (However, Tom only found a young lady on the porch who was there to tell patients that the doctor and his family had been called out of town for the day.)

At that moment, Dr. Bowen drew up before his house.

He and Mrs. Churchill found Lizzie once more on her feet, but she had not yet left the door. She stood by the stairs to the cellar and the back bedroom, a danger spot if the murderer had not already escaped, but she seemed too stunned to have thought of it.

"Dr. Bowen, Father has been killed."

"Where is your father?"

"In the sitting room."

Dr. Bowen started off through the dining room. Lizzie took a few steps after him, turned, and came back into the kitchen. She looked faint. Mrs. Churchill got her to sit down in a rocker.

Andrew's body was on the sofa. He had been dozing when he was killed; his cheek rested on a stout cushion, which propped his head just above the level of the arm of the sofa, even with the frame of the door.

His long legs sprawled off the sofa sideways to the floor. He had changed into his customary short house-jacket, but not to the slippers that he always wore with it; his feet were still in their elastic-sided Congress boots.

There was little left of the exposed side of his face. One eye protruded, sliced through. Conscientiously, if needlessly, Dr. Bowen felt for a pulse. Then he stepped back into the dining room, where he found Bridget and Miss Russell standing together.

He said, "Murdered! He has been murdered!" He pushed past them into the kitchen and said, "Addie, come in and see Mr. Borden!"

Addie declined. "Oh, no, Doctor, I won't want to see him. I saw him this morning. I don't want to see him."

Dr. Bowen turned to Lizzie. "Have you seen anybody around the place?"

"I have not."

Then, for the third time the question: "Where have you been?"

"I was in the barn looking for some iron."

She did not mention the groan, the distressing sound. It was as well; the medical examination proved that Andrew would have passed from his old man's doze directly into death from any one of the ten blows upon his head.

Instead, she began again the rambling talk of enemies, yet this time with a difference. She did not remind Dr. Bowen of the family fear of poison. And when in response he only asked where her mother was, she told him about the note, but not, as she had told Addie, that she thought she had heard her come back into the house.

Dr. Bowen asked for a sheet to cover the body. Bridget went for the keys on the mantel. (Her brogue was so heavy that the court stenographer took down *the keys* as *the case;* the transcript is corrected in pen and ink.) But she was afraid to go alone up the back stairs and through the back bedroom to "Mrs. Borden's room," where the linens were kept. Mrs. Churchill went with her; Dr. Bowen did not offer them his protection.

Just as he was covering the body, the first policeman arrived. It was the day of the annual police clambake at Rocky Point; Marshal Hilliard (our chief of police was called Marshal) was operating with a skeleton staff. He sent an inexperienced young officer, Allen by name, to check up. Officer Allen had a sensitive temperament; he took one look at the body and fled, saying that he must put in his report. Asked in court for a description of the body as he first saw it, he could only say, "I noticed how *small* his ankles were compared with the size of his feet."

However, Officer Allen did first check the front door. The night lock and bolt, which Bridget had recently unfastened for the day, were *both fastened again.*

Officer Allen also took a moment on his flight to impress a very large man who was passing by to stand guard at the side door.

Charles Sawyer, though so large, and as it turned out both remarkably unobtrusive and faithful, was of a temperament rather like Officer Allen's own. He was, as he described himself in court, "a kind of ornamental painter, fancy painter." From his post outside the screen-door he could see into the back entry. He could not protect himself from a murderer emerging by way of the stairs that led to the attic, but once he had got into the entry and bolted the door on the flight that led down to the cellar, he felt a little safer. He forced himself to hold his post.

At the same time, Phoebe Bowen stopped by for a word with her husband. His office was in his house, and his wife "kept the telephone."

Lizzie was still in the kitchen rocking-chair. Her eyes were closed, and the pallor that had first startled Addie Churchill had not left her face. Until Mrs. Bowen saw her chin quiver, she thought that Lizzie had fainted. Addie and Alice were hovering over her. Mrs. Bowen, seeing that she was not needed, did not stay. While her memory of Lizzie's costume changed in the ten months before the trial, one memory remained constant. Lizzie's hands lying in her lap had looked freshly washed, perfectly cared for, immaculately white, not at all as if she had just been scrounging for scrap iron in a dusty barn.

Miss Russell did not notice what Lizzie wore; she was too anxious over Lizzie's condition. She did, however, see that the blouse had pulled loose from the skirt in front, as it does when a woman lifts her arms to comb her hair or to reach something on a high shelf. She assumed that Lizzie had pulled it out in a first attempt to loosen her clothing, that instinctive gesture of a fainting woman in a tight-laced age. She began to loosen Lizzie's clothes still further and Mrs. Churchill to sponge Lizzie's forehead.

Lizzie said, "I am not faint."

Miss Russell had been in the dining room with Bridget when Dr. Bowen had asked the now familiar question. At this point, she repeated it in her turn, and when Lizzie only murmured something about the barn she asked, "What did you go to the *barn* for, Lizzie?"

On this fourth run-through, Lizzie became more specific: "I went to get a piece of tin or iron to fix my screen."

(At the trial, Miss Russell emphasized it: "She said, '*my* screen.' " The emphasis was pointless, since a search, carefully overseen by Lizzie's lawyer, had revealed that *no* screen in the house was loose or in other than perfect shape.)

The coal stove in the kitchen was unbearably hot. Miss Russell suggested that Lizzie rest on the dining-room sofa. As Lizzie lay down, she asked Dr. Bowen to send a wire to Emma in Fairhaven. With curiously directed thoughtfulness she asked him to put it "gently," as "there is an elderly person in the house who might be disturbed." It did not apparently occur to her that Emma, too, might be rather disturbed.

As Dr. Bowen left, Bridget suggested that someone go to the Whiteheads' for Mrs. Borden. (Where else, after all, could Mrs. Borden be?)

Lizzie ignored her. Now that Dr. Bowen was out of the house, she repeated for the first time what she had said to Mrs. Churchill just before he joined them, but this time she put it more definitely: she was "almost positive" that she had heard Mrs. Borden come in. Wouldn't they look for her in the house?

It seemed unlikely. She had not been found in the rear of the house, and if she had come in and gone plodding up the front stairs, Lizzie would not have been *almost* positive—she would have known.

Yet they humored her. Bridget hurried up the front stairs, with Mrs. Churchill close behind her. At the turn of the staircase they could see under the guest-room bed to its further side.

The old white calico showed up, even in the darkened room. Bridget ran in and threw open the shutters.

Abby lay face down in a pool of blood. Her big body almost filled the narrow space between bed and bureau. Her head and the nape of her neck were a bloody nightmare. Her "switch" of false hair and an old handkerchief of Andrew's that she used for a dusting rag lay beside her.

Mrs. Churchill came down white and mute.

Miss Russell asked, "Is there another?"

"Yes. She is upstairs."

Lizzie remarked that she would have to get right over to Oak Grove Cemetery to see about things. Her eyes were dry and her voice disturbingly matter-of-fact, as if shock had set her at one remove from actuality.

Mrs. Churchill soothed her. "Oh, no, Lizzie. The undertaker will see to everything for you."

⟫ 13 ⟪

Officer Allen reappeared. He was buttressed by officers Doherty and Wixon, with Officer Mullaly following hard on their heels; but upon learning that there was *another*, he fled back to headquarters without a confirming glance. This time Hilliard took pity on him and excused him from further duty on the case. He himself was chained to his desk that day, deploying his skeleton staff, but he located the Assistant Marshal, a state inspector, and two more officers, Harrington and Medley. Marshal Hilliard did well on that day, when the town's best murder coincided with the yearly clambake.

The Western Union office was only two minutes from the house by buggy. Dr. Bowen got back to the house as the first three police officers arrived. He was accompanied by the city physician, Dr. Dolan, whom he had met on the way. The three officers and the two doctors studied the bodies.

Officer Mullaly was the first to leave the group; he had little interest in criminal pathology. (His court evidence shows him, in truth, for a rather dim-witted young man, though vastly obliging.) Now he asked to see the lady of the house, explaining somewhat needlessly that "it was the Marshal had sent him." Mrs. Churchill took him to the dining room, where Lizzie lay on the sofa. He asked what property Mr. Borden had on him, and learned that it was "a silver watch and chain, a pocketbook with money in, and a gold ring on his little finger." He also asked if there were axes and hatchets in the house; Lizzie told him that there were, both, and "the girl would show them to him."

(The Providence *Journal* first used Dr. Bowen's diagnosis of a butcher's cleaver; Mullaly's guess was correct. From the state of the heads anyone could have seen that the weapon had not been just a knife.)

Bridget took him to the cellar. She produced two axes, one of which had dried blood and hairs on it—a cow's, as it eventually turned out. She went into the fruit cellar, a dampish place, and brought out a claw-headed hatchet, which also bore brown stains (they soon proved to be rust). Then she remembered a box set six feet high on a jog in the chimney. She reached it down and brought out a couple of dusty hatchets that had obviously not been used for a long time.

At that point, Officer Mullaly's powers of criminal investigation gave out; he bore Bridget's harvest into the laundry room and stood guard over it, waiting for further instructions from authority.

Bridget left him, but she did not go back to the others. She sat down on the bottom step of the back stairs inside the screen-door. She was within arm's reach of Mr. Sawyer and she was by nature a talker; but neither of them spoke a word.

Officer Wixon remembered the battlefields of the Civil War. Before Dr. Dolan pointed it out he noticed how Andrew's blood still ran bright and fresh while Abby's was ropy and coagulated; the murderer had hidden in the house for quite a while.

But how had he got away? The front door had been bolted on the inside, and it was unlikely that a murderer would have walked out past the overhanging windows of the Churchills' house, so close, to make a getaway on a busy main thoroughfare like Second Street. Wixon went out of doors and headed toward the back lot. The hasp of the barn door was fastened on the outside; obviously the murderer was not there. Wixon walked back toward the pear trees. Suddenly he caught a glimpse of a man's straw hat behind the high fence. He ran, climbed the woodpile, and got over the fence, tearing his hands on the barbed wire.

The hat covered the head of a laborer sawing wood in the stone-yard that lay behind Dr. Kelly's cottage and lay directly behind the Bordens'. Two other laborers, stonemasons, were also at work. One sinner among them confessed that he had stood upon a saw horse that morning to swipe a pear from an overhanging bough, but it was obvious that the group had committed no graver crime against the Bordens and that nobody could have struggled over the fence unobserved.

Officer Wixon, his palms lacerated to no useful end, returned to the kitchen.

Just then, in accordance with Andrew's last request, John came home to dinner. He came, as mentioned, with alibi oozing out of his ears.

He had spent the morning on Weybosset Street with his sister and a niece "whom he had only seen for a moment or two since his return from the West." He could account for every moment he had spent away from the house. He had even memorized the number of the horse-car that took him home and the number on the conductor's cap. He had noticed any number of little things that could readily be checked. Indeed, he had provided himself with an alibi so much too perfect that it made him at once the prime suspect.

A crowd of neighbors had begun to gather as Uncle John came back. Small knots of people stood staring at the house and talking. But at that point his phenomenal gift of observation failed him utterly. He did not notice them. He did not notice the many male voices sounding from the open windows as he walked beneath them. He did not notice the bulky Mr. Sawyer, still standing guard at the side door and waiting for young Officer Allen to return and let him go home to his dinner. The side yard was narrow, but Morse brushed past Sawyer without seeing him.

He walked to the back lot and stood for some time under the pear trees eating pears, two or three it was first reported by an interested officer who looked down on him from the rear kitchen window, though at the trial Morse claimed that it was about half of one. The point is unessential; the problem is not quantitative but qualitative. Clearly John Morse was far from anxious to go in and discover what was going on.

Two hours or so had been enough for a man of moderate intelligence to realize that his alibi for the death of Abby was not very sound. It is good to think that in time John Morse's sense of real loss on discovering that Andrew had also been killed was somewhat mitigated by his realization that the alibi that had shown for pinchbeck as he downed his pear was, in fact, pure gold.

Eventually, he brought himself to approach the door, to explain to Mr. Sawyer that he was Andrew J. Borden's brother-in-law and be admitted, to pass the mute and statue-like Bridget on the back stairs, and to enter the kitchen. He learned that Andrew was dead, but it was some time before he learned the comforting fact that he was so freshly dead. He walked off in silence. He had liked Andrew; in fact he had been Andrew's only real friend. I do not think that it was fear alone that made him want a few minutes by himself.

But Abby was in the guest room, Andrew in the sitting room, and Lizzie in the dining room. Informal use of the never-used parlor would have been a pointed gesture. It really left no place to hide. Morse returned to the kitchen, where he explained himself volubly to all who would listen.

For two days the public suspected John Morse; then they lost interest. The unwilling police were eventually forced to admit that Morse could not have been on Weybosset Street when he was and have killed old Borden. Nobody has ever wasted a thought on him again. And by Saturday, Lizzie herself would be making headlines in a new and most unexpected way.

Meanwhile Dr. Dolan continued to study the bodies. A police

doctor, he was at once convinced that Abby must have died at least an hour earlier than her husband; not only was her blood thickened, but also even in that heat her fat body had begun to go cold.

Dr. Dolan wondered, too, if there would necessarily be enough blood on the murderer to catch the eye as he now walked the streets. Abby had apparently been hacked by someone who stood astride the body after the first blow (probably the one on the nape of the neck) had felled her. Her blood had spurted forward and not high or wide; there was none on the bedspread just beside her, and of the wall in front of her head only the skirting board was stained. The man would surely have got blood on his trouser legs, but quite possibly nowhere else.

He left the guest room and returned to consider Andrew's body again. Blood had dripped down on the carpet, but there was not a drop on the table near his head. It had all spurted back against the wall, and the pear-shaped drops, their small end toward the doorjamb, showed why the woodwork had received only one splash, at the level of Andrew's propped-up head; the trajectory of the blood had been away from the door. A man need not even have stood sheltered by the wall and have swung awkwardly around the doorjamb to receive no more than one splash, just below the waist.

Nor would that splash have fallen on the clothing in which the man escaped from the house. Andrew's Prince Albert, folded double, was over the arm of the sofa. To prop his long body higher, Andrew had first folded an afghan and put a pillow on top. The Prince Albert was wedged down between pillow and afghan under the ruined head, as if the murderer had pushed it down inside the fold.

Dr. Dolan thought hard about that coat. Even an untidy man would not have wadded it in like that; he would simply have tossed it to one side. And Andrew was not untidy. He was famous for his meticulous neatness and for his methodical habits and his miserliness. There was a coat rack in the hall, a step away; it was unthinkable that a man with a horror of unnecessary presser's bills would not have hung his coat there.

On the other hand, that tall man's long Prince Albert *put*

on back to front, would have shielded a man of average height to well below the knee; the murderer had almost certainly got no more blood on himself from the second murder.

Dr. Dolan went back to the kitchen. Though he eventually talked about all this in two courts, he found nobody to share his interest; instead, much wishful thinking was spent on two raincoats, Abby's "gossamer" and Lizzie's "American cloth," a kind of oilcloth. Plainly, Lizzie could not have worn the Prince Albert when she killed Abby, for the Prince Albert had been seen downstreet at the time. And after the murders she was immaculate.

(On the hill, it was also long considered a relevant fact that Dr. Dolan was Irish, and, as such, biased and untrustworthy.)

Dr. Bowen took only a moment to look at the bodies, so little time, indeed, that he did not even observe, as Officer Wixon the war veteran had, that Abby had died first and by a considerable margin. He assumed—and told the reporters—that Andrew had been killed first. He was in fact thinking less as a doctor than as a long-term neighbor. To one who knew anything of fat, housebound Abby Borden, that story she had told Lizzie about going to visit a sick friend would have shown itself at once for a transparent lie. He began to wander about the house looking into wastebaskets, for it was worth considering that on the day she was killed Abby had been up to something that she wanted to hide from the family.

He could find nothing. At last he began to sound out Lizzie. She was always forthright about her dislike for Abby and would be quick to tell anything that she knew.

Lizzie agreed that it was strange, so strange that she had spent some time that morning looking for the note herself.

Dr. Bowen asked, "Did you look in her pocket?" (Her handbag, he meant; he was antebellum in his speech, and he used the word as in "Lucy Locket lost her pocket, Kitty Fisher found it.")

This, you observe, was an odd question. When a woman goes out, she takes her handbag with her. Moreover, one curious enough to search that small house of many rooms to find and read a letter sent to another could scarcely, in the course of the search, have avoided finding a large dead body as well.

Lizzie did not find the question odd. On the contrary, she admitted promptly and unblushingly that she had even looked in Mrs. Borden's "pocket" with simple intent to read her private correspondence. (However, no commentator on the case ever has found either the question or the answer odd—or worth reporting.)

Dr. Bowen's question may well have been some sort of absent-minded automatism, but Lizzie's answer apparently rang a bell in his mind. He looked at her and fell silent.

Miss Russell (whose friends all remembered her as exceptionally gentle and percipient) said quickly, "Well, then, she must have put it in the fire."

Perhaps Lizzie's pallor had given way to that mottled flush that betrayed her states of inner excitement. In any event, Dr. Bowen suggested rather abruptly that she would be better off lying down in her room. As for himself, he was now going home.

Mrs. Churchill also said, "Lizzie, I am going home now."

Miss Russell took Lizzie through the sitting room, where the sheeted body lay, and upstairs past the guest room, whose door was now closed. Lizzie was silent on the difficult way, but at the door of her room she spoke, placidly.

"When it is necessary for an undertaker, I want Winward."

Winward did all the *best* funerals. Nobody on the hill would have had anyone else, though Miss Russell and Mrs. Churchill, in their modest circumstances, might well have thought him overpriced. Lizzie thought of that sort of thing.

However, it seemed to Miss Russell, who did not think of that sort of thing, that Lizzie was in some more than normal state of shock. The doctor should not have left her, dinner time or no.

She sent Bridget off to fetch him back, and sat down to wait.

⇛ 14 ⇚

Dr. Bowen came back. Alice led him upstairs. Lizzie was just coming out of Emma's little room, the cubby that could be entered only through her own. She had changed into her pink-and-white striped dress, the other new "wrapper"; she was tying the ribbon bow at the neck of its pretty shirred blouse.

Lizzie's defenders, confused by the word "wrapper," present this change from streetwear to housewear as a change to a negligee in which to lie about half-swooning. Her accusers see it as a guilty change from the bloodstained Bedford cord in which she had been lying about during the past hour under the eyes of hovering but strangely unobservant friends. Both notions, of course, are based on that all-obscuring false either/or, cotton *or* silk.

As I see it, the change is self-explanatory. In the first place, that bengaline silk must have been as hot as hell; and in the second place, Lizzie was no longer going out. Your provincial Yankee on coming home from any public occasion will automatically change to "save" her "best dresses."

(Incidentally, when you read Lizzie's own description of her morning, you will observe that it was just as odd for the bengaline produced in court to have been spic-and-span from a morning's wearing as it was that hovering friends saw no blood on the Bedford cord. The bengaline *should* have been creased, sweaty, and streaked with thick dust from the hayloft.)

Yet to date, nobody has ever wondered why she should have been coming out of *Emma's* room. Her bengaline was hung away with all her many dresses in the big walk-in closet on the landing, and she never kept anything in Emma's tiny closet—in fact she had one of the same size in her own room.

The bloodstained Bedford cord was not in Emma's closet, as you will discover; but I think I know what was. I know it from my memory of the days when ladies' dresses swept the floor.

In those days, a run in a stocking did not show; one gave the least thought to one's leg- and foot-wear. The record shows that Lizzie wore black cotton stockings. A woman in trailing skirts, a frightened abstracted woman changing her clothes, could well have overlooked bloodstains on her stockings until they began to stiffen and stick, bloodstains on shoes until she began to change her stockings. Neither would anyone else have noticed them. Yet once Lizzie had noticed them, felt the drying blood stick, she would not have found them nice to wear. She could not risk opening her door with them in her hand; but she could have rolled them for the time being in something—a blanket, say—and put them on the floor of Emma's closet. Let us bear the suggestion in mind, and wait for a piece of hitherto disregarded evidence.

Dr. Bowen gave Alice the nod, and she left him alone with Lizzie.

We shall never know what they said; but since we know what Dr. Bowen subsequently did, let us consider a possibility.

His mind had been running hard upon a missing note, a note that obviously had been explained with a lie. The sisters had never made any secret of the cause of the five years' cold war in the family—the gift of the Whitehead house. A discovery of the proposed Swansea place transfer, a virtual repeat, would have made many think twice.

But Dr. Bowen liked Lizzie; he had seen her immaculately clean, right after she had found her dead father; her odd response to his questions about the note must have struck him, but he was totally disposed to believe in her innocence. In view of these facts, would it be surprising if Lizzie decided to tell him that her father had planned to meet her stepmother at the bank that day in order to make a piece of property over to her; that he had sent Abby a note telling her when everything was ready at the bank so that she wouldn't have to wait around; and that when she found them dead with the note at Abby's side, she had panicked, torn it up, and thrown it in the trashcan by the kitchen entry door—where someone might still find it and have terrible thoughts about her and her parents?

Naturally, Dr. Bowen was never eager to give any explanation of why he destroyed possible evidence, but I think that you will presently find these suggestions worth serious consideration. All we actually know of that private talk, however, is that he gave Lizzie a mild dose of Bromo-Caffeine, a proprietary tranquilizer, and left her just as the Rev. Mr. Buck of Central Congregational came hurrying to her side.

Assistant Marshal Fleet reached the house a few minutes later with the State Inspector and other officers. Since Lizzie had discovered the crime, he went upstairs for a word with her. Young Officer Medley, a rookie in the detective force, came with him.

Fleet knocked, and Alice let him in. Since he was in civilian dress, he introduced himself to the ladies and Mr. Buck. John Fleet was a well-educated, well-bred man with a quiet presence; those who knew him found him a surprising person, he was so far from the common notion of a small-town policeman.

He asked Lizzie when her father had come home.

She told him that it was about half past ten or quarter to eleven. He came in, sat down in the sitting room, and "took out some papers"; she saw that he was "feeble" and "assisted him to lie down": daughterly touches that sound like a rerun from a sympathetic pastoral talk just ended. Then, she said, she started some ironing, but left it at once and went up in the barn.

The stable beside the house was small; it doubtless had a hayloft under its steep-pitched roof, but that seemed so odd a place to have gone on a broiling-hot day that Fleet was not quite sure that he had understood her.

Lizzie repeated: "I mean *up* in the barn, upstairs, sir." She had stayed there for about half an hour. Then she came down, found her father dead, and called Maggie. Fleet asked if Maggie or the visiting uncle might not be involved. Lizzie told him that one had been napping and the other out.

He asked if she could think of anybody who might have killed her father and mother.

"She is *not* my mother, sir, she is my *stepmother!* My mother died when I was a child."

At once, as if Fleet's ill-worded question had disturbed her in a way that needed words, any words, for release, she burst into a rapid-fire story, which she never told again. That very morning *at nine* a man came to the door and quarreled with her father. He sounded like an Englishman. (A Lancashireman, a mill-worker, the word meant in our part of the world.)

As she finished, Miss Russell said, "Tell him all you told *me*."

Lizzie gave her a curious, long look. Then she merely told her previous story of the man who, two weeks back, had tried to rent a store. Alice waited, but nothing more came. Nothing about poison, nothing about that fantastic robbery.

Fleet, as it happened, knew more about that robbery than Alice did. He knew how anxious Andrew had been to have the investigation called off. After a moment of silence, Fleet excused himself and went downstairs. He went to the cellar and made sure that its outer door, the one in the rear wall of the house, was bolted on the inside. Perhaps he had found himself remembering a nail in a lock, of which neither he nor Miss Borden had spoken.

Officer Mullaly was still standing guard over the hatchets and the axes. Fleet asked where they had all come from, and lifted down the box from the chimney jog again.

Lying among the dusty tools was a hatchet-head. It was not dusty, as they were; it seemed to be covered with white ashes. Fleet took it from the box and compared it with the tools that remained there and with the dusty hatchets that had come from the same box.

All the other contents of the box were simply dusty, and far more dusty on the top, exposed, side, than on the bottom, as one would expect when things had lain long in an open container. But the hatchet-head was coated on *both sides* with white coal-ash like that of the ash-heap beside the furnace. It looked as if it had been washed and then dipped while still moist into the ashes by someone who wanted to make it match the dusty contents of the box. It did not match. But the job, though so far from perfect, had at least been overlooked by Bridget and Officer Mullaly.

Something else about the hatchet-head was yet more striking: it had been freshly broken off. The wood showed that unmistakable brightness of a newly sharpened pencil-tip. Detectable blood, in those days, could be washed from metal under cold running water; not from wood. In an hour or so—and the murders had taken place at least that long apart—blood would soak into the wood; it could even leave a stain that would show up noticeably after a washing. A hatchet-head, freshly broken off. . . .

There was a fire in the kitchen stove that could burn a stick. There was cold running water in the laundry and in the sink room—probably out in the barn, too. One smart tap could have broken the handle off. Ash is strong, but it snaps: a baseball bat is ash, and think how it will snap in two and fly across the park.

Several people had noticed John Morse's strange abstraction as he returned to the house, a house he probably knew from attic to cellar. And whoever concealed that hatchet-head knew the house well; that box of dusty tools, up there above the level of a man's eyes, was not found by chance.

Fleet had a good deal to think about as he walked upstairs.

He had further reason to think of the household—and at the start, of Morse—a reason commonly overlooked. Finger-printing had not yet been made legal in Massachusetts; it was still considered an infringement of privacy, of civil rights, discussed just as we nowadays discuss the legal uses of wiretapping. A mad maniac would have had to be very mad indeed—mad in a way that would almost certainly have insured his immediate apprehension—to carry away the weapon rather than simply drop it at the scene of the crime. But a household hatchet, taken from a place where no outsider would have found it, when two axes and another hatchet had lain out in plain sight—that was another matter. A hatchet-head newly broken off, disguised in clumsy counterfeit dust, hidden . . . And a shabby, red-eyed old man who had just spent the night in the house. . . .

≫ 15 ≪

Officer Medley, meanwhile, had gone directly from Lizzie's room to the barn. He was an intelligent young man, just starting out on the career that in time would see him become a detective of high reputation and such an excellent Marshal of our police that even our Mr. Phillips had to accord him the highest praise, despite his earnest attempts to discredit this, Medley's first step on the ladder.

He had gone to the barn because Miss Borden's casual statement that she had spent half an hour in its loft had struck him as most surprising; he wanted to look at the place. It was a one-horse stable with room for both a carriage and a sleigh; in other words, a two-car garage. There was still an old sleigh in it, which had not been sold off with the horse and carriage. Just inside the door, along with an old vise and some yard and carpentry tools, was a smallish wooden box of assorted scrap, bits of broken metal, door knobs, old locks, a folded sheet of lead. Steep ladder-like steps without rails ran up to the hayloft.

Medley climbed them part-way and stared about, his head and shoulders above the floor of the loft. Under the steep-pitched roof a man could stand upright only in the small strip in the center. The sun was overhead, and the air in the loft was ovenlike. There was nothing in the place but a pile of hay and a workbench, which had one or two boards and a wicker basket on it, apparently full of odds and ends like the box down by the door.

Dust lay thick on the floor, on everything; five minutes in that place would leave you streaked with sweat and grime. Medley stared at the floor. He bent forward and laid his hands, palms down, in the dust. He backed down the ladder until his eyes were at the level of the floor, and looked. His hand-prints showed plainly, but elsewhere the dust lay undisturbed; neither feet nor trailing skirts had crossed that floor for a long time.

Medley hurried back to report to Fleet. Fleet was busy and preoccupied; he thanked him, assured him that he would check up promptly, and instructed him to catch the 12:29 to Providence and come back with State Detective Seaver. But Fleet let himself be detained by other things too long; he did not get to the loft until mid-afternoon. The heat was still stifling and the dust still thick, but others had been there first, and Medley's palm-prints were obliterated.

One other officer questioned Lizzie that day. Mr. Buck had just left Lizzie to fetch her Mrs. Holmes, her spiritual mother at Central Congregational. Officer Harrington had just finished his own examination of Mrs. Borden's body; as he stepped out onto the landing he saw Miss Borden's door ajar, and asked Miss Russell if he might come in for a few words.

Alice closed the door after them as he entered. Lizzie stood facing him at the foot of the bed. With Mr. Buck gone from the room, her manner was not quite the same. To Officer Harrington's request that she tell him what she could she answered shortly: "I have nothing to tell you, sir."

He asked when she had last seen her father, and she replied, "When he returned from the post office with a small parcel in his hand and some mail. He sat down to read the paper and I went out to the barn. I stayed there for twenty minutes and returned and found him dead."

It is interesting to watch Lizzie's inch-by-inch censorings as she has time to think. She spoke of the robbery to nobody but Alice, of poison to nobody after her first words to Addie. Now "some papers," of which she spoke to Fleet, have shown themselves a dangerous notion and become "the newspaper," and her stay in the loft has been shortened by ten minutes.

Harrington asked if she had not heard anything. The stable was only a step from the kitchen door. Could she think back? Perhaps a door had slammed?

"No, I was up in the loft."

Her manner puzzled him. ("It was cool," he said in court, but was checked by an objection sustained.) He shifted to more general questions. Could she think of anyone who had a motive to kill her father? Did she suspect anyone?

"No ... I do not."

She had paused before she answered. He said, "Why hesitate?"

She told again about the man for whose unspecified purposes her father did not want to let a store. He had come twice; the last time was two weeks before. In this version she heard them not at the door but "in another room." And with a conscience we may respect she cleared the loud-voiced English hatter Mr. Clegg. His Tuesday call would be discovered, and in talking to Fleet she had carelessly implicated him. Yet now she took pains to do as much for him as she had done for Bridget and even for Uncle John, for she ended, "But before they separated I heard my father say, 'When you are *in town again,* I will let you know know about it.' "

From that time on the "enemy" remained an out-of-towner whenever Lizzie spoke of him. A cramped, false world made Lizzie Borden, but she had her code.

However, as she told this story her manner was so distant that Harrington interpreted it much as Alice had interpreted her calm request for the superior services of Winward. He felt called upon to caution her, since she would certainly recover and want to say more, perhaps to contradict her present statements to her own undeserved detriment. He told her that "owing to the atrociousness of the crime," she might be confused, and that she should wait until she was in better condition to tell what she knew.

Lizzie gave him a stiff little bow. "No, I can tell you all I know now as well as at any other time."

Harrington tried to make himself clear; wasn't it, for example, difficult to place the time she had spent in the barn so accurately? Mightn't it have been fifteen minutes, or half an hour?

Lizzie said, "No, sir. I was there *twenty minutes.*"

Officer Harrington bowed himself out.

As he came into the kitchen, Fleet was in conversation with Dr. Dolan and the state inspector. The other officers stood together, waiting for instructions. Dr. Bowen stood apart from the rest, in the door of the kitchen entry at the head of the cellar stairs.

He was busy at an odd task, which caught Officer Harrington's eye. The scraps of a penciled note, torn very fine, were in his hand, and he was trying to fit them together like a jigsaw puzzle and read them.

Officer Harrington asked what he had found.

Dr. Bowen said, "Oh, I guess it is nothing."

He crossed the room hurriedly and stood by the stove, which stood against the further wall. He went on trying to read. Harrington, bending over, saw the penciled word *Emma* on a scrap torn from an upper corner.

Emma, Harrington knew, was the elder daughter; his curiosity was heightened and he asked again.

Dr. Bowen's reply was of a remarkable vagueness. "Oh, it is nothing, it is something, I think, about my daughter going through somewhere."

He lifted the stove lid and dropped the scraps upon the burning coals.

Thrust far back in the stove, Harrington saw a roll of papers, charred through but still holding their shape; a roll of about the shape and size that an Irish servant might well have described as being "the same as a paper or a book." A stick laid on that fire would have burned away, but paper, as you have noticed in your own fireplace, is often surprisingly stubborn. It will burn through and still hold its shape until a touch crumbles it.

The torn-up note was not the only paper that had been burned that day.

Dr. Bowen at once fell into general conversation with Dr. Dolan.

Perhaps Dr. Dolan also noticed this episode, though he never testified in any way that might have embarrassed his colleague. In any event, just before he left the house he, too, asked for a word with Miss Borden; and it was only to inquire if she knew what had happened to the note that came for her mother. Lizzie told him that her mother had burned it in the stove. She said so matter-of-factly, without comment. Once more the belated caution was working. She never again suggested as she had to Dr. Bowen that she found her stepmother's story at all unusual or that she had looked for the note herself.

In connection with all this paper-burning, it is well to mention here that the broken lock that Andrew had picked up from Mr. Clegg's floor and dropped in his pocket was found on the mantel. It had been rolled in an unaddressed white mailing wrapper like those that lay in a stack, the top few addressed to Andrew, on a small table in the sitting room. It was a strange way for Andrew to have wrapped a lock, a long roll that could almost have been taken, at first glance, for a roll of documents. Yet, despite the prosecution's attempt—by way of Bridget's evidence—to cast doubt on the notion that what Andrew brought home in his hand was really the lock, I have never seen it doubted by later writers. Even those most convinced of Lizzie's guilt have accepted it for just that, up to this day.

Why Andrew—granted that he got an odd urge to *wrap* the lock he had just pocketed—did not ask Mr. Clegg to spare him an ordinary bit of wrapping paper is a question never raised. I have actually seen it suggested, however, that Andrew rushed to the post office, where unaccountably unrecognized by so many who knew him by sight, he cast his thrift to the winds and *bought* a single unaddressed mailing wrapper so that he might take the lock from his pocket and carry it the couple of blocks home in style!

We do know why there were mailing wrappers *in his house*. The family subscribed to the Providence *Journal,* a solid, conservative, well-written sheet, to which my own family also subscribed. To insure its proper delivery, it came in a wrapper bearing the subscriber's address. This wrapping, if done by the dealer, cost extra. The thrifty method was to supply the newsdealer with wrappers that one had preaddressed.

This Lizzie did for her father; she was justly proud of her handwriting, for every scrap of it that has been saved is as bland, inhuman, and void of character as the sample lines that used to be printed at the top of the old Palmer-method copybooks.

She did this at the big desk in her room. Not only did she sit up there by preference, but also there was no proper place to write in the sitting room; The tables with their crocheted table covers had no function beyond holding a kerosene lamp or a never-filled fancy vase and similar genteel clutter.

But that morning the paper wrappers had got downstairs from the desk in Lizzie's room. We shall meet them again at the inquest, for like the hat on the dining-room table, they were details upon which nobody wasted much thought but Lizzie, whom they haunted. She dragged them in, clues to a sorry story that has been buried for seventy-five years in that sea of sand, her inquest testimony.

It is possible—though there is no proof of this on the record— that the first suggestion of penny-pinching Andrew's having bought that stylish wrapper for his broken lock at the post office came from Lizzie herself. It does accord with her style— or, rather, her lack of style—as a liar. For she very much wanted to explain why the paper wrappers happened to be downstairs, and though many witnesses had been at the post office who knew Andrew by sight, and not one had seen him, Lizzie herself is on the record as saying firmly, not once but *three* times, that he went there that morning before he came home to die.

Yet, to do Lizzie's intelligence justice, she had a point in so laboring her explanation of those paper wrappers. The D.A. never got wind of the Swansea place transfer; but doggedly and in the face of overwhelming evidence, he did cling to the end to the notion of a missing will.

⇛ 16 ⇚

Before mid-afternoon, State Detective Seaver arrived. It had already become necessary to post a guard before the Bordens' fence. The street was packed solid. When the news reached the mills, an amazing number of workers walked right off the job, to stand in Second Street and stare.

It was a strange crowd that filled the block. There were sometimes a thousand gathered at one time, but they were hushed, almost noiseless, just standing and looking at the house.

Seaver walked about studying the set-up. No signs of struggle, of panic, of attempted flight—only two people slaughtered, an hour or two apart, one asleep, but one awake and equally unprotesting. A search of the house and barn under his direction uncovered no weapon other than those that had been already found. Finally the only two rooms that had not been searched were Lizzie's, Emma's, which opened out of it, and the upper hall closet to which Lizzie had the key.

Fleet hesitated to disturb Lizzie again, but at last he went with two officers, Wixon and Doherty, and tapped on her door.

Dr. Bowen opened the door about eight inches and stood in the opening, as Fleet put it, "as if he was holding the fort. . . . I didn't know but what Lizzie might be sick or something the matter, he was so afraid about it."

Dr. Bowen asked if the search were necessary, closed the door, consulted with those inside. Then he opened it again with obvious displeasure. Fleet explained that a brief look around was necessary. Lizzie asked him to be quick: "All this is making me sick."

According to Alice Russell, who was also in the room along with Mrs. Holmes and Dr. Bowen, they were quick. They glanced behind the curtain that hung before the washstand, but examined nothing. They looked under the bed and felt it, and repeated the same process in Emma's room.

A bundled-up blanket lay on the floor of Emma's closet. They had to push hard on the door to close it again, but they did not examine the bundle.

(Alice mentioned this at the trial, as she mentioned the fact that Lizzie was just coming out of Emma's room when she first brought Dr. Bowen back to her. Alice's conscience forced her to *mention* things at the trial, but not to *stress* them; for she loved Emma Borden, and felt for her. And that quietly mentioned bundle on the floor has received no comment in print from that day to this.)

Now the police asked Lizzie for the key to the big closet on the landing, and she gave it to them. Both Alice and Mrs. Holmes followed the police into it, to oversee the search. A dustcloth covered some of the dresses less often worn; the police felt along the walls, made sure that nobody was in hiding, and returned the key to Lizzie.

Once more Fleet asked Lizzie if she still thought that she had been in the loft for a full half-hour. Perhaps she remembered how positive she had been with Officer Harrington about her stay of twenty minutes exactly, for she answered: "I don't say half an hour; I say twenty minutes *to* half an hour."

Earlier, he had only asked her when she had last seen her father; now, being careful to use the right word, he asked her when she had last seen her stepmother. Lizzie replied that she had last seen her *at nine*, making the guest-room bed.

(This was the only time she ever admitted to having seen Abby anywhere but downstairs, waving her feather duster according to her invariable after-breakfast routine. It was a slip, like the man at the door "this very morning *at nine*." *At nine*, when a neighbor to the left saw the front door opened and slammed in a young man's face.)

Fleet then tried to take his leave by the door to the rear of the house; Alice explained that it was bolted on the far side. The police disturbed Lizzie no more that day, and while they eventually came back and searched the house thoroughly, they asked her no further questions. Though the defense tried hard to obscure the fact, their questions had been brief, tactful, and given only in the presence of her friends.

We owe what else we know of the afternoon to Alice Russell.

Not once but twice after the police left her room, Lizzie took the key and slipped out to the hall closet, as if to reassure herself that the police had left it in order. Alice did not stress this detail in court, as she did not stress the bundle on the closet floor, but, again, she was impelled to *mention* it.

Alice was Emma's intimate friend, not Lizzie's; so from time to time she tactfully left Mrs. Holmes and Lizzie alone and moved about downstairs, tidying up. She brought up Lizzie's hat, and some handkerchiefs that had been lying beside the ironing board on the dining-room table. There were five or six of these,[1] two or three only sprinkled and not yet pressed. Lizzie told her to hang them on the rack in Emma's room.

Mrs. Holmes left in the late afternoon. Emma did not get back until evening. If she had left Fairhaven at once she could have been by Lizzie's side before one. Perhaps Dr. Bowen's telegram had been overcautious: not to "disturb" the "elderly person."

The police set a guard to make sure that the maniac did not attempt reentry during the night, and went away. It was after suppertime when the large and faithful Mr. Sawyer, still at the back door, spoke timidly to the officer on watch. He was very tired, he had not even got his noonday dinner, and Officer Allen had not yet come back to set him free.

It was the first murmur to come from that pathetic, outsized Casabianca. He was released, with apologies.

Bridget was afraid to sleep in the house. The policeman took her across the street to sleep with "the girl at Miller's" in the other half of Dr. Bowen's house. Alice Russell offered to stay with the sisters for as long as they wanted her.

That night, and the next, she slept in the Bordens' room. For the first time in five years, the door into Lizzie's room stood unlocked.

For the first part of the night it also remained open. The three women retired within comforting speaking distance of one another. It was only after an oddly disturbing occurrence, which took place before Alice had got to sleep, that she closed the door between her room and Lizzie's.

A full understanding of just how odd the occurrence was demands a brief, nostalgic digression on the uses of the slop pail.

One younger than I, who has never lived in a country house with only one toilet, might be struck by an omission from Bridget's carefully detailed account of the murder morning: nobody coming downstairs went to the water closet. Andrew emptied his slops on the grass and went out to garner pears. Morse stayed in the sitting room from six to seven unseen, though to visit the cellar w.c. he would have had to pass Bridget in the kitchen.

---

[1] Alice's count; Lizzie said eight or ten—a small ironing, either way.

Mrs. Borden also ignored the cellar on first rising. Only Lizzie ever claimed to have used it that morning, and she made the claim only under pressure of circumstances, at the inquest.

The reason for this general indifference was simple. A covered china chamber pot stood under every bed. Customarily, in the morning the contents were poured into the slop pail, the pots rinsed from the washstand pitcher, and the rinsings also poured into the slop pail. One used the water closet for two purposes: to defecate, and to give menstrual napkins a preliminary rinse—if, that is, either operation had to be performed by day. Otherwise, the covered pot and slop pail were more thoroughly cleansed and emptied when the room was made up in the morning.[2]

The birdseye linen napkins of that time I remember well as the burden of my budding womanhood. They were slightly longer than a baby's diaper, and thicker. Once given their preliminary rinsing in the water closet, they were stored away, usually in a container kept under the set-tubs in the basement, to await their proper washing. In a house like the Bordens', which had no hot running water, this entailed not only bringing out the scrub board but also heating up the copper on the washroom stove as well. This was a part of the task that many of that day, wholly lacking, it seems, in empathic fastidiousness, left to the servant.

But all this, I repeat, was daytime work. Slop pails were tall, their covers tight and weighty, and napkins soiled at night could soak in them as well as anywhere else.

That night, Alice heard Lizzie going downstairs alone; going quietly, as if she did not want to disturb Emma's rest. The bodies, sheeted, now lay in the dining room. Alice joined Lizzie quickly and carried the lamp for her, since Lizzie was carrying the slop pail.

Lizzie went into the water closet, and after a moment or two came out and started toward the laundry room.

Officer Hyde, standing guard outside the cellar window, had

[2] On the night that Abby and Andrew were continuously and actively sick neither went down to the w.c. They had a slop pail. Lizzie told of hearing them vomit into it.

seen the lamp going downstairs; now, as he looked in, he could see both women.

At the door of the laundry Alice shrank back and went no further; the Bordens' bloodstained clothes lay in a heap on the laundry floor. Alice was shaking; to Hyde she looked badly frightened. Lizzie did not hesitate. She went to the sink, where she rinsed out the slop pail. Alice did not look in or watch her there, but the policeman saw Lizzie stoop and thrust something, he could not see what, into the cupboard below the sink.

Then they went back upstairs.

Alice closed the door between their rooms and read the newspaper by lamplight for a little. In her testimony she did not indicate that she did so to steady her nerves, or mention the fear that the policeman had observed. She merely said that she herself had waited outside the washroom.

Yet Lizzie had been in a strange mood the night before, when she rushed in on Alice saying, "I am afraid that someone will *do* something." Is it possible that it had occurred to Alice that a woman could cleanse herself of blood very easily by dipping birdseye linen napkins, so absorbent, into a pitcher of cold water on a washstand? Not her dress, no; but at least her hands and arms, her face, the front of her hair. . . . It is hard to sleep with the voice of blood in one's room.

It is also hard to think everything out properly at a moment when one has been taken by surprise, as Lizzie was when Andrew came home so soon. A hatchet could stand concealed by unsurprisingly stained napkins in a tall slop pail unless it were being most carefully—and indelicately—searched for; and when Lizzie, in her hat and silk dress, went downstairs to greet her father, she had not yet, by her own account given later, *put a stick on the fire.*

Incidentally, one does not freshen a coal fire by laying a single stick—or several—atop it; one shakes it down a bit, adds coal, and opens the draughts. But Lizzie was better at remembering details than at explaining them away; she was also better at remembering them than at judging whether or not they needed to be mentioned and explained away.

Fortunately for Lizzie, her narrative style was so lethally dull that nobody has ever bothered with those details.

We still need those details with which to reconstruct the death of Abby; Lizzie will give them to us in four days, at the inquest. But Dr. Dolan, with his ruminations about the Prince Albert wadded under Andrew's head and the trajectory of Andrew's blood; Fleet, with his study of the hatchet-head freshly snapped from its handle, dipped moist into white ashes so as to look almost like the dust on the two other hatchets in the box where it lay, and set high on the chimney jog; Alice, with her story of the slop pail; and Officer Hyde, who saw Lizzie stoop like a woman routinely placing her fresh-washed menstrual napkins in their container beneath the set tubs—routinely, except that she did it by night—these four have given us almost as much as we need for a reconstruction of the death of Andrew.

People have made much of those Judas-like hoverings with which Lizzie coaxed Andrew to take a nap. She told Fleet about them; so far as we can trust her uncle Hiram C. Harrington—which is not far—she also told him about them the next day. She denied them at the inquest, and I think that her denial was the truth, though it was very likely triggered by Uncle Hiram's dry comment that she was not usually "given to such daughterly attentions." Indeed, such hoverings would have startled Andrew, for they were not a demonstrative family.

But I disbelieve them because I believe that Lizzie loved Andrew Borden. She could have killed him; it was the only way she could keep his love from changing to horror. I do not believe that she planned even one step of the way ahead; I only see her as taking advantage of an opportunity.

Andrew came home looking for Abby. She was not downstairs; all the rooms except for the always closed-off parlor were visible through the open doors. He moved away from Bridget at her window-washing into the dining room, for Lizzie was coming downstairs dressed for the street, and he wanted privacy when he questioned her. Lizzie, as Bridget said, "spoke very low," but she told him that Abby "had gone out. Somebody was sick."

He did not believe her, and went up the back stairs to find Abby, where she must surely be, in their bedroom. The bedroom was empty. Could Abby have simply changed her orders to the young man with the buggy and fled to Mrs. Whitehead's? With Lizzie so calm, that could not have seemed likely. If there had been a row, it would now be his turn to hear a word or two —when Lizzie was angry she did not get over it quickly, and she did not try to hide her feelings.

As he moved back from the dining room to the sitting room, once again to avoid Bridget, who had just come in upon them with her handbasin and stepladder, Andrew Borden must have been a deeply puzzled man.

He began to go through with the automatic gestures of home-coming, which he had forgotten in his first abstraction. He changed the Prince Albert for the cardigan jacket on the hall rack; however he did not as usual change from his elastic-sided Congress boots to his house-slippers. He came back and sat down in his rocker. These are attested facts.

Then, I think, he moved restlessly to the sofa.

He was seventy, it was hot, he was convalescent from what sounds like twenty-four hour intestinal flu; he folded the afghan to prop the pillow higher, turned sideways, stretching out those long thin legs, with their delicate ankles, laid his cheek on the cushion, and dropped off, in mid-puzzling, into an old man's snoring nap.

So he was found. And what is likelier than that he signed his death warrant with the first of those snores?

Lizzie had shown eagerness to get Bridget out of the house for her "day off." She warned her to lock up when she left, since Lizzie intended to go out first. The prosecution thought that she wanted Bridget away so that she might murder her father. I think that she only wanted to give Bridget, whom she liked, who liked her, an alibi for the death of Abby like that which she still hoped against dead hope to provide for herself—for Lizzie was strangely long in realizing that the time of Abby's death could be medically determined.

I do not for an instant believe that when Lizzie came downstairs dressed for the street she was proposing either to lull her father to sleep or to pursue him, a long-legged man still active for his years, with a hatchet.

He fell asleep not knowing what had happened.

But Lizzie knew that he could not fail to understand what had happened if he woke and found Abby. She was beside herself. He was asleep, Bridget had gone upstairs to lie down, she was alone with him. The temptation was terrible, and Lizzie, who loved Andrew too much, Lizzie who was known to dread disapproval over even the most trivial matters, Lizzie who could not bear rebuff even from a child, could not withstand it. She could not let him wake, find out, *look* at her.

A blind anguish must have driven her as she stole out into the hall, locked and bolted the front door again, slipped up to her room for the hatchet in the slop pail; as, coming back down, she saw the Prince Albert on the hat rack, reached out and, sheltered out of sight of the door, slipped it on back to front like a huge butcher's apron, listened once more for Andrew's rhythmic snores, and tiptoed closer.

A strength born of terror could have held her up after she had given those blows, so much weaker and more uncertain than those that killed Abby and half as many; until she had washed and broken the hatchet in the barn, thrust the stick into the burning coals, and tried to make the new-washed hatchet-head match the contents of that seldom-used box of tools high on the chimney jog.

A panic caution could still have supported her while she thrust the incriminating roll of papers into the back of the stove, fumbled in the pockets of the Prince Albert for further possible incrimination, found only the broken lock—and finding it, realized that it had to be the explanation of what he had brought home in his hand; while she hurried to snatch up the stack of mailing wrappers, only a few of them as yet addressed, from her desk; while she fumbled out an unaddressed one as she came back downstairs, with which to make that absurdly unconvincing and never questioned simulacrum of "a paper or a book"—or a roll of documents.

She could have done so much, and done it quickly; and she had half an hour to do it in. But she had loved Andrew; she could not also have found the strength to go out downstreet in one final attempt to create an alibi.

Andrew was dead. She knew what she had done. She could only lean on the wall and keep herself spotless—so unconvincingly spotless for a loving daughter who had just found a father dead in his blood.

Immaculate—tragically unconvincing, lacking all dramatic sense. Yet, to her great good fortune, she would be tried by people as lacking as she was in creative imagination.

That is how I think it happened. When you have heard her out at the inquest you may judge for yourself. But here and now, I think we should do her a favor that even her warmest defenders have never done her; we should really think about her final alibi: that fresh and cool, untouched by dust or sweat, she had spent from twenty minutes to half an hour in a dusty hayloft, a place where, as she herself admitted at the inquest, the windows were closed and the heat intense.

It has always been assumed that she made this fantastic claim because it was the only spot from which she could not see the murderer escape by the sole door that was not bolted on the inside. This is not true; the D.A. overlooked something. She could have claimed that, like Bridget, she felt ill and went upstairs to lie upon her own bed for a little nap. At the inquest she claimed (falsely, as Mrs. Churchill and Bridget proved) that the guest-room door was shut throughout the morning; this would have served to explain how she had lain down in her room without seeing Abby's body as she passed.

Why did she choose the so much less plausible alibi? Lizzie was far from being the ludicrous fool she is often painted by those who find murder amusing. She knew that dirty loft and its heat. She was too sensible to try to twist the facts about it, or make it sound a likely loitering place. At the inquest Lizzie knew that this alibi was so hopelessly implausible, absurd, that she made no effort to better it. She only repeated it, stubbornly, over and over.

I grant you that Lizzie had good reason *to have gone* to the "barn." It had running water; water, which still could not wash away all of Abby's thickened blood from the wooden handle. Bridget was upstairs but she might come down unexpectedly, perhaps to empty her slop pail after vomiting again; whether or no she came down, Bridget might have heard running water and a hatchet-handle being broken from its head.

But, does that explain Lizzie's *admitting* that she was out there? The running water, the vise, the heavy hammers, are the sort of details that haunt her testimony as dangerous possible clues; it was not like her to say that she had been out there where the police had found them.

Yet she had good reason to say so. Though the prosecution furiously refused to believe him, the ice-cream man who sometimes made deliveries at her house had seen her coming back from the barn wearing the bengaline with its dark blue background. Her hand, held close to the sweep of her long skirt, would have held the stick and the hatchet-head hidden; he did not see them. But, he had seen *her*.

He had seen her; and Lizzie, quick-eyed with fear of being seen as she took those few steps from stable door to kitchen entry, surely knew that she had been seen. *She had been seen coming back from "the barn" just after her father was killed.*

It was dangerous to mention that place, with its running water and heavy tools, but the risk of having a lie unmasked was greater. She did not, for long, even dare go on saying that she had only been in the yard. She had been seen coming back from the barn, and she must admit it and think of some innocent reason for being there.

Let us think back, and watch her alibi unfold in the growing fear: "I was in the yard—the barn—*upstairs* in the barn." I find it hard to watch that slow realization of necessity, to watch that harsh fear grow, and to withhold all pity.

Those who believe Lizzie guilty have always found her alibi laughable. I do not.

⇒ 17 ⇐

The crowds jammed Second Street throughout the next day. The deaths had been grisly, and Andrew, rich enough in fact, was reputed to be far richer, a legend nurtured by his miserliness, his sharp dealing with equals, and his hard dealing with tenants. So many laborers declared themselves a holiday in which to stand and stare at the house that the mills had to shut down.

Dr. Bowen, waking with those crowds beneath his window, had a delayed reaction. He remembered what the appalling shock of the murders had apparently also driven from Lizzie's mind, since she had not mentioned it to him. It must have shamed him to remember how he had laughed at poor Abby Borden when she rushed to him with an upset stomach, babbling of poison threats. He went at once to make his belated report to the police, who quickly detailed officers to question the local pharmacists about sales of poison.

They struck oil with surprising ease.

Smith's drugstore, at the corner of South Main and Columbia, was only a few minutes' walk from the Borden house. Eli Bence had been its pharmacist for over fourteen years. I knew him by reputation as a solid, somewhat stolid man, who was prosperous and well thought-of in his middle age; I am told that at the time of the trial he was equally undramatic, his sole eccentricity being that he shaved his whole face clean, like the new generation of Harvard students.[1] Lizzie's latter-day defenders sometimes try to blacken Mr. Bence's name; her defense knew better than to attempt it. He was patently, formidably, honest and unimaginative.

---

[1] His photograph in Porter's *The Fall River Tragedy* bears out this eccentricity; of the many whose pictures are there, he is the only man with an undecorated face.

He knew all the Bordens by sight except for the seldom-seen Abby; and Andrew Borden's dressy, pale-eyed daughter Lizzie was almost as unmistakable as gaunt old Andrew himself.

That hot Wednesday mid-morning he was standing in the door of his shop wth two acquaintances named Hart and Kilroy when Lizzie approached them and asked him to step inside. She had a sealskin "cape" with her—that is, a collar with a semi-circular shoulder flare. I still have one like it in my attic; it was my grandmother's. They were the popular "little fur" of the period, small enough to be turned lining side out and carried through an August street in an inconspicuous roll.

She asked for "ten cents' worth of prussic acid" with which to clean its edges. It was a startling request. So far as Mr. Bence knew, prussic acid had no use except in minuscule amounts in certain doctors' prescriptions. Summer furs were then unknown, they were in a heat wave, and the great selling point of sealskin is its natural immunity to moths (insect eggs do not hatch in it). Furthermore, the stuff was not even sold as a poison; people who wanted to get rid of rats or unwanted animals bought arsenic.

Mr. Bence refused Lizzie's ten cents.

Lizzie protested. She had *often* bought ten cents' worth of prussic acid to clean her sealskins.

Mr. Bence merely said, with flat finality, "Well, my good lady, it is something we don't sell except by prescription, as it is a very dangerous thing to handle." [2]

Lizzie walked out of the shop.

The police, having heard Mr. Bence, came back to begin a far more thorough search, this time for a bloodstained dress. Dr. Dolan came back to do a partial autopsy in the dining room, where the bodies still lay. Amazingly, in that heat, they had not yet been taken to the city morgue, let alone to Winward. And Lizzie sent for the family lawyer, Andrew J. Jennings.

Mr. Jennings was very neat, not tall, and in those days wore a pointed beard. The Providence *Journal* characterized him more than once as "nervous," and he was that, I think. But he

[2] Bence's deposition, shown to the judges only, at the final trial (full transcript).

was also upright. My family always spoke of him with admiration and sympathy.

He had total faith in Lizzie at the time of the murders; but faith did not make him foolhardy. Obviously, as few people as possible should learn of Lizzie's silly mistake about the uses of prussic acid, and as many as possible should learn of her true attitude toward her parents.

His first advice that day seems to have been sound.

The sisters put an advertisement in the local papers offering five thousand dollars' reward for the apprehension of the murderer; this, at the buying power of 1892's tax-free dollar was far more than it sounds today. They also quickly invited Mr. Almy to be Andrew's chief pallbearer. Mr. Almy and his close friend and partner Mr. Milne were joint owners of the Fall River *Evening News,* and the *Herald,* which was the morning voice of the establishment.

I remember Mr. Almy and Mr. Milne. When I lived on the northeast corner of French and High, they lived respectively on the southeast and southwest corners: Mr. Milne gray and silent; Mr. Almy ruddy, loud, and likeable. Mr. Almy was related to the Almy who had been half of Almy and Borden, Undertakers, in the leaner days. Both he and Mr. Milne were friendly in-group neighbors of Mr. Jennings.

The Fall River *Globe,* unfortunately, was edited by Democrats; a similar invitation to its editors was impossible. However, it was a morning paper. On that day, rumor did not drip down to the masses, though its fumes rose to the hill.

Mr. Buck also hastened to Lizzie's side, as did Mrs. Holmes, this time with her banker-husband in tow. And so, for the only time he was ever known to visit the house, did Mr. Jerome Borden, who was, with the possible exception of Mr. Hezekiah Brayton, the town's ranking socialite, the pinnacle of the hierarchy. He had to fight his way through crowds to get to the house, but he came as soon as the rumor about Mr. Bence reached him.

His call was a showy indication of the prompt huddling-together that I mentioned at the start, as if our families were all on trial together. (That I broke out of this huddle after a mere forty years away from Fall River perhaps can be explained by the admission that my mother was actually an outsider, always; in fact, a *Bostonian*. Tainted blood will tell.)

Hiram C. Harrington, the blacksmith uncle with whom Emma had stubbornly kept in touch, also called that day; it is to be feared that his motives were less pure.

Lizzie often had to excuse herself from the police search to speak with her callers, but Mr. Jennings stayed on hand to oversee the whole procedure. And throughout, Lizzie was highly cooperative; at one point she helped the police open a tricky lock on a trunk and asked, "Is there anything else I can do for you gentlemen?"

But by the end of the day, the police had found no blood-stained garment. The search squad left, saying that they would not return next day until after the funeral.

Lizzie's defense took Mr. Bence very seriously; they managed to exclude his evidence from the final trial. Her latter-day defenders show more ingenuity. Speaking as a local, and as one older than she likes to admit, I find the most startling suggestion among those recently published that which claims Mr. Bence was approached with a request for this unusual insecticide by a lady who was en route to New Hampshire, via the New York boat, which docked in Fall River.

The lady had jumped the gun on fashion by some forty years; as a present-day New Yorker might carry a mink stole, she carried a sealskin shoulder cape for cool northern evenings. (Girls, then, used cloth jackets, old ladies' cashmere shawls, for out-of-season chill.) She found moths in it; since it is so well known that moths do not breed in sealskin, one can understand that she was shaken.

She was extremely shaken. The New York boat had a prepaid connection with "the boat train" to Boston, from which travelers to New Hampshire transferred to the train from North Station, the train made famous by the whale in the *Just So Stories* who said: "Change here for Nashua, Manchester, Keene, and all stations on the *Fitch*burg line!" However, the hypothetical lady passed up that prepaid connection; she traveled by hack or horse-car to a part of Fall River at considerable remove from both boat and railway depot to rid herself of moths by the drastic means of prussic acid.

This hypothetical lady vexes me. Why didn't she take the waiting "boat train"—only a fifty-minute ride to Boston—and do her shopping around North Station? I have decided, with a provincial's resentment, that it was because she thought the rules for selling such volatile and dangerous poisons would be more lax in a hick town.

Well, as I suggested at the start, people have always tended to become emotionally involved with Lizzie. Her defenders, that is; her accusers have usually preferred to smirk. Both, I suppose, are natural reactions, if you are writing about a legend and not a real woman who lived up the street.

That evening, John Morse attracted attention for the last time. He was the popular suspect, still, with that staring, heavy-breathing crowd in the street—the horse-trader uncle from out West. He must have known it from his morning paper, though he did not know that the police had detailed an armed guard to watch over his movements until his long alibi was all checked out.

The Providence *Journal*, the paper of Andrew's choice, was a conservative old sheet, its front page given over to national and international news. That the Borden murders held the lead column, sometimes four lead columns on its front page, for many days was a tribute to the family's position.

Dr. Bowen had told the reporters that he was "positive" that Mrs. Borden had surprised the murderer at "his bloody work," and had been pursued upstairs, cornered, and slain. (This, as I have pointed out, was a mistake that Officer Wixon—no medical man, but one who remembered battlefields—had not made, even at the start. Dr. Bowen must have been *highly* preoccupied with Abby's story of an anonymous poison threat, since it was so obvious that she died first; Andrew's blood, you recall, was still running fresh.)

Lizzie was referred to with deep sympathy as "the poor girl" who "discovered the terrible deed."

But the visiting horse-trader uncle was not made to sound

attractive or confidence-inspiring, so unkempt and countrified with his "bloodshot eyes, the veins in them prominent." Worse, the reporter had picked up the one flaw in his alibi.

The whole family were bad liars, and there had been something awkward in Uncle John's throw-away line about the niece who had just happened to drop in at his sister's house on Weybosset Street, a niece whom he had not seen for more than a moment or two since his return from the West. Why bother to mention *that?* The reporter decided to get a word with the niece in private, and her account of dear Uncle John, quite different, included a casual mention of their pleasant drive to *Swansea* two weeks before.

Uncle John may have hoped that the wind was soon due to change. He also knew that it had not yet changed and that the crowd outside the house still fully shared the bias of that reporter. They were watching for *him.*

However, he had to get to the post office to mail a letter. The policeman on guard at the gate would have mailed it for him. Yet Uncle John, no impulsive young daredevil but a cautious old Yankee, preferred to expose himself to a crowd that in a flash might have turned into a dangerous lynch-mob. Even a fool would have known the danger.

Uncle John elected to go out alone and carry his letter to the post office himself. Strangely enough, nobody has ever wondered why. The sole explanation of this reckless act that I can recall is that he "wanted a breath of air." It seems insufficient; there was air in the back yard, and a policeman to guard the front gate against intruders.

To me—in the light of our new knowledge about the Swansea place deal and our not totally unsupported assumptions about the hanky-panky in which Andrew had involved Uncle John—it seems that a more convincing suggestion lies ready to hand.

It seems likely to me that John V. Morse felt it worth bodily risk to make sure that the young man who had driven the buggy and delivered the note "from Mrs. Whitehead" understood that it would still pay him well to keep quiet, despite recent dramatic developments. Initially, upon learning he had somehow got mixed up in something big, the young man might keep quiet in fear of getting himself "involved." Morse could not hope that this would last. Mr. Jennings had already suggested running an advertisement in all the papers for the sender of that missing note or the messenger who carried it. (Soon a national weekly was offering five hundred dollars for the name of either—a large sum for a young farmhand of that time.) Uncle John must have found it of the essence to make that young man down in Westport understand that any offer would be bettered by John V. Morse.

Yet he would not have wanted the police to carry such a letter. He knew that he was a suspect. The newspaper had also told him that his ill-conceived gratuitous lie about the niece he had taken over to Swansea was now discovered. It is unlikely that Mr. Jennings, Lizzie, or the police had confided in Uncle John about Mr. Bence: it was possible that, for all he knew, that afternoon's search might have been for his nonexistent suitcase and bloody change of clothes. He must have feared that his outgoing mail would be of interest to the police, and if it were discovered to consist of bargainings over the price of a certain silence, how would that look?

(If, until now, the simple desire for "a breath of air" has sufficed to explain John Morse's Friday night trip to the post office, his trip on the following *Monday*, made—as we shall learn shortly —in flat-footed defiance of a specific request from the Mayor, has never been mentioned, let alone explained.)

In the dark, Uncle John managed to slip out of the house, pass the guarded gate to the side yard, mingle with the crowd, and reach the post office unobserved.

He was not recognized by the crowd until he emerged from its lighted door. At once he found himself being chased by an angry mob, estimated by the police as being in the neighborhood of a thousand people.

He must have been vastly relieved to find that the suspicious police had been keeping tail on him all the time. Officer John Devine got him safely home.

⋙ 18 ⋘

Mr. Borden's honorary pallbearer had been well chosen. On the day that the funeral was held, neither the morning *Herald* nor the *Evening News* found Mr. Bence newsworthy. And the Bordens, of course, did not read the *Globe.*

They did, however, read the *Journal,* and the loyalties of the hill did not bind the leading conservative newspaper of the metropolis, Providence.

Its headlines ran: ENVELOPED IN MYSTERY . . . A CHAIN OF CIRCUMSTANCES FAVORABLE TO THE CRIME . . . DETECTIVES THINK IT IS THE WORK OF A WOMAN.

A cautious sheet, the *Journal* mentioned no names when it reported the attempted purchase of prussic acid by "a woman." But it did what it could to make up to Morse for having spoken slightingly of his bloodshot eyes and his little lapse of memory about his niece: Mr. John Vinnicum Morse's whereabouts at the time of the crime had been fully substantiated, and Mr. Isaac Hastings, with whom he made his home in South Dartmouth, spoke of him most highly.

But without putting it into so many words, the *Journal* also stressed the extreme likelihood of the murders' being an inside job. It detailed the murderer's amazingly fortunate timing: Emma away; the maid out washing windows; the visiting uncle's call on a sister, though on his visits he generally spent the morning around the house and yard; Lizzie's happening to spend just the requisite time, neither more nor less, in the loft of the stable. It told of the neighbors, laborers, hired men out of doors on every side who had chanced to be looking away as a bloodstained, axe-bearing maniac went past.

Mrs. Holmes, after her Friday call, had given the Fall River papers an interview, which contained an interesting touch. That day the police had examined all the screens, and by her report Lizzie had gone both for a piece of tin or iron to fix a screen— as she had been told the day before, like everyone else—*and* for a piece of lead with which to make a fishing sinker.

Lizzie herself never mentioned anything *but* the fishing sinker again.

That fishing sinker had Lizzie's Uncle Hiram C. Harrington bubbling over with malicious glee. He, too, gave the papers an interview on the same day, and it was, to put it gently, nasty. His call on Lizzie delighted him in many ways, but no part of their conversation delighted him more than the fishing-sinker touch. This was not simply because he considered it a barefaced lie; he himself was demonstrably less than bound by facts in that interview, and I think that he would have accorded a grudging respect to a good lie. But, as I shall explain directly, he knew, and all his local readers, acquainted with Lizzie or not, knew at once, that it was a lie manufactured with ten wooden thumbs —hilariously implausible.

However, in the course of time and in the great world, Hiram C. Harrington's joke fizzled, and he won himself a curious, anonymous immortality. For on one point in the Lizzie Borden story at least both her attackers and her defenders are agreed: Lizzie was most enthusiastic about fishing.

As he told it, "She told me that she helped him to get a comfortable place on the sofa.... She pressed him to allow her to place an afghan over his body, but he said that he did not need it." (One hears him chortling at this heat-wave touch, which I expect was his own invention.) "She went directly to the barn to obtain some lead. She informed me that it was her intention to go to Marion on a vacation, and she wanted the lead to make some sinkers; she was a very enthusiastic angler. I went over the ground several times and she repeated the story."

This is the sole source of that bit of information that I have seen so repeatedly stated: Lizzie, an outdoor type, was keen on fishing. At the inquest she admitted that she owned no fishing apparatus, though she had seen some "lines" over at the farm "about five years ago"; but Hiram C. Harrington's printed word outweighs hers.

The word "lines" is interesting. I was a grown woman before I ever saw a fishpole. In our part of the world—Lizzie's and mine —professional fishermen trawled the deep waters with nets. The rest of us fished the shallows of the tidal inlets using a small wooden hand-reel, like four clothespins fastened together in a square, with the fishline wound around it. We let it out idly over the side of the rowboat and took in scup and tautaug—fairly edible—and chogset, to be tossed back. It was a child's, an idling man's game; even in men it woke no strong enthusiasm, and *ladies* had outgrown it. Harrington was relishing, for locals, a joke that any local would have enjoyed. (Even the District Attorney, a New Bedford man, knew better than to ask Lizzie if she owned a *fishing-rod.*)

However, what amazes me about the persistent myth of Lizzie the angler is not ignorance of obscure facts about fishing in that time and place, but blindness to the construction of Harrington's sentence: not "she is" enthusiastic, but "she was," continuing *her* story: thus implying: "she *said* she was."

He went on with zest about that alibi, as well he might have done, since even in my day, hook, line, and sinker came complete for a dime, and if you lost your sinker a nickel would buy you a small fistful of them. He was gleeful—and I am sure, laying it on—as he told of her claim to have spent the time in the barn "cutting the lead into sizable lengths." Yet he was doubtless accurate enough when he gave her time as twenty minutes—corrected, after she had thought, to a possible thirty. And he was probably truthful in reporting that she did not answer when he asked if she had looked for her stepmother and who had found her.

But vastly as he relished the lie about the sinkers, he obviously relished another even more. When he asked if she had any notion of who could have done it, "she said calmly" (a phrase that in our part of the world routinely prefaced an outsized whopper), "A year ago last spring our house was broken into while Mother and Father were in Swansea and a large amount of money was stolen together with diamonds. You never heard of it before because Father didn't want it mentioned so as to give the detectives a chance to recover the property."

She would repeat that last line for the court record; Harrington reported it straight. But there is small wonder that he enjoyed it as much as he enjoyed the bit about the fishing sinkers. Truth can be more implausible than fiction.

Hiram Harrington's interview was long, and most of Lizzie's detractors have found it useful. He talked irresponsibly and at length about what he saw as the obvious motive for the crime—money—and of family quarrels over money that had been "kept dark." Only Lizzie had quarreled, as she was "contentious," Emma "retiring." Of Emma, who refused to drop the Harringtons when Andrew quarreled with Uncle Hiram and Andrew's fortune increased (a double barrier in that financially stratified society), he said firmly, "I am convinced that Emma knows nothing whatever about the crime." Lizzie, the "Congregationalist moving in the best social circles" was clearly portrayed as a greedy social climber.

One who knew the structure of the town would find his interview useful only as the accidental self-portrait of a bitterly envious and resentful man in a society in which Yankee blood *alone* did not ennoble—Lizzie was *in* and the blacksmith uncle was *out*.

Between Mr. Bence and Uncle Hiram, the papers carried little to calm Lizzie on the day of the funeral. They bore the news that Andrew had died intestate, leaving the sisters his sole heirs, but the girls knew that already.

Yet they contained a tribute to Lizzie. After the search for the dress ended on Friday, a reporter from the Providence *Journal* talked to an officer who said that he admired Miss Borden's nerve; she was not the least bit scared or worried and she had seemed the same even the day before. "Most women would faint at seeing her father dead, for I never saw a more horrible sight and I have walked over battlefields where thousands were dead and mangled. She is a woman of remarkable nerve and self-control, and her sister Emma is the same though not so strong."

It was a tribute that Lizzie could have done without. Trembling and swooning was expected from the ingenue in late-Victorian melodrama.

The funeral was scheduled for the early afternoon.

The coffins were placed end to end in the dining room.[1] They were of unfinished wood, masked in black cloth. On Andrew's body lay a wreath of ivy, on Abby's a bouquet of white roses and ferns. Winward had been wisely chosen. Only the back of Mrs. Borden's skull had been shattered, and Andrew had one cheek cuddled into the pillow when he died. Now, turned good side up, Andrew appeared only to repose in a deeper sleep, and the press reported that both looked "wonderfully peaceful."

Mrs. Holmes came to the house early, before the other mourners. Lizzie took her to look at Andrew, at rest with her gold ring on his little finger.

Suddenly, Lizzie bent down and kissed him.

Abby's sisters both came to her funeral, Mrs. Whitehead and the sister who lived in New Haven. Andrew's sister, Mrs. Harrington, did not. Besides the four still living in the house, Lizzie, Emma, Alice, Uncle John, there were only Emma's friend Addie Churchill, Lizzie's friend Mrs. Holmes, who was joined by her husband, and Dr. Bowen, who brought his wife. And, of course, Mr. Almy. Twelve in all, and of those, only two sisters and a brother-in-law were contemporaries come to mourn the two who were dead.

But there were two clergymen. Mr. Buck of Central Congregational shared the services with Mr. Adams, in whose church Andrew had bought his rarely used pew as a gesture of spite.

And there were undertakers' assistants to carry the coffins, so two hearses and eleven hacks made up the procession to Oak Grove, even though Alice and Mrs. Holmes stayed at the house in case the police search should be resumed before the sisters came back.

Lizzie emerged from the house "leaning on the arm of Mr.

[1] Providence *Journal*; a witness, ten months later said, "The sitting room."

Winward." She did not wear black, and even Emma did not wear the customary mourning veil.

A crowd of between three and four thousand had got as close to the house as possible, and the whole line of route to the cemetery was packed, as if for the funeral of a national hero. But the cemetery itself was left decently uncrowded; only a small group of the uninvited were gathered near the open graves.

The coffins were set down. Mr. Buck read: "I am the resurrection and the life . . ." Then Mr. Adams prayed, less for the deceased and the bereaved than for the souls of their fellow townsmen, "that all should be delivered from mistake."

As he fell silent, a shabby old woman pushed forward from the small huddle of the uninvited and knelt by Mrs. Borden's coffin, weeping, rosary in hand. She was led away. She had once been a servant of the family. Abby and Lizzie had one thing in common, at least; those who worked for them liked them.

The moment had come for the bodies to be lowered into the graves, but instead there was a silence, a bending-together and whispering to the clergymen, and the coffins were put back into the hearses.

A telegram had just come from Harvard Medical School asking for the two skulls. The bodies were placed in a receiving vault, and the funeral party disbanded.

⇨ 19 ⇦

Captain Desmond of the detective force and young Medley, who had visited the loft, did in fact get to the house slightly before schedule. At their request, Alice and Mrs. Holmes showed them through the second floor again. They opened the beds and glanced into a few of the bureau drawers; Alice noticed that the blanket was still on Emma's closet floor.

Lizzie, unknown to Miss Russell, had gone back to hooking her bedroom door again; as the party of four moved from the back of the house to the front, the hook got pulled loose, although nobody noticed this until evening, when Alice saw Lizzie screwing it back into place.

I was delighted to find this trivial item in the trial transcript, for at the inquest Lizzie had said that the upstairs was always kept locked "until Thursday when *they* broke the door open." [1] This had disturbed me as an infraction of the rules, for as I have told you, while Lizzie *manipulates* facts, she does not invent out of whole cloth, and Thursday, I knew, everyone knocked and waited. It was a relief to find that the seeming exception to her rule was no exception.

Incidentally, I have read this cited as an instance of police brutality: "Lizzie's room was *broken into*." Similar instances of brutality are notably lacking from the record.

Throughout the previous day, John Morse had asked several times for permission to bury the Bordens' bloodstained clothing behind the stable. As number-one suspect, he was curtly denied. Now, on returning from the curtailed funeral, he apparently felt strongly that *something* should be buried that afternoon, and, having lost status, he was allowed to dig the clothes under properly, while Dr. Dolan stood by and supervised.

It was now three, and the search for a bloodstained garment began again. Assistant Marshal Fleet and State Detective Seaver headed it, Desmond and Medley assisted, and Dr. Dolan followed them to identify possible bloodstains.

Mr. Jennings also came, and since he feared that the police had been biased by Mr. Bence's story, he had hired and brought along detective help of his own, one O. M. Hanscom, a Pinkerton's man from Boston, not to help with the search, but to keep an eye peeled for police trickery.

The five-man squad combed the house from attic to cellar. They moved furniture, upended mattresses, and went through every drawer, box, and barrel in both house and barn.

They were terribly anxious, for Marshal Hilliard had made it plain to them that the Fall River police were in a forked stick. Since the *Globe* and Providence *Journal* had come out that

[1] Providence *Journal*.

morning, the crowd in the street had grown and its temper had changed; if Lizzie were not taken under protective arrest there was real danger of an ugly incident. The police would be blamed for it, and most hotly blamed by Lizzie's own—and it was amazing how promptly all those who had real influence in the town had shown themselves to be her very own. Our huddling-together was real, and powerful.

Hilliard himself wanted to make an arrest; the past two days had shown more and more clearly that sole opportunity had rested with Lizzie, or with Lizzie and Bridget working together. He both feared for Lizzie's safety and doubted her innocence. But he also knew that the group who would blame him if any ugly incident occurred would be the first to bring a charge of false arrest if he took her in custody without the bloodstained dress to show as evidence. It must be found.

And it had to be there, for with two exceptions no member of the family had left the house. Uncle John had gone to the post office and got mobbed, and a policeman had taken Bridget across the street for two nights to sleep with "the girl at Miller's." Bridget's pitifully small wardrobe [2] had been examined the first day, and since she was only on happenstance, neighborhood good terms with the girl across the way, it was vastly unlikely that the girl was passing up five thousand dollars—a fortune to a servant in those days—to conceal *Bridget's* smuggled-out bloodstained dress.

(Bridget would not sleep in that well-locked, police-guarded house, for fear, she said, "that the *man* would come back and kill them all." [3] She named as a possible suspect "the Portuguese from over the river," by which she meant the Swede who ran the farm "over the river" and came to do outside chores. He had brought the bloody axe to the house with which to chop wood after he had used it to dispatch an ailing cow. But I was told by a servant who knew her that she suggested the Swede to disarm Uncle John, whom she suspected for several weeks—indeed, until

---

[2] At the trial it came out that it was "two or three dresses," *not* "half a dozen," as the defense had suggested.

[3] Quoted to Pearson by the officer who escorted Bridget to the inquest.

after the preliminary investigation at which she heard Lizzie's inquest testimony. Until then, the cops could say what they liked, but she knew what Lizzie had always thought of Uncle John and she was terrified that he might go berserk and finish off the job he had begun. (While this is only kitchen gossip, it has to me a certain likely ring.)

No, the bloodstained dress had to be in the house, and to save their own skins, the police had to find it. Fleet, Seaver, Desmond, Medley and Dr. Dolan exerted all their care, experience, ingenuity, to find that bloodstained cotton dress.

They did not find it. To Lizzie's defenders, this has always proved that they examined the blue "wrapper" and found it bloodless. To her prosecutors, it has proved that either the search was sloppy or the five-man squad managed to conceal their findings from Mr. Jennings and O. M. Hanscom.

It proves neither. It proves that they were men. Men saw no details in the inquest testimony to suggest to them that Lizzie had changed her dress. Men did not find its dazzlingly simple hiding place, though that hiding place was almost shouted aloud in court by the head of that five-man squad.

Do you remember the old riddle: "Where does a wise man hide a leaf? In the forest." Do you recall *The Purloined Letter?* Do you also remember that after the police had satisfied themselves that no murderer was hiding in the big hall closet, Alice Russell saw Lizzie, not once but twice, take the key and go out to it alone, as if to make doubly sure that the police had left it in order?

Here, verbatim, is Detective Seaver's court account of his search of that closet after Lizzie once more unlocked it for him on Saturday afternoon:

"Captain Fleet was with me, and I commenced on the hooks and took each dress, *with the exception of two or three in the corner* and passed them to Fleet, he being near the window; he examined them himself, he more carefully than myself. And I took each garment and hung it back, all excepting two or three which were heavy or silk dresses in the corner."

(They are looking, you see, for a cotton.)

"Those *were* silk dresses, I am very sure, heavy dresses, and they stood there and I did not disturb them at all. I didn't see any light-blue dress with diamond-shaped spots and paint around the bottom of it or the side."

(Brown paint, the hue of dried blood, as I only learned from the housepainter's evidence when I finally got my hands on the final thousand pages of the trial—Volume II, the sheep that was lost and was found.)

The twice mentioned oversight of those dresses at the back of the closet is so pointed that it looks almost as if Seaver wished to test his degree of culpable negligence by offering the court a chance to point out what he had realized in a delayed reaction— or at his wife's suggestion: a dress can be hidden inside another dress.

Jackets and pants being what they are, it is hard to conceal a man's summer suit inside a winter suit. But every woman has at one time or another vexingly mislaid a dress simply by having hung *another* dress over it on the same hanger. *Mrs.* Seaver would have taken down those "heavy or silk dresses" at once, automatically seeing them for what they were, likely, efficient hiding places for a dress of summer cotton.

Mr. Seaver and Mr. Fleet wore suits; their minds didn't work that way. And after all, a suspect's own dress closet to which she has just courteously handed over the key *is* an unlikely place in which to expect to find a dress stained with her stepmother's gore.

When the police admitted defeat, Lizzie was tired. She asked for a day's rest. The Pinkerton's detective, O. M. Hanscom, agreed to spend Sunday checking up around the town and not return to weary the household further until Monday morning.

I am not surprised that Lizzie wanted that respite. She lived not in the day of James Bond but of Sherlock Holmes; a *private* detective was generally assumed to have powers lacking in the dull minions of the law. And O. M. Hanscom had learned that afternoon that a missing cotton dress was important.

The police got ready to take away such evidence as they had.

Desmond and Medley went to the cellar for the only weapons that could possibly be held suspect: the big axe, which had been used to kill a cow; the claw-headed hatchet with the brown rust-stains on the handle—for both must be tested in the laboratory [4] —and last, and likeliest, the hatchet-head. Likeliest because it had been newly broken from a wooden handle, which could not, like metal, be washed free of detectable blood under running cold water; likeliest because it had been disguised with white coal ash to look (approximately) dusty again after it had been washed, and then hidden, high on the jog in the chimney, in that box of dusty tools that had contained two other *genuinely* dusty hatchets, which matched the rest of its contents and had clearly been up there unused for a long time.

Captain Desmond went into the water closet for a sheet of the Providence *Journal* from the thrifty stack beside it. He wrapped the broken-off hatchet head in it carefully.

Just then, State Detective Seaver came down to the cellar, asking to see it; he had heard Fleet's description of it, but up to that time he had not examined it closely himself.

He unwrapped it and saw that Fleet had been right. Seaver, who had begun life as a carpenter, knew wood. The break, as he said in court, was "a very bright break, a new break"; and the white furnace ash was altogether different from the dust on the tools in the box and the other hatchets that had lain with them.

He fell into discussion of these details with Captain Desmond, while young Medley rewrapped it for them. Both Desmond and *Seaver*, that is, examined that heavily suspect hatchet-head, and both Desmond and *Medley* wrapped it in the same wrapping. And, amazingly, this dull and trivial fact would be used with enormous brilliance and ingenuity by that dazzling trial lawyer, ex-Governor George Robinson to confuse a jury and consolidate the myth that *the weapon was never found.*

It was a necessary myth, and he knew it. Upon it, and upon the missing bloodstained dress, along with Lizzie's well-known

---

[4] Dr. Dolan, unlike Fleet and Seaver, first suspected the axe.

father-fixation, would hang the whole significant body of the defense.

Lizzie had withdrawn to her room. The departing police asked Mr. Jennings to see her and request the clothes she had worn on the murder morning. He brought them the heavy, dust-free, unwrinkled silk bengaline and a starched white underskirt. There were no shoes and stockings, but the weary police forgot to point it out or to ask for them until the D.A. prompted them a week later. Then she turned over a pair of black strap slippers (*ties* she called them; I called mine ankleties) and a pair of black stockings, which she admitted had been washed.

If the blanket on Emma's closet floor ever held a pair of unwashed stockings or a pair of shoes that were *not* ankleties, the former had doubtless received their preliminary rinse and the latter been blackened and put away before the police search first began on the afternoon of Friday, the day after the crime.

It would, however, have been indiscreet to remove the blanket against which the police had pushed in such kindly haste when Lizzie said that "all this" was "making her sick." It was certainly better to have it look as if it *belonged* on the closet floor.

⋙ 20 ⋘

When Fleet came back with no bloodstained dress, Hilliard was desperate on the horns of his dilemma. He called the District Attorney, Hosea Knowlton, to ask advice about making an arrest. Knowlton offered to take the earliest evening train from New Bedford and confer with him. Then Hilliard went to Mayor Coughlin to talk about the increasing danger of an incident. The Mayor suggested that they both drive to the Borden house and tactfully request the *entire* household to stay safe indoors.

The request would scarcely seem too pointed, after Morse's narrow escape the night before; but it was arranged that Hil-

liard would do absolutely no talking beyond a courteous greeting and farewell. Both saw that it would be better for the legal
future of the case if the call bore not the faintest suggestion of
house arrest, merely a generalized warning and the Mayor's assurance of continuing police protection.

The crowd had closed the way to traffic when Hilliard and the
Mayor turned into Second Street. Even though their authority
was recognized, they had a hard time getting the horse and carriage through.

Miss Emma showed them into that rarely entered room of
state, the parlor, and brought Lizzie and Uncle John to them.
Alice Russell stayed upstairs in her room, and Bridget had been
escorted across the street for that night and her coming Sunday
off. (She had it in her mind, she later admitted, not to go back
—understandably, since the alarming Uncle John had apparently settled in. She learned, however, that she was not free to
choose.)

The Mayor at once suggested that it would be "better for all
concerned" if the family stayed inside for the next few days.
Emma nodded, taking it for granted. Lizzie, on the other hand,
showed surprise.

She asked, in a quick, excited voice, "Why, is there anybody
in this house suspected?"

She had called in her lawyer as soon as the police had heard
out Mr. Bence and returned to search the house. Her morning's
Providence *Journal* had told her why "a woman" was suspected.
That afternoon she had watched her dresses being examined for
bloodstains. And on the evening before her uncle had been
mobbed.

It was a striking question.

The Mayor said, "Well, perhaps Mr. Morse can answer that
question better than I, as his experience last night, perhaps,
would justify the inference that somebody in this house was
suspected."

Lizzie stared him down. "I want to know the truth."

He hesitated. She made her repetition a demand: *"I want to
know the truth."*

The press would often comment on the crimson mottling that

darkened her sallow face in moments of tension; it heightened the effect of her huge, protruding, pale eyes.

The Mayor cracked, and in so doing provided the legal loophole that excluded her inquest testimony from the final trial—one which took only a little stretching to let Lizzie through: "Well, Miss Borden, I regret to answer but I must answer—yes, you are suspected."

A friendly court was to rule that from the moment of this, his reluctant answer, she was "virtually under arrest."

As a result, much of Lizzie's preliminary testimony, before she was taken into custody, was excluded on the grounds that she had not been formally warned of the danger of self-incrimination. (Mr. Jennings' legal counsel was technically not enough.)

Lizzie's tension vanished. Her answer was flat, quiet, and as striking as her initial question: *"I am ready to go now."*

There was little that Emma could do to cover for her, but she did her best. She said, "Well, we have tried to keep it from her as long as we could."

The Mayor struggled to make Lizzie understand that nobody wanted her to go anywhere. It was no easy task, since it had to be done without putting it into so many words or even indicating that there was any reason for him to say so. One feels for him, since this could be managed only by a seemingly casual change of subject, and the moment was scarcely one to spark general conversation.

This, then, was the moment chosen by Uncle John to speak up for the only time that evening. His remark gives an indication of what was on *his* mind.

Throughout the call, Uncle John seemed barely aware of Lizzie, and did nothing to help Emma make Lizzie's strange question seem a natural one. He had his own troubles. He had not dared another trip to the post office that day, and tomorrow was Sunday. But by Monday a reply would have come—or so he could hope—a letter from the young man who had helped him carry out Andrew's fool scheme to keep Lizzie off the scent. The reply would say whether—now that double murder was part of the package—he would feel it his duty to speak out or, for a price, continue to keep still, and say nothing about having been *asked* to keep still. It's one thing to agree to getting an old lady up to a bank without somebody's finding out about it and quite another to keep still about a crime. Though there was a chance: for the young man might also dread to "get involved."

Yes, Uncle John had cause for self-absorbed anxiety. For a letter from that young man, if it fell into the hands of the police, would be *written evidence* that he was being bribed to keep still about something that had some relation to the murders. And the Mayor and the Marshal had told Uncle John to stay home!

Abruptly, then, Uncle John spoke for the only time that evening: "How will we get our mail?"

The Mayor promised to have it brought to the house. Uncle John heard the offer in silence.

(I should not have known how promptly he flouted the Mayor had not a reporter from the Providence *Journal* been amused to note how, once Mr. Bence's revelation about the prussic acid had been made public, a man who was nearly lynched by a mob on Friday did not so much as rate a second glance from the many who recognized him at the post office on Monday morning.)

The Mayor rose to go, assuring them again that they need only report any annoyance from the crowds to the policeman on duty to receive all the protection that the force could provide.

Lizzie did not respond. Emma thanked him, and as she showed him out, along with Hilliard, she assured him more than once, "We want to do everything we can in this matter."

She then went directly upstairs to her friend Alice and asked if she would be willing to exchange beds with her that night.[1]

So far as we know, Emma never again used the little back bedroom that opened out of Lizzie's. Emma was a loyal and rigid woman with a great will to believe; but I find it hard to doubt that from that evening she was a woman in deep inner conflict, a conflict that she always labored to conceal from herself.

The Mayor and the Marshal went on to the hotel, the Mellon House. Dr. Dolan and State Detective Seaver joined them, and they met in a private room to confer with the D.A. Knowlton

[1] Trial transcript, Alice's testimony. The rest of this chapter is drawn from Hilliard's and Mayor Coughlin's testimony.

told them that they had insufficient grounds for arrest and ordered an inquest to be held, beginning on Tuesday.

Reporters had observed the visit to the Borden house and the subsequent meeting with the D.A. Rumor spread from mouth to mouth and phone to phone. The public expected an arrest that night, or by the following morning at the latest.

That night Lizzie faced a problem. A missing dress had been brought to the attention of a private detective, and he was coming on Monday morning, to detect.

I know well enough what I should have done in her shoes. I should have lain awake that Saturday night until the house had been still a long time. I should have felt my way in the dark, on tiptoe, to the big hall closet, then down the stairs to the narrow cupboard in the corner at the far side of the stove. Coal and wood were kept there, but I should not have risked the noise of making up a fire. I should have thrust a rolled-up dress far back and to one side of the high shelf where the heavy kettles stood. I should have shut the door on it gently and tiptoed back to bed to wait for tomorrow's first good chance.

My recent visit to the Second Street house, which I had not seen for many years, made all the written evidence about the dress-burning clear to me, vividly clear, in a way that I found amazing.

A friend of mine is also a friend of the present owner, who lives in it and also owns and manages a local press; the print shop adjoins the Borden house and is built on the land that once was the narrow side yard and site of the Kelly cottage—the sitting-room side. (When we were introduced, Mr. McGinn looked at me and grinned, saying to my friend, "You needn't tell me why you brought her here. *I know the look.*" My gratitude to his generous patience with those who have *the look* is very great.)

In my visit to that house I came to understand many passages in the trial transcript that I had only thought I understood before. But it was when I looked up at the high shelf of that cupboard, now seen in hard fact but already vivid in my imagination, that I experienced a sharp and singular identification with Lizzie. The kitchen has been remodeled; the stove no longer stands where it is shown on our floor-plan, yet I knew where it had been. In my mind it was there. I stood beside it in the corner, looking up at that unchanged high shelf. The closet door opened out, screening me from the only window (now blocked by the adjoining press), through which my head and shoulders would have been visible from outside the house if the closet door had been shut.

When I had actually stood at the door from the sitting room to the dining room lifting my arms and letting an imaginary hatchet fall on an imaginary, propped-up head, I saw how easily the thing could have been done by someone sheltered in a Prince Albert like the one I remembered my grandfather as wearing on daytime, top-hat occasions. I noticed how the blouse of my own suit pulled up from the skirt in front, as Alice found Lizzie's. But the exercise was intellectual; my spirit held apart from the game.

Not here. I stood in that corner knowing that it was now Sunday morning, that Bridget was across the street at Miller's, that Alice had gone to church, Uncle John was skulking in his room, and Emma, in the sink room, the whole length of the kitchen and width of the dining room away, was washing dishes. If I hurried, I could be done before she was beside me.

The safe corner. It was completely hidden from anyone outside; no window, no door afforded a glimpse of me there, briefly safe, doing what I must. I shall never forget that strange, hallucinatory moment of false recall; for one moment I *was* Lizzie, hidden but still frightened, knowing that I must be secret, quick. Before Emma should leave the sink or Uncle John come downstairs, I must burn that dress stained with Abby's blood.

Forgive this incursion of self. It has served, I hope, to give you the lay-out of the kitchen and the details of that sorely needed opportunity. Lizzie had a first-rate place and moment for a little quick work beside the kitchen stove. And this must all be stressed if you are to appreciate, in due time, the so different picture of that kitchen as conjured up by the defense at the trial.

Indeed, Alice Russell's own evidence slightly confuses the picture, for at one point she elides her story, saying, "Emma turned," directly after speaking of her at the sink, thus creating a false picture of a sink in the kitchen and the two sisters first found in the same room—a false picture that the defense was quick to observe and use.[2]

Let us come back to the bare facts as sworn to by Alice Russell —after she had concealed them for four months. Nobody blamed her for hiding them so long; for all knew that she was as gentle as she was honest, and that she loved Emma Borden.

Alice had got breakfast for the family that morning and dressed to go out. But she changed her mind and did not go to church, where she would meet people and have to talk. She spent a short time in her cottage on Borden Street and came back to Emma again.

It was mid-morning, but Emma was not her own energetic self; she was still in the sink room with the breakfast dishes. She unhooked the screen-door for Alice and followed her up the entry into the kitchen. Lizzie was in the corner between the stove and the open door of the coal closet, with the skirt of the Bedford cord dress in her hands.

As Alice put it: "Miss Emma turned toward her and said, 'Lizzie, what are you going to do?' Lizzie said, 'I am going to burn this old thing up, it is all covered with paint.' "

Lizzie held the skirt in such a way that Alice saw no paint.

It was an odd situation. Alice walked out of the kitchen and left the sisters alone, saying nothing. Though she did not mention it at the trial, she must have been very conscious that the police had spent two days searching the house in vain for a brown-stained housedress.

Lizzie apparently paused in her occupation, for when Alice came back to the kitchen a little later she had not yet finished. Perhaps Emma had checked her, briefly, for when Alice came in, Lizzie was just reaching down another piece of the dress from the high shelf. She began to rip it apart.

Alice said, "I wouldn't let anybody see me do that, Lizzie, if I were you."

She may have been thinking of Uncle John's presence in the

[2] Floor-plan.

house, or it may have been only the automatic reaction of one who lived in a house with windows at the usual distance from the ground. Lizzie took one step further back within the shelter of the closet door and went on tearing the fragment of the dress. There was still a little more of it left on the shelf.

Once more, Alice left her alone with her sister.

Mr. Jubb, Mr. Buck's assistant, took the service at Central Congregational that morning. He spoke with fervor of "a life which has always been pure and holy." He prayed: "Help us from giving voice to innuendoes and insinuations which we have no right to utter." He also prayed eloquently that the press, which covered the service, might be granted sufficient grace to play the case down.

In his sermon he inveighed against the murderer: "Why, a man who could conceive and execute such a murder would not hesitate to burn a city!"

In the afternoon, Emma scrubbed the sole splash of blood from the doorjamb where Andrew's head had rested. It had been measured off at three feet and seven inches from the floor.

Mr. Hanscom called on Monday morning. He wished to talk to the household privately, one by one, and he was shown into the parlor. He spoke first with Miss Russell.

From her talk she hurried back to the sisters, who were in the dining room; unlike the sitting room, it had no door into the parlor. They could speak privately.

She said, "I am afraid, Lizzie, the worst thing you could have done was to burn that dress. I have been asked about your dresses."

Lizzie said, "Oh, what made you let me do it? Why didn't you tell me?"

Miss Russell left her with Emma and went upstairs.

Mr. O. M. Hanscom left the Borden house immediately thereafter and did not come back to it.

BOOK THREE

WHY LIZZIE WAS ACCUSED: *The Inquest*

WHEN no arrest was made and the word went out that the inquest would be held in private, there was a stir under the hill. As the Providence *Journal* put it, there was "a change of opinion as to the final outcome" since the friends of the Borden family had begun to "make their influence felt." As our maids would sum it up later: "Ah, God, it's great to be rich!"

This was unfair to Judge Blaisdell. He had known Lizzie since childhood, and he was kind; but he was not stretching the law in her behalf. In Massachusetts, such inquiries may be held in private when there is any chance that their premature publicizing may be prejudicial to a witness.

In fact, the judge leaned over backward to stress the fact that it was an inquest, not a trial. He ruled that Lizzie, like the other witnesses, should not be represented by counsel; he did not warn her or any witness of their rights. Clearly, she knew them, since she had been in constant consultation with her lawyer since the day after the crime; and clearly she could not avail herself of them and refuse to testify without damaging her image as an innocent bystander.

The reaction to all this care for justice was strikingly different before and after the event. When it was first learned that the only witnesses to the whole process would be the city physician and a state detective, there were mutterings about money and influence; later, the inquest would be represented as a corrupt judiciary's dark means of trapping Lizzie into self-incrimination by three days of confusion and mental torment.

Yet, aside from Lizzie's remarkable performance, the inquest was a run-of-the-mill affair, meriting neither the earlier nor the later criticisms.

The witnesses were the household, the friends who came to the house directly after the murders were discovered, Mr. Bence, and Hiram C. Harrington—who was called only because Lizzie named him as a possible suspect. (The only name, to her credit, that she ever did name, and in his interview he certainly asked for it.)

All were questioned briefly except for Bridget and Lizzie. Bridget got the works. She was called as first witness and examined from early morning until four in the afternoon, almost twice as long as any other witness was questioned at a stretch. On the final day she was recalled for the better part of the morning and until three, an hour and a half longer than Lizzie's longest questioning. Knowlton was never satisfied that she was not involved.

On the first day, Lizzie was on the stand for an hour and a half, on the second for the whole afternoon, and on the last day for an hour-long review.

We can now penetrate that press blackout. We have Lizzie's testimony entire, which is fortunate, since she was not put on the stand again and her testimony, unlike that of the others, could not even be briefly quoted at the trial. For the rest, counsel for both sides pounced upon every variation between the testimony given at the inquest and that given at the trial. The quotes tell us something, though the variations were few. At the inquest, Emma was unhappily honest about the cause and nature of the five years' cold war; at the trial she did her clumsy best to undo the harm. For Lizzie's sake, Bridget did a little good-natured lying at the inquest about that household strain, and she said that Lizzie was crying when she found her father, though everyone else had found Lizzie too stunned for tears, as, guilty or innocent, she might well have been.

It was not because of her kindly lies that Knowlton suspected Bridget's complicity and subjected her to the longest questioning undergone by any witness, longer than Lizzie's by hours; you will understand why, when you study Lizzie's testimony.

One witness was not asked back for the preliminary, the Grand Jury, or the final trial. Hiram C. Harrington doubtless overflowed with willingness to talk of the money troubles that were "kept dark" and of Lizzie's "contentious nature"; but Knowlton was both shrewd and a man of conscience. Mr. Harrington was plainly not unbiased.

The police sent a hack for the sisters each day; Lizzie's friend Mary Brigham always rode with them. Throughout, she was as faithful as the Rev. Mr. Buck and Mrs. Holmes.

Bridget went afoot, with a policeman at her side. When he came to the door for her on the first day, demanding her by name, she thought that she must be under arrest and began to cry. But at the end of her long first day's questioning, she was allowed to bundle together her two or three dresses—all her worldly goods, that is—and go to stay with a cousin who lived on the far side of town. (Even from that distance, however, she still had to walk; no hacks for the humble.)

The papers had next to nothing to report. They noted that only Emma appeared to shrink from the huge crowds that waited outside the court each day. They remarked that after Lizzie had testified on the second afternoon, the officials "looked more peaceful." And they reported that Knowlton had hired a professional safecracker to open Andrew's safe, in which he had kept his papers, preferring it to a box at the bank.

(It was a phenomenal safe, which took two days to crack. Lizzie had told Knowlton that to her belief Andrew had made a will; she doubtless wished it were true, since any will that did not disinherit Emma could only have weakened that money motive at which Uncle Hiram so light-heartedly hinted.)

This was lean fare for a waiting public. It was eked out by investigations of numerous suspects, none of which proved more fruitful than Bridget's first suggestion of "the Portuguese." that is, the Swede, with his perfect alibi. For example, Andrew had been threatening one Mr. Walker, journeyman tailor and alcoholic, with eviction; but at the time of the murders, Mr. Walker had been, for once, sober and on the job under his boss's eye. Peleg Brightman, a paperhanger who sometimes worked for Mr. Borden, was seen digging in his back yard, and an inspired neighbor decided that he was burying the hatchet; but his hatchet was found on his kitchen shelf and his alibi found watertight. And so on.

There remained the young man who had loitered on the sidewalk. Some considered him a mystery, though many believed that he was only "Mike the Soldier," a drunk given to walking off his hangovers in the vicinity. Dr. Handy's firm statement that his neat, pale young man bore no resemblance to Mike the Soldier was largely shrugged off, and many continued to laugh for years about "Dr. Handy's wild-eyed man." Those who did not embraced the unknown youth for the mad maniac who, to judge from Dr. Handy's report, had *twice* got in and out of the house unnoticed, waiting outside from one murder to the next. Since poor Dr. Handy had never said that the young man was wild-eyed, an apparent lunatic, or even drunk—indeed he had stressed the opposite—he remained for the rest of his days equally vexed by those who had mocked him and those who had accorded him overearnest faith.

Mr. Jennings was permitted to see the transcript of the proceedings each day at their close. It must have puzzled him. On the Wednesday evening, when the authorities were said to look "more peaceful," he took the stand that he maintained to his life's end.

He said to the reporters, "I might say things that would do no harm, but I have decided to say nothing, in order to stop any stories that might arise from what I say."

It was not until four on Thursday afternoon that the inquest ended and the press had any news worth the writing.

Lizzie was under arrest.

≪ 22 ≪

Five days before, the District Attorney had prevented that arrest and called an inquest held before the kindly old man who had known her since childhood. At the preliminary investigation old Judge Blaisdell found her probably guilty, and wept pronouncing the words. A Grand Jury heard her testimony read aloud and voted a true bill against her, twenty to one. A jury of the superior court were prevented by the defense from hearing that testimony. As previously mentioned, every official copy of the inquest disappeared from the files in short order. Clearly, what she said was dynamite.

Yet, think of this: forty out-of-town reporters heard it read aloud in Fall River, at the preliminary, and reported it patchily with the mild remark that it had "variations." Once a jury was locked away, the New Bedford *Standard-Times* printed it entire. Far from rocking the world, it received next to no attention at the time; and *it has never been carefully studied since.* If it was dynamite, why?

The answer is simple: as a liar, Lizzie was phenomenally dull. One can scarcely overstate her supernal power to bore.

And, by a remarkable paradox, it is through this lethal dullness that she provides a singular excitement: she explains the whole *modus operandi* of the crime.

While Lizzie could not invent details, little touches to give a story life and credibility, she was overmastered by actual details, unnoticeable details which she is driven to mention and explain away. Every *object* that she mentions had solid physical existence, and none is mentioned without purpose. For example, she claimed to have read an old magazine, a *Harper's Weekly*,[1] taken from the kitchen cupboard, as she sat beside the hot stove. The old magazines, it turned out, were hoarded in that cupboard; and she did not mention that *Harper's Weekly* just to hear herself talk.

Through months of going over her words with a fine-toothed comb I found a single exception to this: there is *purpose* in her mention of sewing a button-loop on the sleeve of a dress, or as she first put it, with typical dimness, "basting a piece of tape on a garment"; but the specific dress was not identified. For Lizzie this would be so wild and atypical a flight of fancy that I think she must have found a button-loop loose on the bengaline as she dressed for the street. I mention it not for its own importance, but because it is the exception to that rule of actual

[1] She calls it *Harper's*, which everyone did; this gives a confusing picture of its size and thickness, which were relevant.

things mentioned with comprehensible *purpose.* (Its purpose you will presently see.)

Even that fishing sinker, not thought up under pressure in a courtroom but the slow growth of twenty-four-hours' leisure in which to consider and invent, shows this same limitation. Why was she in the barn? Questioned, she thinks of actual objects in the barn and remembers a box of scrap metal. What use could scrap metal have? "To fix a screen." But when the screens are proved sound, her mind is still hung up on that box of scrap metal. What else was in it? Old doorknobs . . . no. Some folded lead. What is made of lead? Why, fishing sinkers. And there it rests, the best she can do for herself. The box was not in the part of the barn where she remembered it as being— a basket was there—but it was real, and the tin, the iron, the lead were all found in it—all real.

It was this tic, combined with her compulsion to mention and explain away incriminating details that might well have gone unnoticed, which made Lizzie's testimony, *for me,* unthinkably exciting; these qualities, combined with her denial of Bridget's testimony—testimony so far from injurious to her that the defense cited it at the final trial, while its denial, though also made with comprehensible purpose, would, if it were believed, actually have cleared Bridget and given Lizzie herself sole opportunity for the murder of Abby.

The excitement, however, is of a special sort, the excitement of a challenging puzzle, to be worked out with the puzzle-lover's stubborn joy. Simply to read, this testimony is both confusing and excruciatingly dull. So, to my grief, I must largely summarize, not quote. To my grief, for the impact of that whole drab waste, that shifting sea of sand is, essential to an understanding of Lizzie. It is strange to study the mind of one who is at once so unimaginative and so wholly out of touch with reality. Yet though she plods and cannot invent, she is never really unintelligent, except when it comes to people. In fact she is often shrewd. But out of touch—just out of touch.

Her testimony might affect few readers so. But I think that anyone would be fascinated by Knowlton's gentle, inexhaustible patience. He was crisp once, irritated once, and once shocked into real anger; these three moments of human weakness are all, I think you will agree, more than understandable in their context. It is his steady, quiet patience that strikes one as **nearly** superhuman.

To clarify matters, let us consider the subjects that Knowlton wanted to find out about one at a time, instead of covering the whole field of each session as it occurred. So we begin with the general background and Uncle John.

At the beginning, Lizzie's testimony went smoothly.

She did not know what her father was worth, and believed that he had made a will. She knew of nobody on bad terms with him, except for a stranger from out of town who had been at the door two weeks back and Hiram C. Harrington. Her stepmother's property was a half-house, formerly the property of Mrs. Borden's father; it was, she implied, inherited. She had never had any trouble with her stepmother.

Questioned further, she admitted to "a difference of opinion" five years back, but without "hard words," and ever since they both had "very kindly feelings, very pleasant."

(Lizzie did not explain that "difference of opinion" until the last day, when she knew that Emma had spilled the beans. The story, when she told it, sounded so bewilderingly trivial that Knowlton asked, "Is that all there is to it, then?" I doubt that he ever quite believed the ludicrous, tragic truth.)

Next Knowlton asked if she had thought of her stepmother as a mother. She said, "Not exactly, no," though in some ways they were like mother and daughter. Asked what the "some ways" were she replied, "I decline to answer." Asked if her father and mother seemed fond of one another, she paused so long that Knowlton asked, "Why hesitate?" Then she said, "So far as I had any opportunity of judging."

Knowlton changed the subject and asked what she had worn on the murder morning. She replied, "I had on a navy blue, sort of a bengaline or India silk.... In the afternoon they thought I had better change it. I put on a pink wrapper." Yes, she had put on the navy blue when she first got up and no, did not change until afternoon.

Other than by these three questions, Knowlton did not mention the dress until the final day, when he brought it up once more. It had gone to Harvard Medical School and he had not seen it. It sounded unlikely housewear, but he distrusted the description. Pongee was popular at the time, a light summer silk that could be washed; a rich man's clothes-struck daughter could conceivably have worn it about the house on a hot day. Lizzie, as it happened, wore pongee that afternoon.

For the second time, as briefly as the first, Knowlton brought up the subject:

Q: Was the dress that was given to the officers the same dress you wore that morning?

A. Yes, sir.

Q: Something like that? [Pongee]

A: No, it was not like that, it was a silk and linen; some call it bengaline silk.

The subject was dropped for good. (Some writers have seen in this painstaking mention of the stout flax warp on which the better grades of silk bengaline were woven evidence that the dress was suitable for sitting by a hot stove on a heat-wave morning. They were not writers who came from a family that had manufactured looms for three generations and had an inbred fascination with textiles. Nor were they women.)

We have now covered as much of Lizzie's evidence as she gave before the first mention of Uncle John shot it straight to hell. So before we pass on to such complexities, it is as well to mention here the two other points on which, like those just considered, Lizzie gave straightforward evidence.

On the last day, she was asked if she had gone to the cellar with a slop pail on the night after the murders. Lizzie could not remember having done so. She was also asked if she had tried to buy prussic acid from Mr. Bence. She said, "I did not."

Smith's drugstore, Knowlton told her, was at the corner of South Main and Columbia. She knew where that was?

Lizzie replied firmly, "I do not."

He had mentioned a main intersection a few minutes' walk from the house she had lived in since childhood; the drugstore had been there more than fourteen years. He dropped the subject.

To Knowlton, when the inquest began, Uncle John was still a possible suspect; for all he knew, the police had been too easily satisfied with his alibi.

To Lizzie, the name of Uncle John must have been terror.

Uncle John was bound up with the precipitating motive, the Swansea place, and with its prototype, the Whitehead house, five years before. His visit of three months back had coincided with the beheading of the pigeons and Detective Shaw's private conversation with her. God knows, anything connected with the "peculiar spells" had to be concealed. And on the afternoon before the murders Uncle John and her parents had talked by the open window just under her own; it must be made plain that she had heard nothing.

One who knows the background is not surprised by Lizzie's panic evasions about Uncle John's three most important visits, five years before, three months before, and five days before. To Knowlton they must have been bewildering, coming as they did so sharply on the heels of her well-controlled answers about the rest of the family.

Lizzie had just finished telling Knowlton that she wore "a sort of bengaline or India silk" on the murder morning. He next asked when Morse first began to come to their house for visits: "I don't mean *this* time."

At the name, her responses went askew.

A: Do you mean this time that he came and stayed all night?

Q: No. Was this his first visit to your house?

A: He has been in the East a year or more.

Knowlton asked if he had visited before he came back East to stay. Lizzie remembered that he had "in the winter that the river was frozen over and they went across, some fourteen years ago, was it not?"

The freezing of a New England river is not the sort of front page news that is long remembered. Knowlton said crisply, "I am not answering questions but asking them."

Lizzie could not remember the date. Questioned further, she said that Uncle John had been there once since, that he had *not* been there since, and, again, that he had but she did not remember when. Urged to give her best remembrance, she said, "Five or six years ago—perhaps *six*."

She was yet vaguer about his recent visits. "Really, I do not know, I am away so much myself." (Abroad, and all.) But she soon tripped herself by mentioning her recent stay in New Bedford as her sole lengthy absence in the past year.

Knowlton came down to the present. At what time of day had Uncle John turned up on this visit?

"He stayed there all night, Wednesday night."

"My question is, *when* he came there?"

"I don't know. I was not at home when he came. *I was out.*"

(In this first panic she has even forgotten that she must cover not having had any opportunity to see Mr. Bence.)

Uncle John was there, but she did not see him. That evening she went out again to pay a call; she locked up for the night when she went to bed, but she did not glance into the sitting room. When she came down in the morning, he was gone.

There was clearly something odd about this shadowy uncle. Knowlton ran over it again.

This time, Lizzie remembered Mr. Bence. She had *not* been out when Uncle John came. "I was in my room all day, not feeling well." (But she did not hint that Abby had felt sick, let alone thought herself to have been poisoned.)

When did she hear his voice? "Around suppertime." Then, remembering that he left for Swansea at three, she corrects it: she heard him first "around three." (No long talk, ever, beneath her open window.) She went down to no meals that day and only went out in the evening in the hope that the fresh air would make her feel better. She did not hear him again or know where he was. Next morning she saw only her mother and father and "Maggie," and talked with them all.

About Uncle John? "I did not mention him."

Nor had anyone. Uncle John was a character to think about.

It was also something to think about that Lizzie had mentioned neither her parents' illness nor the anonymous poison threat, which Dr. Bowen had reported. One would think that a girl unjustly suspected would want that anonymous threat remembered—and a murder threat just preceding a murder is a natural thing to mention at an inquest.

Knowlton, a wise investigator, let it pass. He had read an interview with "the girls at Marion," that interview that so quaintly gave it as more probable that "Lizzie would commit a murder than that she would lie about it afterwards." He asked why she had not joined her friends at the seashore. She explained that she had been getting ready for a roll call of Christian Endeavor which was to have been held on the Sunday after the crime.

(Fall River's well-to-do almost all leave town for the hot months, the men commuting from nearby watering places. It would have been a skeleton meeting to which Lizzie had allotted an awesome minimum of two weeks and three days' solitary preparation.)

Knowlton merely asked a few questions about Emma and returned to Uncle John. Why had Lizzie not stepped into the sitting room to say good-night when she came in from her evening call?

"I had no reason except that I was not feeling well and did not come down all day."

"No, you *were* down. When you came in, from *outside*."

Such good-nights were not the family custom.

Had she gone up the back stairs to avoid notice?

No, because of the locks, which had "always" been like that "until Thursday when *they* broke the door open."

For a third time, Knowlton tried to make sense of Uncle John, but Lizzie's answers became yet more confused.

She heard his voice because she always kept her door open in hot weather; she did not, because she always kept it shut; it was open but she shut it because she wanted to take a nap and the voices "annoyed" her. She came down to no meals; she came down to both dinner and supper with her parents.

It was panic. She had been in all day, out morning and evening, upstairs all day, down for two meals; her door was open, shut, and alternately open and shut. And it did not directly concern the murders—only Uncle John.

Yet after that first day of the inquest, even Knowlton lost interest in Uncle John.

And now, at long last, we are able to reconstruct the murder of Abby Borden. To do so, we needed Lizzie's own help. The slop pail and the brown-stained dress that was burned were not enough. They did not, for example, answer that important though seldom asked question: "Why did Abby let herself be hewed down with no outcry? Why did no neighbor hear a scream?" Now Lizzie will help us understand.

In comparison with what she had to say about Uncle John, Lizzie's testimony on Abby is calm and consistent. She saw her for the first and only time flicking her feather duster in the dining room; Lizzie went into the kitchen and neither saw nor heard her again. As Lizzie put it, "That has always been a mystery to me."

Her first-day evidence on Abby is brief: Uncle John took up most of the time. Though brief, it gave Knowlton food for thought.

When Lizzie came downstairs, her father was in the sitting room reading the Providence *Journal,* her mother was in the dining room; Bridget, with the long-handled mop in her hand, was just entering the kitchen for her pail, and she dropped a word about washing the windows and went out at once. Lizzie did not feel up to coffee, but thought she might have eaten half a banana.

Even if we grant that Lizzie retained only the dimmest memories of the early morning through her brownout and was simply playing it by ear, the discrepancies between this story and Bridget's are worth thought.

In the first place, by setting her father in the front of the house and not, as Bridget remembered, up in his room, she made it impossible for Bridget to get in at the front door and slaughter Abby just overhead in the guest room until he left the house. (This was important to Knowlton, who saw Bridget as the only other possible suspect, once he had satisfied himself that the police had eliminated Uncle John.) In the second place, Lizzie did not breakfast with Bridget in the kitchen, but saw her only in one passing glimpse: Bridget, that is, had *no real chance to notice what Lizzie had on*.

To continue this first version of the story, which was elicited by patient questions, drab grain by grain. As Lizzie passed Abby in the dining room, Abby told her that she had already made up the spare room, but that she was going up to put fresh slips on the two small pillows that stood at the foot of the bed. (They were used as cushions, for the guest room-sewing room bed also doubled as an upstairs sitting-room sofa. According to Alice, the girls always entertained their friends there.)

Abby also said that she was going to close off the room, because she was going to have company Monday. (This never substantiated "company Monday" would have been a singular event in poor Abby's life, almost singular enough to account for her shutting that much-used room off from common use four days ahead of time. But, you note, the invention, though clumsy, is not purposeless. It explains why Lizzie did not see Abby's body before it was found. And Lizzie also had an errand upstairs to explain, as you will see.)

Changing two pillowslips is not a lengthy business. Knowlton asked Lizzie if she had any idea of what might have kept Abby up there so long. Lizzie then remembered that Abby had said she was about to run up some new pillowslips on the sewing machine. But questioned, she admitted that she had not heard the sewing machine. (The old treadle-Singer made a racket; Bridget would have heard it, too.)

After further questions had made it increasingly obvious that Abby could not have got back to her own room without being seen, Lizzie amended, "Except for two or three minutes when I first came down, I went to the water closet."

This was sound. At first Lizzie had been careful not to mention being in the entry near the cellar stairs, where Bridget saw her "appear" (out of nowhere, as it seemed to Bridget, since Lizzie had not been downstairs or had time to get down from her room). Yet Bridget *might* have mentioned that "appearance," and it was now explained, even to its proper timing, for she had already placed Bridget as just coming back from the barn "when I first came down."

But now, abruptly, as if mention of the cellar led into it, she added that she also, *right then*, carried some clean clothes upstairs.

Note this well. The clothes, like all the details, were real. They had been, as Bridget explained at the trial, sorted in stacks on the dining-room sofa that morning for the family to take to their respective locked rooms. Lizzie mentions nothing without purpose. She sees the fact that they were taken upstairs before the murders as an incriminating fact to be explained away—to be riskily explained away, since it would be so much better to insist that she did not go upstairs at all that morning. If she speaks of that errand, she sees it as something very much worth mentioning.

However, she reiterates, she could not see into the guest room: "The door was shut. She said that she wanted it kept shut to keep the dust and everything out."

But for question after question Lizzie implied that Abby must have been either there or in her own bedroom. She went to striking lengths to avoid mentioning the arrival of a note, which might have called her from the house. The substitute inventions become increasingly labored.

"Yes, sir, I know what she used to do there sometimes; she kept her best cape for the street there, and she used to go up occasionally and take it into her own room. She kept a great deal in the guest-room drawers, she used to go up there and get things and put things." (Passing through the first floor like a ghost.)

Eventually, Knowlton was forced to ask Lizzie directly about the note. This made it plain that he had been told about it, and she admitted it: Abby told her that somebody was sick and asked her what she wanted her to buy for dinner on the way back.

(According to Bridget, the change in the diet was planned. This time there were to have been potatoes in the mutton soup. It has been remarked that right here one would prefer to trust Lizzie.)

Knowlton's next question is obvious: then, why had Lizzie not believed that Abby was out?

Why, she had believed it. But she did not know *where* Abby was going, did not know who the note was from, and had not seen it herself.

This ended her first day's questioning about Abby.

On the second day, Lizzie tried to make it seem that Abby waddled out to market almost every morning and sometimes dined out, thus showing both note and absence for commonplace matters, not at all, one would say, the sort of thing to set a girl searching the house for that note, even in her stepmother's "pocket," as she had so promptly and indiscreetly admitted to Dr. Bowen.

In the hour-long questioning on the final day, Lizzie returned to saying that she had thought Abby was making pillowcases in the guest room—by hand, though, not by machine. And when Knowlton reminded her of the note again, she so belatedly thought to explain Abby's old white calico in which she died.

"I said to her, 'Won't you change your dress before you go out?' She said, 'No, this one is good enough.' "

To one who grew up in provincial mill-town society, this touch is the clumsiest of all Lizzie's lies. The thing is anthropologically impossible. *Even* for a social equal, Abby would have changed to go out; but if—as I have seen it suggested—poor lonely Abby, so ungiven to corporal works of mercy, had been called to a *humbler* bedside, she would have found it flatly unthinkable that she go out dressed beneath her station and "not looking right." And nobody in that whole taboo-ridden society could have known it better than Lizzie Andrew Borden.

There you have the Abby story in bare essence. Let us see what we can make of it.

Andrew, let us assume, is upstairs, as Bridget remembered, when Lizzie comes down; he leaves the house while Bridget is out behind it vomiting. Lizzie is already sleepwalking in her attack, aware and not aware. While Bridget is outside and Andrew had gone, Lizzie steals to the cellar and takes down the box of hatchets.

(Did Bridget sadly mention to Lizzie, as she sat over her coffee and cookies, that *herself* has took a notion on a day like this to get the windows washed? This would, at least, have been in character for many a Bridget.)

In the cellar, Lizzie can hear Bridget come in and the order being given again; she can hear Bridget go through the house shutting down the windows and start off to the stable for her mop. (By Bridget's own account, you may remember, she took the other equipment out first and did not come back in for her pail.)

Cautiously, Lizzie slips up to make sure that the screen-door is latched—for a little, only a little—and "appears" to Bridget, who tells her she will get her water from the barn. Bridget then goes to the back lot and falls into talk with "the girl at Kellys'."

Abby has gone upstairs. Lizzie slips down for the hatchet, conceals it under her stack of laundry, and unlatches the screen-door. (Not only must a murderer have had a chance to enter; Bridget must not rap for admittance at an inconvenient time.)

It is now nine, the hour when a neighbor saw the front door slammed in a young man's face, when Lizzie told Fleet on the murder day (and never repeated it) that a man came to the front door, when she told Fleet (again for the only time) that she had last seen Abby making up the guest-room bed.

The doorbell rings. Lizzie calls up to Abby that a note has come for her and she will bring it, since she is already on her way up with her clean wash.

The note—Andrew's final reassurance that Emma and Lizzie will never know—she tears fine and drops in a trash can, perhaps one at the foot of the cellar stairs, perhaps outside the screen-door. Harrington first saw the doctor trying to fit those scraps together as he stood by the entryway across the room from the stove.

She runs upstairs, carrying the clean clothes. As Abby straightens up from smoothing the bedspread, Lizzie flings the clothes behind her in one gesture connected with the first blow. As Abby falls dead, Lizzie slams the wooden shutters closed. The Harvard surgeons described the nineteen further blows as weak and ill-aimed for a man's, but they were hideously persistent.

Did the seizure pass away when that orgasm of hate was spent? I think that it did; that Lizzie saw with surprise the clothes still clean on the floor behind her—except, perhaps, for one tiny, unobserved spot on a starched white underskirt. (For she may, though this minor point has never been suggested, already have burned an underskirt before she was caught burning the Bedford cord. It is not significant, though I have found it interesting that so *little* blood got on her underskirt.) I think that she saw with surprise that there was only one tiny drop of blood on the bedspread, and none on the fresh fancy-work covers on the cushions propped up against the footboard.

There was cold water in the washstand; stained birdseye linen napkins would need no explaining that week. Her hands, her arms would be clean before she refolded and laid away that clean wash, whose presence put away upstairs she was compelled by guilty fear to mention, to explain. Only Lizzie would have thought that anybody would ever question it.

And so she explains the long-term mystery of why Abby uttered no outcry at seeing a stranger—or even Bridget or Lizzie —hatchet in hand, coming in at the door with a look of intent. For not even they did carpentry or chopped kindling; the Swede did that.

Lizzie knew why. And, being Lizzie, she saw it as a wise precaution to mention the fact that she had gone directly from the cellar to the second floor, *at nine, with an armful of clean clothes*. An armful of clean clothes covering a hatchet.

You know the rest. The hatchet could stand concealed in the tall slop pail. And when she was perfectly cleaned, face, hair, and all—that curly red hair needed only a little wiping off at the front—she could change to the dress that was so perfect in its verbal, point-for-point description: ribbed fabric, two-piece, half-train, figured, its colors navy and pale blue.

And her father never came home before dinner time.

⇥ 23 ⇤

In Bridget's story of the murder morning, as you remember, after Andrew came home, Lizzie went for a little sleeve board and began to iron a few handkerchiefs in the dining room, while they talked together. By Lizzie's first account she was engaged in this ironing *before* her father left home, shortly before nine. She changed the story quickly; she was only getting ready to iron, as her "flats" were oddly unwilling to get hot. So, she sat beside a coal stove in a kitchen chair for an hour and three-quarters (to figure from her timing of Andrew's return) just waiting, not opening dampers, shaking it down, adding more coal, or even getting herself and her heavy dress out of the heat.

The fire in the stove she sometimes described as good, sometimes low. (Dr. Bowen, you remember, found it still burning in the afternoon.) But through her long, patient wait beside it the sole encouragement she gave that fire was to lay a stick, a single stick, upon it *just* as she started to the barn loft. In other words, the hatchet-handle (which might not have burned all away, and so have been noticed as an oddity, wood lying *above* the coals) had to be allowed as short a time in the stove as possible.

Her only time upstairs that morning was five minutes or less, in which she basted a button-loop on a sleeve when she carried up her wash. (This was just enough time to let Bridget go through the house closing the windows, in case only her absence from the ground floor and not her subsequent "appearance" at the screen-door had been mentioned.)

But this happened early; she was down in the kitchen sitting by the stove and reading when her father came in. She did not know where "Maggie" was, but she must have let him in because he said that he had forgotten his key. (Apparently, at this point she is concentrating so hard on the detail of that night

184

bolt, twice found locked by daytime, that she overlooks the unlikelihood of her not having seen Maggie with her stepladder walk past her in the kitchen, the only way Maggie could get to the front door. The day latch on the door, it was found before the inquest, did not always catch. If her father *could* have got in with a key, an intruder could conceivably have got in without one.)

Understand, we are reporting Lizzie's first evidence about her father's return (Uncle John has taken the greater part of this initial hour and a half). To clear our minds about the first murder, we took up most of the first-day questions about Abby out of their proper time sequence. Here is the next sequence:

Q: Where was Maggie when the bell rang?

A: I don't know, sir.

Q: Where were you when the bell rang?

A: I think in my room upstairs.

Q: Then you were *upstairs* when the bell rang?

A: I don't know sure, but I think I was . . . as I say, I took up these clean clothes and basted a little piece of tape on a garment. [Just stated as having been at around nine.]

Q: Did you come down before your father came in?

A: *I was on the stairs coming down when she let him in.*

Throughout the years, Lizzie's defenders have persistently, laboriously distorted the inconvenient fact that within that *first moment or two* of being asked about her father's return, Lizzie said that when he came in she was in the kitchen, that she was in her room, and that she was on the stairs.

Knowlton tried to clear her mind and to calm her.

Q: You remember, Miss Borden—I will call your attention to it to see if I have any misunderstanding, not for the purpose of confusing you—you remember that you told me several times that you were downstairs and not upstairs when your father came home? You have forgotten that, perhaps?

A: I don't know what I have said. I have answered so many questions and am so confused that I don't know one thing from another.

Lizzie's defenders have always been partial to that sentence; it is effective, quoted out of context. But it was Fall River's own

Mr. Jennings who first presented Lizzie's statements that she was upstairs, downstairs, and on the stairs when Andrew returned, *not* as her initial memory of the situation but as the inevitable results of a tricky three-day grilling. I hereby give credit where credit is due.

These lies, however, could be any woman's panic response to a need to conceal the fact that she had been up near Abby's body; they lack the ineffable Lizzie touch.

Not so her explanation of what she had been doing in the kitchen when Andrew came home. It has never been mentioned before, and it is a beauty:

On the first day, Lizzie said that she had been reading an old magazine from the kitchen closet—where they were, in fact, hoarded. As an afterthought, she added that she also went into the dining room for the newspaper; she did not *read* it, she said, but she did bring it out there, just to have handy. It was the "only time" she left the side of the stove where she sat in the rocker waiting for her slow-heating flats except for the early trip to the w.c. ("only two or three minutes") and the subsequent trip with the wash ("not more than five minutes").

Bridget had described the roll of papers in Andrew's hand as being the size and shape of a magazine or a newspaper; Lizzie has left an *old* magazine near the stove [1] and then for good measure she has got the daily paper out there, too. In most houses, what could be likelier than someone's rolling up the one or the other and sticking it into the stove as she tidied the kitchen—the handiest place to get rid of it? It would account for a roll of papers, if it had been seen there.

In most houses. In the Borden house, old magazines were hoarded; old newspapers were saved both to start fires and for sanitary purpose. Moreover, if the documents had safely burned away, it was ill advised to labor an explanation of them, and even, perhaps, if they had not. Lizzie seems to have given all this considerable thought after her first hour and a half of testimony.

On the second day the magazine and the newspaper have van-

[1] A thin one—*Harper's Weekly*.

ished for good. She was not reading that morning; when her father came home, she was eating a pear, to pass the time away. And her brief departure from the side of the stove was not to the *dining room* for a subsequently neglected newspaper, but to the *sitting room,* where *she addressed a few paper wrappers.* (In her final one-hour wind-up she claimed to have addressed them to oblige Abby.)

She must have been delighted with this brilliant stroke. Chances were all against the papers in the stove not having burned safely away; how silly, really, to have worried about that part of it! But those paper wrappers, which she had forgotten to put back on her desk—the duplicates of that in which her father had brought home an old lock—ah, that had really needed explaining away!

Actually, you know, she was no fool. The unskilled clumsy lies show a real grasp of real probabilities. It was only by chance that the papers did not burn all away, that the lock was accepted without question, and that the coincidence of paper wrappers in the sitting room struck nobody.

Knowlton did not comment on the substitution of a pear for an old magazine and a newspaper. I doubt that he noticed it, for the sea of sand made very heavy ploughing that day.

He did, I am sure, notice one striking improvement on her story of the day before. Her father had not left the house at shortly before or shortly after *nine,* as she had alternately set the time in yesterday's testimony. He had stayed downstairs with her *"until ten or a little after."* In that railroad-flat layout, with its locked and bolted front door, he had sat for an hour and more since they last saw Abby alive—within sight of the front stairs, within sound of the guest room. He could not—as Bridget might—have been an accomplice, for he, too, had died. Knowlton did not yet have the final results of an examination of the stomach contents, which when it came made it impossible for the two deaths to have occurred so close in time; but even so, Lizzie had already given him enough to think about.

It did occur to him strongly that day that Bridget might have been an accomplice; and he never wholly relinquished the notion. It is easy to see why.

Lizzie had gone home the night before to find "Maggie" gone, bag and baggage. Girls from the south of Ireland, I have observed, often quit the service of those they like best without notice; it avoids unhappy words. Lizzie could never have understood such excess of tact; she must have been terrified. Had Maggie, after all, decided to tell that Lizzie had changed her clothes? She must make it yet more clear that Maggie could not have seen her, early or late.

When Knowlton asked on that second day where Bridget had been when her father came home, Lizzie answered firmly and without hesitation: *"Maggie had come in and gone upstairs."*

He reminded her that Bridget had opened the front door. Lizzie remained firm; she had not seen her. She did not know where she was.

Knowlton reminded her that Bridget had been washing the windows inside. Lizzie still had not seen her: "She might have been in one room and I in another."

In time, the defense treasured the picture of that cozy, domestic chat, Lizzie at her ironing and Bridget beside her washing windows; but Lizzie's own denials of having seen Bridget at all went on so long, so clumsily, in such blatant disregard of the physical possibilities in a house with that layout that Knowlton was reduced to pleading, "Miss Borden, I have been trying to get the story of that morning from yourself and Miss Sullivan and I have not succeeded. Do you desire to give me information or not?"

Lizzie stuck to her guns. She had not seen Miss Sullivan; by obvious extension, Miss Sullivan had not seen her.

Since Bridget had said nothing even faintly detrimental about Lizzie, in reference either to breakfast or to Andrew's return, small wonder that an intelligent man perceived that she must, instead, be holding something back—and something that Lizzie was in panic fear that she had not held back. Small wonder that he recalled Bridget for a grilling, not as long as her first but still considerably longer than any Lizzie ever got.

To the end of the case, he suspected a complicity, and one far darker than that which I see as the truth. I have sometimes wondered if his amusement was not tempered by wistfulness when he read one of his many letters after the preliminary investigation, a demand from an embattled Protestant that he cast "Bridget Sullivan and her Confessor" into prison and *force* them to confess. The letter ended: "Beware of Jesuits!"

Lizzie's story of her last moments with her father was also strikingly unlike Bridget's. They had not mentioned Abby, or the note, and she had not seen him take his key and go upstairs. He came in and sat down in the sitting room. She left her place by the stove and joined him.

"I asked him if he had any mail. He answered, 'None for you.' He had a letter in his hand." (It was as well that some torn-up letter should be provided for Dr. Bowen to find and burn. A *real* letter, that is, had to be accounted for.) [2] "I asked him how he felt. He said, 'About the same.' I asked him if he wanted the window left that way, if he felt a draught. He said, 'No.' That is all."

Further questions brought out that she watched him change to his jacket (which he did) and his slippers (which he did not) but that she did not help him or "touch the sofa in any way." He had been home less than five minutes when she once more tested her recalcitrant flats and paid her sole and (very unusual) attention to a coal fire—by laying a single stick on top of it, "in the hope that some few sparks would kindle it."

She then went directly to the loft. With striking formality, she put on a hat for her two or three steps from kitchen to stable door.

The hat accords with her style of lying; its presence, forgotten on the dining-room table, had to be accounted for. But—that *window?* Lizzie is so starkly uncreative. Was I wrong about those first rhythmic snores as Bridget went upstairs? Could an awful thought have struck Lizzie even as she saw Andrew first settling for his nap? The next-door windows were so very close. The least groan or outcry, should he have had the chance to emit any, as he did not, would have been heard next door.

Is it possible that Lizzie murmured something about draughts

2 She had more than one *possible* reason for her unsubstantiated triple insistence that he went to the post office.

and tried to close the window, only to hear Andrew demand what the devil she thought she was doing in that stifling heat?

In Fall River when I was young, we never closed windows *against* the heat. I only learned to do that sensible thing in later life.

She went to the loft at once to find lead for a sinker. Yes, there was lead in a basket down by the open door, but there was a boxful of old things upstairs.

(She has unintentionally transposed the actual positions of box and basket, as they were both found, but they and their contents are as real as all the other *things* she mentions.)

Did she find any lead, did she bring any back? No, she brought back nothing but a chip of wood that she picked up off the floor. (Details, those haunting, overmastering details! If a chip had chanced to fall from a broken hatchet-handle to the kitchen floor, who would have noticed it at such a time?)

How long was it since she had last been out to the stable? Not for *three months*. (Once more, the helpless addiction to fact: not, that is, since the death of her beloved pigeons.)

This much evidence, so quickly summarized, took long questioning to elicit. Now Knowlton sharpened: why had she chosen that particular moment to go to the barn for a fishing sinker for a possible afternoon's fishing four days ahead? (Miss Russell had told him when Lizzie was going to Marion.)

A: I was going to finish my ironing. The flats were not hot. I said to myself, 'I will try to find that sinker; perhaps when I get back my flats will be hot.' That is the only reason.

Grain by grain the fishing story continued. The family had some fishlines at the farm, but "some time ago"—which turned out to mean "five years, perhaps"—she had found no sinkers on them. She had not intended to use *those* lines, anyway, but buy new ones. She owned no apparatus for fishing of any kind, no, but she intended to go out *that noon* and buy a hook and line. (She had several times mentioned feeling ill that morning, but this would at least explain why she was dressed to go out.)

But, she added warily, she was not *sure* that they would go fishing Monday. (This is one of her odd, sudden cautions; "the girls" would have been startled at being asked if they, too, "angled.")

She had heard her father say that there was "lead with a hole in it" somewhere in the barn. She described—and accurately—the contents of the box that she falsely remembered as upstairs "on that workbench-like"—old locks, old doorknobs, some folded sheets of lead.

It had been full, but not very large. Clearly this could not have taken her fifteen minutes, or much more than three. How else had she spent her time?

A: I went to the west window over the hay and the curtain had slanted a little. I pulled it down.

Q: What else?

A: Nothing.

Yes, that was all she did. No, the window was not open.

Q: Hot?

A: Very hot.

(On this point, Lizzie's defense distrusted her as strongly as they distrusted her denial of the cozy chat with Bridget. It is one of the Articles of Belief that Lizzie was wrong, and the loft was pleasantly cool.)

But she stayed there at least fifteen minutes. (The minimum to which she can finally narrow it down from the original half an hour.)

Her memory improves: "I ate some pears there. . . . While I was looking out of the window, yes."

One almost hears Knowlton gulp.

Q: I now call your attention and ask whether all you have told me—I don't suppose you stayed there any longer than was *necessary*?

A: No, sir, because it was very close.

Q: I suppose the hottest place on the premises?

A: I suppose so.

Yet she still sees the downing of the pears as a necessity. She ate them, not, as she had first remembered, after looking at the box, but as soon as she got to the loft; three of them, in fact. (Which on top of the one just finished in the kitchen makes four.)

She had spoken of feeling sick. Did she feel better, then, "in that hot loft, looking out of that closed window, eating all those pears? She assured Knowlton that he had misunderstood her. She felt perfectly well, she had only told her mother that she did not care what kind of meat she chose for dinner.

At long last, Knowlton began to push hard.

Q: I ask you why you should select that place, which was the only place which would put you out of sight of the house, to eat those three pears in?

A: I cannot give you any reason.

He rephrases the question. She replies that she was also out of sight of the screen-door "for *only* about two minutes" while she picked up the pears.

Somehow, that limiting of the time she might have spent both out of sight of the door and in cool believable shade to "only two minutes" grudgingly spared from her desperate alibi as she had first conceived it strikes me as a wonderful example of the blind stubbornness for which Lizzie and Andrew alike were always famous.

Q: I ask you again, why you took those pears from the pear tree.

A: I did not take them from the pear tree.

[She has goaded him into his second lapse from perfection; this time he is not simply crisp but obviously vexed.]

Q: From the ground. *Wherever* you took them from. I thank you for correcting me. Going upstairs to the rear of the barn, the hottest place, and standing there, eating those pears that morning?

She has the bit in her teeth. Having set him right once, she does it again: "I *beg* your pardon. I was not at the *rear* of the barn, I was at the other end, that faced the street."

Knowlton's jaw must have dropped.

"Where you could see anybody coming into the house?"

"Yes, sir."

Incredibly, she stands firm. The murderer did not have a possible fifteen or twenty minutes in which to make his lucky getaway. If he did not do it in the two minutes, *"only* two," when she was under the pear trees, or the "three or four" while she was looking through the box, he had no other chance. For the rest of the time, Lizzie, in her sweltering eyrie, had eyed the yard.

Knowlton simply gave up and dropped the whole thing for good. He only asked her one last time if she might not have taken a little longer away from that window than she seemed to think. She admitted it as a bare possibility, since she had pulled over some boards to get at the box. (The real boards, which lay on the worktable beside the basket of scrap metal.)

Knowlton led her story back to the house. Her answers came oftenest in two or three words at a time.

She went through the kitchen to the dining room, where she took off her hat and laid it on the table. She started through the sitting room on her way upstairs.

Why? "To sit down."

What had become of the ironing? "The fire had gone out."

She saw her father lying down on the sofa.

Q: Describe anything you noticed at that time.

A: I did not notice anything, I was so frightened and horrified. I ran to the foot of the stairs and called Maggie. . . . I said, "Go for Dr. Bowen, I *think* father is hurt."

Q: Did you know he was dead?

A: No, sir.

Knowlton had studied the photographs. It was too much. For the only time in that long, patient investigation he was the man the defense would try to paint him as having been throughout. He fired the questions at her one by one.

"You saw him? You went into the room? You looked in at the door? Saw his face? You saw where his face was bleeding? Did you see the blood on the floor? You saw his face covered with blood? Did you see his eyeball hanging out? See the gashes where his face was laid open?"

Again and again, "No, sir."

"Nothing of that kind?"

"No, sir."

The transcript reads: *Witness covers her face for a minute or two; then examination is resumed.*

It was gently resumed. Knowlton changed the subject and did

193

not ask her to speak of her father again. But at least he knew that her account of that casual strolling in to go upstairs and sit down was wholly unlike any description of the discovery that she had given to the other witnesses.

Her testimony on the household hatchets, given at the end of her Wednesday afternoon questioning, was also unlike that which she had promptly given Officer Mullaly on the murder day.

To Knowlton she denied knowing whether or not they had ever owned a hatchet. Her father killed some pigeons in May or June, she added abruptly, but she thought he wrung their necks. She remembered asking an odd question: " 'Why are their heads off?' I think I remember telling someone that he had twisted them off."

This is tragic pure essence of Lizzie—impelled to *mention* that death in this context so that she may deny the thing that seems to her so hauntingly relevant, and quite blind to the unlikelihood that Knowlton would ever hear of it.

Judge Blaisdell then asked Knowlton to find out what effort Lizzie had made to notify her mother of her father's death.

She denied suggesting that Mrs. Borden was upstairs, that she had asked or suggested that she be looked for, or that she looked herself. But then she amended these denials.

"I did not do anything except what I said to Mrs. Churchill. I said to her, 'I don't know where Mrs. Borden is, but I wish you would look.' "

Knowlton asked, "Where did you intend her to look?"

Lizzie replied, "In Mrs. Borden's room."

It is perhaps the sweetest example of Lizzie's ineptitude as a liar. Her hearers might not realize that "Mrs. Borden's room" had already been searched; but surely few, even in Lizzie's tight spot, would have failed to realize that Mrs. Borden's marked lack of curiosity about the excitement below had an obvious explanation, and one that made a so casual suggestion of a so limited search pretty funny.

That about covers the inquest. Dark legends of its brutality still hang heavy over the facts. Yet aside from that one moment when Lizzie said she "thought" Andrew was "hurt," she was treated with amazing forbearance and gentleness.

When it was over, Knowlton had not only heard Lizzie repeatedly contradict herself, but contradict every other witness whom he questioned. When a long grilling had shown Bridget to be in agreement with every other witness except Lizzie, he thought he had a case.

You may disagree with him. But at least, unlike most of those with strong opinions on the Borden murders, you have got Lizzie at first hand. You have heard her speak for herself. You have heard what poor Mr. Jennings feared you might hear.

He sequestered the two legal records of this court process. And if a disregarded small-town newspaper had not also taken down a full stenographic record when Lizzie's inquest testimony was read aloud at the preliminary investigation, we should still know only that it had "minor variations," no more. We should know nothing that Mr. Jennings did not want us to know.

BOOK FOUR

How Lizzie Became a Cause

✦ 24 ✦

THE inquest ended at four on Thursday, one week and almost five hours after the murders were discovered.

Lizzie emerged from the hearing and flung herself on the couch in the matron's room. Mary Brigham stayed close by her side. Emma and Bridget sat in far corners of the same room, white and still.

Knowlton and Hilliard drove to Mr. Jennings' house and brought him back. Then Hilliard said to Lizzie, "I have here an order for your arrest. I shall read it if you so desire, but you have a right to waive the reading."

Jennings turned to Lizzie. He said, "Waive the reading."

Lizzie gave him a long look, which the press called cryptic for no better reason, I suspect, than the effect that was given by her startlingly pale eyes. She said, "You need not read it."

Emma began to shake and cry. Lizzie was white and moist-eyed but controlled, her face almost stolid. They called a carriage for Emma; when she stepped outside she looked at the crowds with such obvious suffering that the reporters found it pathetic. The police led Bridget to another room.

It was now half past four. Lizzie had waited out that week with an awful control that baffled strangers and touched her friends to the heart. Now she was alone with the matron, the wait was over. And at long last, she broke.

She sobbed, hysterically and long. She went into a dreadful, protracted vomiting and retching. The matron could not help her; it did not stop. They sent for Dr. Bowen, who sedated her.

She was not put into a cell. The couch in the matron's room was made up for her, and she was "treated with the utmost kindness and consideration." A local reporter was unfeeling enough to point out that never before in the history of Bristol County had a prisoner received such special, red-carpet treatment.

The next day's Providence *Journal* ran a banner headline: AT LAST! LIZZIE BORDEN ARRESTED.

They also published interviews with Marshal Hilliard and Mr. Buck.

Marshal Hilliard said: "She is a remarkable woman and possessed of a wonderful power of fortitude."

Mr. Buck said, "She still retains the same Christian spirit of resignation as at the onset, and her calmness is the calmness of innocence."

Cynics have laughed at the conduct of the ubiquitous Mr. Buck and his assistant Mr. Jubb throughout the trial. They hint that Lizzie's inheritance made her a favored parishioner. I know nothing about Jubb beyond his own words often quoted in the press; he sounds a dreadful Stiggins. But Mr. Buck was a good man, and, I am sure, he was Lizzie's selfless true believer. He had a hard and disillusioning time of it after the trial, when Lizzie gave him one shock after another. And throughout, he lacked good judgment; but he followed his own best lights.

The press watched him come and go on his visits to Lizzie on the day of the arrest and the day after. They noted the flowers that filled her window in the station house. And they waited for the arraignment and the preliminary investigation, which would give them something solid to write up.

Their hopes were once more disappointed.

By Massachusetts law, these proceedings were slated to be held before old Judge Blaisdell. Mr. Jennings entered a surprising and vigorous protest.

"By all the laws of human nature, you cannot help being influenced by the evidence which has been submitted to you," he said at one point. "You might look at things differently from what you do if certain questions that have been asked in the inquest had been excluded."

This was undeniable. If Knowlton had not asked like the others, "Where were you, Lizzie, when it happened?" or "Where were you when your father came home?" the judge might indeed have looked at things differently.

However, precedent is precedent. Knowlton said, "My brother is in error. More than twenty times to my certain knowledge this thing has been done. The inquest was *against* no one. It was to ascertain who committed these murders. It is your honor's duty to hear this complaint."

Jennings was overruled. Knowlton moved a continuation until August 22.

Lizzie went back to the matron's room on the arm of Mr. Buck. John Morse was summoned and released on bail; the money was put up by my former neighbors, Mr. Almy and Mr. Milne, Andrew's pallbearer and his partner. They did not extend the same generosity to Bridget; Mr. Jennings at the time did not foresee the wisdom of such a gesture.

Instead, Marshal Hilliard and State Detective Seaver vouched for her. Throughout that morning they had unofficially and lengthily reexamined her. Now she was called from her corner, pale and vastly confused, and permitted to return to her cousin's house on Division Street until new employment was arranged for her at the New Bedford Jail.

The prisoner spent the night in her flower-filled room. She was taken to Taunton Jail next day by the 3:40 train. Emma and Mr. Jennings came for her in a carriage; Mr. Buck was with them. Hilliard and Seaver crowded in, too. Lizzie's brief crack-up was over, and the reporters found her disappointingly composed.

Readers of the *News* had been sure that she would clear every thing up at the inquest; she had not, and there were crowds in the streets. To avoid them, the carriage did not take the direct one-street way to the depot; in that slant-built town, it had to go up hill and down dale on its zigzag route.

On the railway platform, Lizzie turned white and tottered. The Marshal and Mr. Buck had to support her. She wore a blue high-style dress and her cherry-trimmed hat with its short veil. Mr. Buck carried much reading matter, chiefly religious, though some secular magazines were included.

As Lizzie took her seat by the car window her face appeared

vacant and abstracted. Her party sat motionless, none of them speaking to one another, and Lizzie stared before her. Then Emma drew the window shade between them and the pushing, peering crowd on the platform.

Taunton Jail is small and ivy-grown; of its nine cells for women, five were in occupancy. When Mr. Buck had left Lizzie there he had another word for the reporters about her "calm resignation." He added that her friends would be allowed to drop in, and that she had asked not to be shown any newspapers.

After he had left, Mrs. Wright, wife of the sheriff and matron of the jail, came out to the reporters in tears. She had been a Ferry Street neighbor before Andrew's fortunes rose. Lizzie's name in the newspapers had rung no bell, but those large, pale, protruding eyes, which Mr. Bence had found so unmistakable, she, too, had remembered, and after almost twenty years. She stared, and said, "Why, aren't you the Lizzie who used to play with my Isobel?" [1]

She cried as she told the reporters about it, reporters who would also see her husband's tears at the moment when Lizzie was pronounced not guilty.

This is all the explanation we need for an odd fact usually explained by hints of bribery: namely, that all through the nine months Lizzie spent in Taunton Jail she was taken out almost daily for refreshing strolls in the open air. Her meals, too, were not the common prisoners' fare; they came by carriage from the town's best hotel in a special four-decker dinner-pail. [2] I am sure that no attempt to bribe good Sheriff Wright would have been permitted by able counsel; and it was not needed.

Meanwhile, Mr. Jubb inveighed against Judge Blaisdell, calling the decision that he should sit on the forthcoming hearing "scandalous and indecent." As he was an Englishman who had lived in America only a year, his ignorance of Massachusetts law is understandable.

Central Congregational invited a former minister, Dr. Mason of the Bowen College Church in Maine, to come and preach;

1 Edwin H. Porter, *The Fall River Tragedy* (Fall River: George R. H. Buffington, 1893).
2 Now the property of the Fall River Historical Society.

he assured the congregation: "God is with the poor, storm-tossed girl. He will vindicate and he will glorify."

The women's auxiliary of the Y.M.C.A. held a meeting at which Mrs. Hezekiah Brayton—the only matron in town who could have been considered one up socially on Mrs. Jerome Borden—offered a prayer that the cloud of unjust suspicion might be lifted.

A newspaper took Judge Blaisdell to tasks for the harsh words used in the complaint. Since he had merely read off the form for the accusation of murder that had been in unvarying use since the days of the colonies, he was surprised by the suggestion that Lizzie's case called for a new form of courteous understatement.

With Lizzie in jail and the hearing put off, the murder story lost its lead place in the Providence *Journal* for the first time in ten days; the old paper looked like itself again.

On the eighteenth, one Charles Peckham gave himself up to the Fall River police and made a full confession. He had, he explained, leapt over the barbed wire fence behind the Borden house. He had been wearing the clothes in which he now turned himself in; they had not got stained because the Bordens' blood had stagnated from all the poison they had taken.

The defense did not invite Mr. Peckham to witness at the final trial; however, they invited Joseph Lemay, who only eight days after the murders had seen the murderer with his bloody axe and his unchanged shirt weeping for Mrs. Borden on the edge of a scrub grove of maples.

No effort was spared to keep things quiet for Lizzie when she was brought back to Fall River on the twenty-second. The reporters were told that her train would come in at around two. However, word spread that the stately Mrs. Marianna Holmes was hovering about the depot well before eleven; her civic position and devotion to the cause had made her a figure to be noted. The newsmen gathered just in time to see Emma also waiting as Lizzie got off the train, leaning upon the arm of Mr. Buck.

The secrecy had helped; there was no crowd. Nevertheless, the carriage once more avoided Main Street and took its up-and-down zigzag way to the police station.

Outside the building itself, the crowd was vast; stretching back from both sides of the door, men and women stood lined up patiently for many blocks, as if the intensity of their desires could somehow stretch the walls of the courtroom and gain them admission to the three hundred seats within.

The police cleared an entranceway, and Lizzie passed through the crowd to lunch in the matron's room with Emma and Marianna.

By half past twelve the station house guardroom was already filled with smartly dressed ladies and their escorts, Fall River's best. They were admitted and shown to their seats before the doors were opened to the vulgar herd. Oddly enough, every doctor in town seemed to be there; the case exerted a peculiar fascination over the whole profession.

Forty out-of-town newspapers were represented. The room was quickly packed full, and the crowd outside continued to grow. Inside, there was a hush of anticipation, broken by excited murmurs at each entry: Judge Blaisdell, Dr. Bowen, Mayor Coughlin, Eli Bence.

Blaisdell took his seat at two. For half an hour, nothing happened. Mr. Jennings was in conference with Lizzie; at two thirty, he asked to confer with Mr. Knowlton. The judge looked frequently at his watch. Fifty minutes after he had taken his seat the two lawyers came in. Knowlton had caused the delay. Professor Wood's final examination of the stomachs, which would give the definitive word on the time-lapse between the murders, was not completed. The Government wanted it presented as eagerly as the defense wanted it withheld.

The judge granted a stay of three more days. It was arranged that Lizzie would remain as before in the matron's room.

Which brings us to a consideration of the Government's most thoroughly discredited witness: Mrs. Reagan, matron of the Fall River station house.

»» 25 ««

Mrs. Reagan, so she claimed, overheard a quarrel between Lizzie and Emma; the obvious inference to be drawn from her report of it was that Emma knew Lizzie to be guilty. Lizzie's lawyers and Lizzie's friends pressured Mrs. Reagan to retract. In all likelihood, she did retract under that pressuring, though ten months later she once more vouched for the truth of the story in court.

Before I had studied the case carefully, this Mrs. Reagan bit bothered me. I knew that Lizzie had always got on most easily with her social inferiors; I could not see why Mrs. Reagan would invent a malicious lie about her, or why after Lizzie had learned of the lie she remained on good terms with Mrs. Reagan, as she did. But on the other hand, I was also sure that Emma had never let herself believe that Lizzie was guilty.

Mrs. Reagan's story made sense only after I first realized that Lizzie had changed her dress—and that Emma, who always had her feet on the ground, would surely have felt that their discreet and helpful lawyer, Mr. Jennings, should know about it, too. Lizzie was never fond of Mr. Jennings, but Emma, like the rest of us, respected his sterling probity and trusted his discretion; I have been told so by too many slightly younger members of Emma's generation to have any reasonable doubt of it. Not that she wanted Lizzie to tell him that she had *burned* a dress, no. (Mr. Jennings himself made that clear later.) Only that she had been afraid to tell about finding Abby and had changed for the street, from the cotton cord, which accidentally got stained in the moment of discovery. Bridget knew that she had changed her dress, and no more; Emma could have made herself believe that it was *innocently* stained with Abby's blood. God knows she must have wanted to believe it.

With this in mind, let us begin the story with Mrs. Reagan's account of it in court the following June.

Mrs. Hannah Reagan testifies:

"I am the matron for the Fall River police station. . . . On August 24 (this was the day before the preliminary investigation) Miss Emma Borden came to see her sister. It was about twenty minutes to nine, and I was tidying up the room.

"I let her in . . . and I went into a toilet room about four feet from where Miss Lizzie Borden was lying on a couch, and I heard very loud talk, and I came to the door, and it was Miss Lizzie Borden. She was lying on her right side, and her sister was talking and bending over her, and Lizzie says, 'Emma, you have given me away, haven't you?'

"She says, 'No, Lizzie, I have not.'

" 'You have,' she says, 'and I will let you see I won't give in one inch,' and she sat right up and put up her finger (*witness measures on finger with thumb*) and I stood in the doorway, looking at both of them.

"Lizzie Borden lay down on the couch on her left side and faced the window and closed her eyes, and Miss Emma got a chair, I gave her a chair, and she sat right down beside her sister. They sat there until Mr. Jennings came to the door, somewhere about eleven o'clock. Miss Lizzie didn't speak to her sister or turn her face to her any more that forenoon."

So Mrs. Reagan told it, and surely that terse exchange followed by a two-hour-and-twenty-minute sulking silence sounds more like the typical Borden family fight than the sort of quarrel an Irish police matron would dream up from her own experience.

Mrs. Reagan, according to her story, let Mr. Jennings in. The silence was heavy on the air, and Mr. Jennings, a far from thick-skinned man, seems to have understood it at once. He said to Emma, "Have you told her all?"

Emma said, "Yes, all."

Mrs. Reagan went about her work, found herself cornered by Mr. Porter from the *Globe* and the fellow from the Providence *Journal,* and had, for a change, something more interesting to tell than the usual dull tidbits about gifts of flowers and visits from friends and clergy.

Porter's version of the story is slightly different from Mrs. Reagan's ten-month-old memory, just given. In this, Emma said, in answer to Lizzie's accusation, "I only told Mr. Jennings what I thought he ought to know." The Providence *Journal* had it "what he ought to know for *your defense*."

Emma, another woman, could have had little hope that a court would accept as they did the heavy silk bengaline as a likely morning choice of housewear in which to sit by a hot stove. However, one who has ploughed through the long, drab, reiterative panic of Lizzie's lies about the invisible Maggie who opened the door and washed the windows—unseen, and so unseeing—can have little doubt that this change of dress was a matter that Lizzie felt strongly about keeping under wraps.

As soon as the *Globe* and the Providence *Journal* hit the local stands with the story, Mr. Jennings took the first train to Boston and came back with Melvin O. Adams, a well-known trial lawyer; this was the first outside help engaged by the defense. ("Graceful" is the word by which Col. Adams is more than once characterized in the press, as Mr. Jennings is "nervous.")

A council of war was called at the police station, made up of the two lawyers, Mr. Buck, and Mr. Holmes who, though a banker and kingpin of the laymen at Central, was said to be very much under the thumb of Lizzie's protectress, the full-sailed Marianna.

They drew up the following statement: "This is to certify that my attention has been called to a report *said to have been made* by me in regard to a quarrel between Lizzie and her sister Emma, in which Lizzie said, 'Emma, you have given me away, etc.' and that I expressly and positively deny that any such conversation ever took place and that I further deny that I ever heard anything that could be construed as a quarrel between the sisters."

(You observe that the wording gives Mrs. Reagan every chance to deny her story without embarrassment and pass the buck to the dishonest reporters.)

The Rev. Mr. Buck was elected to bear the paper to Mrs. Reagan for her signature. In words that he heard quoted in court and did not deny, he said, "If you sign this paper, it will make everything all right between Miss Lizzie Borden and her sister."

These are striking words. For consider: an actual disagreement, precipitated by something that Emma had said and Mrs. Reagan had inconveniently overheard could readily have left the sisters angrily blaming each other for the ill-timed indiscretion, with everything far from "all right between" them. But how could a malicious lie made up out of whole cloth have done anything but draw them together in embattled fury against the liar?

Mrs. Reagan asked to be given the paper to take down to Marshal Hilliard. Mr. Buck refused to hand it over, but agreed to show it to Hilliard himself.

Hilliard looked at it. He spoke angrily, first to Mrs. Reagan, "You go to your room, and I will attend to this business. And you, Mr. Buck, attend to yours."

Marshal Hilliard then started checking up. Mrs. Reagan assured him that her story was true, and he sought out Mr. Jennings to say a few firm words about tampering with Government witnesses. Mr. Jennings stormed from the building, waving the prepared retraction over his head. Though by temperament tensely reserved, he seems in that moment to have been beside himself with his sense of injustice.

Almost fifty reporters had gathered, and Mr. Jennings shouted to them: "This is an outrage! The Marshal has refused to let Mrs. Reagan sign this paper!"

The crowd surged forward, notebooks in hand; but Mr. Jennings recovered his discretion, leaped into his carriage, and drove away.

However, he continued to pressure Mrs. Reagan to deny her story, as did the Rev. Mr. Buck, the Holmeses, and Mary Brigham. Mrs. Reagan did not even have the Marshal on her side; he liked eavesdropping, loose-mouthed matrons as little as he liked a concerted attempt to intimidate a possible witness. In the presence of State Detective Seaver that evening, he really did forbid her to sign that paper, as he had been prematurely accused of doing, but he also added a stern warning for the future:

"If you have got anything to say about this, you will do it *on the witness stand in court.*"

I believe that Mrs. Reagan denied her story. Lizzie's closest friends testified that she denied it to them and to Mr. Buck. (Mr. Buck preferred not to testify himself, and was excused out of respect to the cloth.) Mr. Holmes testified likewise.

Three reporters also said she did. One of them, Mr. Hickey, had been discharged from the *Globe* at the time of the trial and had his eye on a berth at the *Herald,* Almy-Milne property. Another, Mr. Caldwell, was a close personal friend of the third, Mr. Manning; and our Mr. Phillips characterized "my friend Manning" as the *only* reporter of all those who came to Fall River, with the exception of "the genial Mr. Archer of the Boston *Evening Transcript*" to treat the case "with even a semblance of fairness."

In other words, the seven who asked for a denial (if they all did) were not wholly unbiased witnesses. Yet I believe them. And not only because Mrs. Reagan had been frightened; I'd be surprised to learn that she did not like Lizzie as much as Bridget and her other servants always did. I think that she blurted out her story, realized the harm she had done, and regretted it—until she learned more at the preliminary investigation and decided to testify.

But it is not for her sake that I find the story interesting; it is for what it indicates about Emma, always so unhappily clearheaded and so deliberately blind.

And, yes, because it also indicates that Lizzie's much touted "calm of innocence" was not shared by her friends.

⇛ 26 ⇚

God knows, poor Mr. Jennings must have found Mrs. Reagan's story important. His rush to Boston to bring the graceful Col. Melvin O. Adams in on the case took place on the morning when the twice-delayed preliminary investigation finally got under way.

Mr. Jennings was cut out to be a family solicitor, not a trial lawyer. While he still trusted Lizzie, I am sure that he was as unhappy as Emma over her stubborn refusal to let the facts about her innocent change of dress be known. And later I do not think that he was capable of a full emotional assent to the trial lawyer's duty to protect his client whether he believes him innocent or guilty. I wish that in-group tact had not kept him from discovering how little anyone blamed him for having been, as we came to believe, the instrument of a pay-off that we did not fully understand. He would not talk, and he never found it out.

And fourteen years after Lizzie's death, his faithful Mr. Phillips was moved to explain that the public had never seen "the mass of documents" because "until the recent (!) death of Miss Borden," Mr. Jennings (who had predeceased her by five years) considered that "their secrecy was important to her defense." Not because they contained anything incriminating, but because "facts which were gathered in her interest" would "meet any new phases of police investigation" and be "important if the trial should be reconsidered by the District Attorney."

Poor honest, intelligent, sensitive Mr. Jennings! How he would have winced to see the cache in the hip bath thus publicized and quaintly explained away as a legal ignoramus' fear of double jeopardy for his ex-client! It would be a strange lawyer indeed who did not know that one acquitted of murder is acquitted for good and all, no matter what damning facts are later discovered.

We have studied the first set of "facts which were gathered in her interest": the inquest.

As for the preliminary, as forty out-of-town newspapers show, it differed from the trial only on three major points: Alice had not yet brought herself to tell about the dress-burning, Mr. Bence was allowed to testify, and Lizzie's inquest testimony was read aloud.

And, yes, there was another difference: Mr. Jennings had a major part in the proceedings. It was not his fault that he was eased aside directly they were over; he had only shown a little too much faith in Lizzie.

When the court reopened after its three-day stay, the crowds in the street were as great as ever. But far fewer from the upper crust were present. Too much had been said in the papers about that earlier assemblage of ladies from the hill.

Bridget came provided with a lawyer, Dr. Kelly's young kinsman James T. Cummings. It has been hinted that Mr. Jennings had felt she might need this legal support since she intended to withhold evidence. I find no basis for the rumor, and she could not have offered much of a retainer on four dollars a week.

Emma wore mourning; she looked drawn and tense.

Lizzie wore blue with red trimmings, and her manner was composed. Throughout the six days of the investigation her lips often twitched and worked together, but otherwise—with two notable exceptions—she remained apparently quite calm and collected.

Dr. Dolan was the first witness. Shown a photograph of the body, he pointed out how it had sagged from when he first saw it; the head was no longer propped high on the arm of the sofa. The Prince Albert, formerly wedged deep beneath the head, had also become disarranged. The rest of his evidence you know.

Next, Thomas Kieran, an engineer, read off the measurements of the house and grounds and the distance to the banks downstreet. He further deposed that Miss Brigham, standing on the landing, had been unable to see a man lying on the floor where Abby had lain. Few newspapers found this experiment worth reporting at the time and none at the final trial; but a recent defense of Lizzie has sharply criticized its deletion in the editing of those two thousand pages. (Dr. Bowen carelessly mentioned that he *could* see the body from the landing.)

Knowlton then recalled Dr. Dolan to ask if he could state positively that the deaths took place at least an hour apart. The medical evidence from Harvard would settle the point with finality when it arrived; Mr. Jennings' excited objection to the question was both useless and impolitic. However, he fought it out until the court recessed for noontime dinner.

This was the day the battle with Mrs. Reagan was at its height. The interested reporters needed to have their attention diverted. During the recess, the graceful Melvin O. Adams called them together and handed out copies of a letter to one and all; the original, he explained, had been mailed to Emma Borden from Waltham on the day of Lizzie's arrest.

The letter was from a man who identified himself as "a Jewish pedler" who traveled about selling handmirrors, shoelaces, blacking, and the like. He said that "when the fatal murder occurred" he had met a bloodstained man not far from Fall River who told him that he had got into a fight with a farmer.

Mr. Jennings, the reporters were told, had telegraphed the Mayor of Waltham, who replied that nobody of the name signed to the letter lived there, though he might have come from Boston.

The press was not overexcited by this newsbreak. Letters of the sort were constantly pouring into police headquarters; Massachusetts and Rhode Island that August seem to have been infested with bloodstained wanderers.

Anyway, Col. Adams had tried.

Mr. Bence was the first witness of the afternoon. When he appeared on the stand Lizzie "evinced extreme uneasiness." He told a plain, unvarnished, and highly convincing tale. Col. Adams, in a lengthy and severe cross-questioning, was unable to make him anything but consistent, placid, and matter-of-fact. True, he could not describe Lizzie's hat or handbag and refused to attempt it, but his very caution told in his favor. Hart and Kilroy thought that Lizzie had the "cape"—that is, the little flared collarette—with her; Mr. Bence would not swear to it, for he had been concentrating on her unexpected request, delivered in a low and somewhat shaky voice. Prussic acid is dangerous to handle and not used for making up home-brewed insecticides; she left him empty-handed. That was all.

The police, on first hearing Mr. Bence's story, had taken him along with Hart and Kilroy to stand below the windows of the Borden house and listen to Lizzie's voice; it was a stupid way to fix an identification, and the defense pounced upon it, attempting to make it appear that Mr. Bence had *only* recognized

Lizzie by her voice heard through the window. The attempt fell flat and the defense knew better than to attempt it at the trial.

According to the Providence *Journal,* everyone was "gravely impressed" by the fact that severe cross-questioning had not at all disturbed Mr. Bence's evidence.

The other witnesses were heard. Except for Alice, who remained silent about the dress-burning, and Phoebe Bowen, who could not remember what dress Lizzie wore on the murder day, all evidence was consistent with that given later, and you have read it in the narrative.

Only Bridget added one unfortunate touch, for she had no way of knowing that the defense would eventually struggle to prove that the Bedford cord became so paint-stained back in May as to make it unwearable thereafter. After denying that she knew what Lizzie wore on the day of the murders, she added, "Wednesday, the day we was all sick, *that* was the day she wore the blue wrapper."

Knowlton's assistant, William Moody, asked if this was one of the two new dresses that had been made in May, and Bridget answered, "Yes."

The report from Harvard Medical School did not come in until the fifth day, when the witnesses had all been heard. It separated the deaths of Andrew and Abby by probably two hours, possibly only an hour and a half. This was unfortunate. But to the joy of the defense, not a trace of blood had been found on the bengaline. It was truly, as Mr. Jennings told the press, "the deliverance of Lizzie Borden."

No blood had been found on the shoes and stockings handed over six days after the crime, either. And there was only one drop on the starched white underskirt, a tiny, easily overlooked drop scarcely larger than a pinhead. (Prof. Wood, in the trial transcript, said that it was six inches from the hem.)

Oddly enough, this drop of blood had come from the *outside;* it was markedly heavier on the outer starchy glaze than it was within.

At the inquest, in a throw-away line with no follow-up,

Knowlton had asked Lizzie if she knew how a bloodstain could have got on her underskirt. She replied, "I have fleas." The answer was quaintly dictated by a Victorian delicacy which the Tampax advertisements now make it hard for us to believe in; but it was, in fact, more convincing than that which her defense later offered, in refined circumlocutions, to the jury. And a female jury would have known it. Over their heavy napkins, women wore ruffled drawers to the knee and short white petticoats under the underskirt; I remember. A widish smear caused by a heavy period was quite possible; a small, clear-edged spot, so placed, would have been wildly improbable even if it had come from the inside, not the outside, of the garment.

However, men judged the case, and have judged it ever since.

(It was, incidentally, a woman who wrote to Knowlton that a *bloodless* dress on a daughter who had just found her father lying in his blood was a suspicious circumstance and not the opposite.)

When the evidence from Harvard had been heard, Knowlton called the court stenographer, Miss Annie White, to vouch for the exact length of time that Lizzie had been present on each day, and that Dr. Dolan and State Detective Seaver had been present throughout.

He then read Lizzie's inquest testimony aloud.

At the end, he said quietly, "This is the case for the Commonwealth."

The newspapers all noted that Lizzie's testimony contained self-contradictions, but it was a drab, wandering, and confused business from which to make a good news story. The New Bedford *Standard-Times,* with a fine sense of legal responsibility, withheld its full stenographic coverage until a jury had been chosen for the trial.

For the last day of the investigation there remained only the summaries.

Many have expressed surprise at their length, Jennings' so full-bodied and emotional, Knowlton's so painstaking in its point-for-point refutations, like summaries addressed to a jury, not simply to a judge who could only decide whether to pass the case on to a Grand Jury who would, in turn, decide whether it should come to trial.

Those who speak so miss the point. The summaries were indeed addressed to that jury who would, in the end, free or condemn Lizzie Borden. They were addressed to forty-two out-of-town reporters who represented forty newspapers and through them to public opinion.

Lizzie would leave the Second District Court of Fall River in the character of a woman suspected of murder because her own testimony gave her sole opportunity for the murder of Abby and no credible alibi for the murder of Andrew—or she would leave it as the victim of a brutal police force and a power-hungry D.A.

For the most part, Mr. Jennings did well.

The God of Reason alone knows why the words "circumstantial evidence" mean, *per se*, faulty evidence to the man in the street, since it stands when witnesses may lie and it is the only evidence upon which crimes done in secret ever can be judged; but the prejudice exists even now, when we revere the scientist, and it was stronger in a day deeply convinced that a man with plain horse sense knew more than any so-called experts with their theories.

It was Mr. Jennings' job to appeal powerfully to that prejudice and splash the damning words on the front page, and he did it handsomely. If Lizzie's dislike of him was confirmed for good that day, and before he left the courtroom he was due to be eased out of any active place in the defense, it was not by his fault.

He believed Lizzie innocent. He could not have guessed how showily he was about to break her down with one strong sentence in her defense: "We have heard a description of the injuries, and I suggest that even the learned District Attorney himself cannot imagine that any person could have committed that crime unless his heart was as black as hell."

Lizzie's mouth shook. Then her whole body was wracked with sudden, convulsive sobbing. She spread her hands and pressed them over her face, but she could not hide the tears that poured over it.

Mr. Jennings, his face lifted in the orator's stance, did not notice; he went on steadily. "Blow after blow was showered upon them. . . ." Lizzie's body shrank and tensed upon the sobs that it could not control and her hands sought desperately to cover her distorted mouth, her streaming eyes.

At last he changed his tack, and she got herself in hand.

The boys after her pigeons in the barn, the daytime robbery of which he had so recently learned, were presented as Lizzie had tried to present them to Alice Russell: evidence of lurking enemies, a history of repeated burglaries.

This was good; but he must have terrified Lizzie when he began to suggest Bridget as a possible suspect, saying often, "Mind you, I don't say that Bridget Sullivan did it." This was a theme avoided by ex-Governor Robinson at the final trial, though he pulled out every other stop; but the case was older then, and Robinson was a shrewd man.

The mention of Bridget led Jennings into the Cordelia theme: the gentle youngest daughter.

"Would it be the stranger, or would it be the one bound to the murdered man by ties of love? And, right here, what does it mean when we say the *youngest* daughter? The last one whose baby fingers have been lovingly entwined about her father's head? Is there nothing in the ties of love and affection?"

Lizzie had got herself in hand. She did not break again. The reporters saw her bite her lips fiercely, but she held on, not sobbing, her handkerchief over her eyes, and as soon as Jennings dropped the subject, she wiped them and sat upright. Her swollen eyelids were red in her white face, but she was steady.

Jennings went on to describe the inquest in the manner that he created and gave its ever returning popularity: "I have stated before that I consider the inquisition of this girl an outrage. Here was a girl they had been suspecting for days. She was virtually under arrest, and yet for the purpose of extracting a confession from her to support their theory they brought her here and put her upon the rack. . . . As in the days of the rack and thumbscrews, so she was racked again and again. Day after day the same questions were repeated to her in the hope to elicit some information that would criminate (*sic*) her. Is there any wonder that there are conflicting statements?"

This was good stuff, worth repeating word for word. It was better with his further addition: "Lizzie Borden who had been under surveillance for days and *compelled to take preparations* to induce sleep."

Before she testified, Dr. Bowen left Lizzie an eighth of a grain of morphine to help her sleep one night, and when that did not work he left her a quarter-grain on two succeeding nights. Dr. Louis Lasagna, professor of pharmacological medicine at the Johns Hopkins Medical School and an eminent authority, assures me that these dosages, given at bedtime, could not have disturbed her mental processes while she was testifying unless given intravenously (they were given by mouth) and continued considerably longer. It did not matter. The phrase "compelled to take preparations," like the rack and thumbscrews and the twining baby fingers, worked powerfully upon popular opinion.

"Do you realize that the poor girl was drugged? They *drugged* her and then spent three whole days trying to trip her up!"

Jennings made only one tactical error in his summary. He cannot be blamed for it. Alice still kept her secret about the dress-burning, Emma had clearly told him little, and O. M. Hanscom had not been permitted to linger about the house.

However, remembering Mr. Jennings as I do, I fear that he did unjustly blame himself for that bit of oratory. It came at the end of a good job, but he was one of those unfortunate souls who remember their mistakes more vividly than their successes.

He had just discussed the hatchet-head. Had the statement from Harvard experts that detectable blood could have been removed with cold running water proved that there had ever been blood on it in the first place? Of course not.

Then, most unfortunately, he warmed to his theme: "Where did she get rid of the weapons? The dress, the shoes that she had on that morning? Are there any shoebuttons in the fire? *Is there any smell of burnt clothing?* No!"

That was his climax, though his final passage was lengthy

and moving. It ended, "Don't, Your Honor, put the stigma of guilt on this woman, reared as she has been and with a character past reproach."

As he fell silent, a hush was on the courtroom. Many had tears in their eyes. According to the Providence *Journal*, Col. Adams looked deeply moved and young Mr. Phillips was weeping openly.

After a long moment of quiet, the whole courtroom burst into a spontaneous thunder of applause.

That afternoon the reporters watched Lizzie enter with quickened sympathies. The myth-makers had not been warmed by the self-control that Hilliard called "remarkable fortitude" and Mr. Buck, "the calm of innocence." In ways that he had not intended to, Mr. Jennings had presented them with the lovable, tormented girl who would really make copy. Her first, showiest breakdown; next, her lips caught in her teeth as he talked about the tiny twining fingers; and even her ashen pallor as he began to suggest the greater likelihood that Bridget Sullivan was the criminal—all were moving. The effect was good.

I am sure that many who wept at the end of Mr. Jennings' plea had not come prepared to weep. He had served her better than either of them ever knew. Though she disappointed her new-found public by returning that afternoon to her familiar stony calm, they could forgive her now. They had seen the suffering girl behind the mask.

She showed feeling only once again, and that in a way no reporter interpreted unkindly. As Knowlton rose, her face flushed to a deep, mottled crimson.

Was it surprising, when the sensitive girl faced her inquisitor?

Knowlton's speech was long, for Mr. Jennings had given him many points to refute, but its tone was quiet and grave. A few brief excerpts drawn from its opening, middle, and close will indicate its temper and quality; its material you already know.

"The straight and narrow path is always full of anguish and does not have the popular vote behind it. . . . When I came to Fall River, I knew no difference between the honorable and respectable Lizzie Borden and the honorable and respectable

Bridget Sullivan. And so Bridget Sullivan was brought here, to what my learned friend calls a Star Chamber, and she was questioned as closely and minutely as any other member of the family. The innocent do not need to fear questioning.

". . . I asked her [Lizzie] where she was when her father came back, and we get this story: 'I was down in the kitchen.' Almost a moment after, Where were you when the bell rang? 'I think I was upstairs in my room.' Were you upstairs when the bell rang? No hesitating, now, no daze: 'I think I was on the steps coming down.'

". . . We are constrained to find that she has been dealing in poisonous things, that her story is absurd, and that hers alone has been the opportunity for the crime. Yielding to clamor is not to be compared with the satisfaction of a duty well done."

When he had ended, the silence was deathly. Judge Blaisdell's gentle old face was sad. Lizzie sat expressionless and unmoving, almost catatonic. Mr. Buck, in a gesture strangely unlike a man schooled by long years to live in the public eye, raised his thin hands and pressed them over his ears.

The moment could not have been easy for Judge Blaisdell. He was speaking not to a stranger but to a girl he had met often in the homes of friends. His voice was low as he spoke, but wholly steady.

"The long examination is now concluded and there remains for the magistrate to perform what he believes to be his duty. It would be a pleasure for him, and he would doubtless receive much sympathy if he could say, 'Lizzie, I judge you probably not guilty. You may go home.'

"But upon the character of the evidence presented through the witnesses who have been so thoroughly and closely examined, there is but one thing to be done.

"Suppose for a single moment that *a man* was standing there. He was found close by that guestchamber which to Mrs. Borden was a chamber of death. Suppose that *a man* had been found in the vicinity of Mr. Borden and the only account he could give of himself was the unreasonable one that he was out in the barn looking for sinkers, that he was in the yard, that he was looking for something else. Would there be any question in the minds of men what should be done with such a man?"

The old judge broke off. His eyes overflowed, he pressed his lips together. Then he went on.

"So there is only one thing to do—painful as it may be—the judgment of the court is that you are probably guilty and you are ordered to wait the action of the Superior Court."

Lizzie went back to Taunton Jail. Unlike the other five women captive there, she continued to be taken out for health-giving strolls in the open air and to get her meals from the town's best hotel.

The press in subsequent months often referred to Taunton Jail as a bastille.

Taunton is a nice little town; on both sides of my family I have roots there which reach down more than three hundred years; I am loyal to it. But I must admit that its bastille, considered purely as a bastille, was substandard.

⇒ 27 ⇐

We Americans like a cause, or, as we say nowadays, a commitment. The world was running pretty smoothly in 1892; our problems in Venezuela were small potatoes, really. We had a lot of free-floating commitment to use up. Lizzie got it.

Before she was drugged and given over to the rack and thumb-screws of the Inquisition, it had been the laxity and timidity of the police upon which public opinion centered; the headline in Andrew's favorite newspaper AT LAST! LIZZIE BORDEN ARRESTED expressed a widespread attitude.

But once the ugly inside truths of her persecution were bared, the attitude changed, and changed dramatically. Worcesterites at breakfast read an editorial that ended with a fervent wish that the cholera that sailors had recently brought into New York harbor would spread to the Narragansett Bay area and wipe out everyone connected with the hounding down of Lizzie Borden. As an expression of public feeling this was strong but not out of step.

A handful of Congregationalist ministers deplored sermons that jumped the gun on due process with announcements that God would vindicate, glorify, or otherwise distinguish Lizzie; they were a tiny minority. Sermons on Lizzie's innocence abounded.

The W.C.T.U. got into the act: how could a famous teetotaler have committed a brutal crime?

The women's-rightsers took up cudgels for Lizzie. They had a positive stake in her innocence, for woman, by their credo, was not simply no less stupid than man; she was a creature of innate moral superiority. Famous lady journalists visited Lizzie in jail, intellectual ladies wrote articles for the magazines, and the rank and file flooded the newspapers with letters to the editor. Even the truly intelligent and admirable feminist Lucy Stone issued a public word in Lizzie's behalf.

Nor did their defense at all put off the anti women's-rightsers, who knew that woman is too pure to sully herself in the arena of politics. An age somewhat disillusioned about woman's mystic power for righteousness can scarcely imagine the Lizzie-as-woman fervor that found its way into print between the preliminary investigation and the Grand Jury trial.

And the only anti-Lizzie story of the period rebounded to her vast advantage.

Its beginnings were unimpressive. An unemployed private detective named McHenry, a Providence man by birth, drifted to Fall River at the time of the murders and hung about the police station. Unable to peddle his services to either side, he decided to write a human-interest story for the papers. He seems to have had thin pickings. He claimed to have hidden under Lizzie's bed and heard Mr. Buck give her spiritual counsel, and Lizzie herself request that a left-over biscuit from her dinner be saved.

However, he had a vastly creative friend, a modern day Defoe named (honestly) Trickey, and Trickey transmuted this meager take into a stunning short novel, which he sold for fact to the Boston *Globe*.

The Trickey version had everything, even sex. Mrs. McHenry had "gained the confidence of the Bordens' servant" and learned that Lizzie was pregnant; Andrew had been heard shouting, "I will know the name of the man who got you in trouble!"

The Government had twenty-five new witnesses, many of them eyewitnesses who had been strolling Second Street just in time to see amazing sights. One, for example, peeked in Mrs. Borden's bedroom window and saw Lizzie in a bloody bathing-cap, waving an axe.

Obviously, the names and addresses of these witnesses sold the story. Few living in the stretch between Fall River and Providence could have doubted the solid reality of Mrs. Abigail Manchester, Mr. and Mrs. Frederick Chace and the rest, or their perfect places of residence, such as "the second Queen Anne cottage on the street below Rhodes Pavilion, Pawtuxet, R. I."

On October 9 the *Globe* came out with smash headlines: LIZZIE'S SECRET. Her secret not only took up the better part of the front page, but also ran on for page after page within. Small wonder that the next day's headlines ran ALL NEW ENGLAND READ STORY ... GLOBES WERE PURCHASED BY THOUSANDS. The purchasers got their money's worth in fantastic overplus.

Col. Adams came to the *Globe* threatening suit. But after two days, when those lovely names and addresses had all proved fictitious, he settled for a front-page retraction.

The *Globe,* as it turned out, had done Lizzie an inestimable service; it had proved, once and for all, what kind of people were against her.

Trickey, having told his story, rushed to the New Bedford Jail, cornered Bridget, and offered her a cut of the swag if she would not deny his story and would flee to Canada with him. Bridget refused and reported him. The same Grand Jury that sat on Lizzie's case indicted him for attempt to tamper with a Government witness, but he had got away to Canada, where shortly thereafter he was run down by a railway train. McHenry returned to the shadows of his chosen profession of free-lance snoop.

But as I say, the incident had performed a function. Attorney-General Pillsbury became ever increasingly aware that the Borden case was unpopular. To give the Grand Jury every chance to refrain from turning in a true bill, he suggested that Mr. Knowlton invite Mr. Jennings to be present to speak for the accused and bring his own witnesses with him.

Mr. Jennings declined this unusual offer. He showed good judgment. If a Grand Jury had still returned a true bill after the Government had so pointedly fallen over backward to give Lizzie the breaks it would not have looked at all well.

The Grand Jury met on November 15. For almost two weeks they heard witnesses on the Borden case; then without explanation to the press they were adjourned to meet again on December 1.

They were adjourned because Alice Russell's insomnia had gone on for three months and she could bear it no longer. When she returned to Fall River after testifying in Taunton as she had before, she decided to go to her lawyer, Mr. Swift. (Another family friend; the study of this case has been for me an endless old-home week.) Up to now, she confessed to Mr. Swift, she had told the truth and nothing but the truth, but not the whole truth. Only she was *very* fond of Emma. What did Mr. Swift think she should do?

Mr. Swift advised her to get in touch with Mr. Knowlton immediately. When the jury reconvened, Alice told for the first time about the burning of the dress. She was wretched about it, I have been told, but at least she began to get some sleep again.

The Grand Jury brought in their vote: twenty to one for a true bill. Lizzie would be tried in New Bedford six months later. The jurymen had been deeply impressed by the absolute impartiality with which the case had been presented to them. They wished to pass a resolution praising Knowlton for his full and fair presentation of matter favorable to the defense.

Knowlton dissuaded them.

Knowlton was at that time receiving a steady stream of mail from all parts of the country, pleading for Lizzie and often denouncing him. By no means all of it was crank mail. Much of it, though founded on scant information, showed intelligence and sound feeling.

Attorney-General Pillsbury coveted no part of it. By custom it was his unhappy duty to plead a capital case of such importance; in April he let Knowlton know that unless he were willing to shelve it and release Lizzie on permanent bail the job would have to be his.

Knowlton himself had small stomach for the job. He had no hope that he could win. On the grounds of the Mayor's slip, it now seemed likely that the defense would be able to keep the inquest testimony out of court—"Lizzie's confession," as he called it in a letter to Pillsbury referring back to their last conference. Furthermore, the defense would be headed by ex-Governor Robinson, a superbly gifted trial lawyer, and there were rumors that Robinson's friend Judge Dewey, whom he had raised to the bench during his term in office, would sit on the case. Knowlton stood to gain neither love nor fame.

However, he said to Pillsbury in the letter just mentioned: "Nothing has developed which satisfies either of us that she is innocent; neither of us can escape the conclusion that she must have had some knowledge of the occurrence." (He was still willing to believe that Lizzie and Bridget had pulled it off together, with Bridget wielding the axe; the fact that Lizzie had provided Bridget with an alibi for the death of Abby seemed to argue that they were in it together, and so, of course, did Lizzie's obvious fear that Bridget would let something slip about the earliest morning and the hour when Andrew came home. Knowlton was never *sure*. At the end of the trial he requested that the judge suggest to the jury the alternative possibility of Bridget's guilt and Lizzie's part as accessory to it.)

But he considered it likeliest that Lizzie was the actual murderer, and he felt that she should be tried. The opinion of a Grand Jury who had been, as he wrote to Pillsbury, *"to say the least,* not influenced in favor of an indictment" should be respected.

As Knowlton saw it, Lizzie was sane and had murdered in cold blood.

The public made the same clear-edged sort of judgment. This, to one turning the crank and reading on and on in microfilm, is the striking thing about all the pleas for Lizzie. They all take it for granted that the murders could only have been committed by a "mad maniac" or by a criminal with a heart of ice. Nowadays many, faced with such a problem, come close to denying the human race any responsibility for its actions. It is astounding how hard the shoe was crammed onto the other foot when my own generation was in its infancy.

Knowlton was convinced of his duty. He was morally impelled to seek a sure defeat, but he was not happy about it. He did not fear cranks; what hurt him were rebukes from the measured voice of intelligent love of justice—which he, too, loved.

(This temper of opinion was subsequently well summed up in the long editorial with which *The New York Times* hailed Lizzie's acquittal. The *Times* exonerated the Fall River police as the "usual stupid muddle-headed sort" who needed "a victim whose sacrifice would purge their force of the contempt" they would incur if they made no arrest. Lizzie was "the nearest and the most helpless" and "they pounced upon her." But the higher-ups, the District Attorney and the Attorney-General, could not be excused so lightly. No. "*They* were men trained in the law, accustomed to weigh evidence . . . they were guilty of a barbarous wrong to an innocent woman. And we hold it to be a misfortune that the victim has no legal . . . means of bringing them to account.")

The Fall River police and Mr. Jennings, as it happens, were as unhappy as Pillsbury and Knowlton.

Like Knowlton, Marshal Hilliard had a strong hunch that Bridget was holding something back. In the six months before the trial he sent detectives frequently to call at New Bedford Jail, where she worked. They learned nothing, and Bridget, questioned in court about these calls, refused to remember anything about them.

Mr. Jennings made similarly frequent and anxious calls. As his ever faithful Mr. Phillips puts it: "Bridget was detained by the prosecution as a material witness for nine long months; . . .

our search for the real murderer was sadly handicapped by our inability to confer with her *except in the presence of those who were working at cross purposes.*" Mr. Jennings, in other words, could never manage to see Bridget alone.

(Mr. Phillips does not explain why that search for the true murderer that Bridget could have forwarded was so lightly abandoned after the trial, when she was again at liberty.)

I believe that Mr. Jennings knew only what Emma had told him—that Lizzie had changed her dress. After he had risked antagonizing Bridget at the preliminary investigation, I believe that she also told him that Bridget was in on the secret. I do *not* believe that Mr. Jennings bribed Bridget to keep quiet about the dress *before* the trial, or suspected that she was being bribed. Emma probably saw to this—and without embarrassing him with any knowledge of it.

Yet he was intelligent. He had read Lizzie's testimony and surely understood her panic: "Maggie had come in and gone upstairs." He was a placid man but he must have made those trips to New Bedford with a heavy heart to assure himself of Bridget's continuing good intentions, surrounded and influenced as she was there by Lizzie's enemies, the police.

He need not have worried. Bridget was an employee at the jail, not a prisoner. Her mail was not intercepted, and both she and Emma knew how to read and write. Emma could easily have made the first token enclosures in cash, and not by check.

I do, however, believe that Mr. Jennings had lost a certain unquestioning innocence; and remembering his temperament and that town of sharp tongues, I believed that he always feared suspicion even where it did not exist.

And the dressy, smiling, self-assured Bridget who came to the trial was scarcely recognizable for that shabby, tearful, bewildered girl who kept her warmhearted understanding silence at the inquest and the preliminary investigation.

BOOK FIVE

How Lizzie's Cause Was Won

IT HAS BEEN said by an eminent jurist that the prosecution did not receive fair trial in the Borden case. Perhaps this is true; the exclusion of Mr. Bence's testimony was certainly a legal shocker. But we should remember that according to Anglo-American tradition, the duty of the court in a capital case is not to hang the possibly guilty but to protect the possibly innocent.

Lizzie's money bought her brilliant representation. In later years she used to say, with admirable realism, "Where would I have been without it?" But trials held outside the capitalist world show that money is only one possible form of influence; she had money, she used it, and I say: fair enough. She had luck; her lawyer when Governor had raised to the bench a man who was abidingly grateful. We all need luck and seldom quarrel with it when it comes our way.

In presenting her trial, I have done my best to suspend judgment, both moral and emotional.

To this end, I have limited myself to three sources: the full trial transcript, and the coverage in *The New York Times* and the Baltimore *Sun*. Though both were strongly pro-Lizzie, they were, as they are, shining examples of responsible journalism. Local papers were often more colorful; I decided with regret that they were also less objective.

With all her faults, Lizzie was no hypocrite. She had needed an image-maker, and she found a great one in George Robinson, whose own image of the plain, honest backwoodsman hid so successfully throughout his career the handicaps of good background, money, and Harvard education.

From the first moment, when he laid a fatherly hand on her

arm and said, "It's going to be all right, little girl," Lizzie felt confidence in him. At his suggestion, she went into mourning for the first time since the murders. He showed restraint; there were no heavy crepe-bordered veils or such excesses, and her clothes were chic—but black, without even a white ruching or a touch of mauve to relieve it.

Throughout the trial she carried a long black fan. Sometimes she unfurled it to hide her face; more often she held it closed and stiffly upright like a small baton, its tip just touching her cheek. The press sketches frequently show her so: "Lizzie Borden in a characteristic attitude."

Her exits and entrances were always made upon the arm of one of the pair who were referred to in the larger world simply as "her clerical friends."

A pro-Lizzie press noted that "her thickish and sallow complexion" had gained a becoming pallor in the past nine months and that "the coarse and heavy outline of her figure" had become "somewhat refined." It also used the word "livid" to describe the odd flush, purpling even the forehead, that her thick skin took on in moments of excitement.

With two brief exceptions, this flush was the sole indication that she was not superbly calm throughout the trial. Lizzie had always been a woman of strong character; but I believe that in the past nine months she had already managed to move a little away from herself, as she remained for the rest of her life. The vulnerability, which Mr. Jennings had caused her to display so showily to the world at the preliminary investigation, was gone.

But she showed another side of herself at the trial. It would be a mistake to infer from Lizzie's panic and plodding at the inquest, or from the phenomenally dull and lifeless letters that she wrote, that she was unintelligent. She was not intuitive or gifted, but she had native shrewdness.

The Baltimore *Sun* spoke of it admiringly:

"Miss Borden always has her wits about her. While the witnesses for the state were telling what she said to them or did in their presence, she was always alert and ready with promptings to her counsel for use in cross-examination. Her suggestions displayed remarkable sagacity...she brought up recollections which greatly qualified what the witness said, put another construction on it...or smashed it altogether."

This liveliness did not appear at once, but it grew by leaps and bounds after the exclusion of the inquest testimony. The *Sun* somewhat overevaluates; but her rapport with George Robinson was definitely a two-way street.

On the night before the trial, New Bedford was crowded with reporters, newspaper artists, and would-be spectators. Huge cables ran from the courthouse to carriage-houses in every nearby backyard, hot lines from the corridor outside the courtroom to the nation's dailies. Temporary fences were up all around the building to control the crowds. They were needed; for two weeks the crush to enter the court each day was tremendous.

Ladies of the better sort seldom go to murder trials for amusement; they did so even less at the end of the last century. The number continually present, day after day, was commented upon repeatedly by the press. Whether they believed her guilty or innocent, it was a woman's crime and women felt intensely involved in it.

Yet despite the crowds, the trial itself was no circus. Up to the pandemonium that greeted the verdict, the proceedings were conducted with dignity, and with remarkable dispatch, considering the number of witnesses to be heard and cross-questioned.

Three justices were on the bench. Chief Justice Mason, a self-effacing old gentleman with muttonchop whiskers, preserved a noteworthy detachment throughout; it was almost as if he saw himself for what in effect he was: a benign figurehead. The consultations, the whisperings, were between Justice Blodgett and Justice Dewey.

Blodgett was an elegant, long-faced, with eyes nearly closed by the heavy, puffed eyelids above and the swelling bags below; his unsmiling face appeared to regard the proceedings with some secret amusement. Dewey was a lively little grasshopper of a man who wore pince-nez and continually waved a large palm-leaf fan. His usual expression was a fixed bright smile, which pointed yet more sharply upward when ex-Governor Robinson was having a little fun at the expense of a witness. The press sketches of the pair look like an illustration for some lost episode from *The Pickwick Papers;* the twosome could not have been better chosen for satiric effect.

One sketch of Dewey bears a caption; "Justice Dewey smiling at one of Governor Robinson's witticisms."

Robinson showed a sense of vaudeville as well as of drama, but like a wise politician, he eschewed wit. Rather, he warmed the jury with his sense of schoolboy fun, which took delight, for example, in the fact that Mr. Porter was a re-porter. Dewey's appreciation of these sportive moments may have been heightened by his personal friendship and his professional debt to Robinson.

Dewey *de facto* ran the show; the rulings given were (with very few exceptions) only such as he warmly approved, and it was he who delivered the remarkable charge to the jury.

Throughout the trial, Lizzie was overwhelmed by "floral offerings" both from friends and from total strangers. The courthouse was daily bombarded with sheaves of fresh blooms. An Associated Press man writing from Fall River observed that while Miss Borden had never been a popular girl before her trouble, she now had far more friends than ever before.

The court convened on the first day at eleven. The prisoner entered on the arm of Mr. Buck, in black, but fashion-plate black; her sleeves exaggerated the new leg-of-mutton style, rising above her shoulders like small black wings, and the drooping brim of her black lace hat made her sallow skin whiter by contrast. She faced the empty jury box and the justices with great calm while a clergyman offered a prayer for divine enlightenment.

Then Mr. Knowlton stepped forward. Lizzie changed color, the purple-red flush suffusing her face so dramatically that the press all noted it.

However, Mr. Knowlton only said that Attorney-General Pillsbury had been taken sick and felt that his presence there might endanger his health; he had asked that his place be taken by Mr. William Moody. Knowlton suggested that the court proceed to the selection of a jury.

Lizzie's flush faded.

One hundred and forty-eight veniremen waited to be picked over. Certain grounds for choice were agreed upon by both sides. No juryman should be young; middle years to bearded age were prerequisite. They should also live at some remove from centers of gossip; Mr. Augustus Swift of New Bedford was accepted, but the rest, to a man, were farmers living in townships at more than a convenient buggy-ride from Fall River. A farmer from Dighton, which considers Fall River its shopping town, was promptly excluded. Nor were any European or Lancashire names accepted; to a man the jury were all good Yankees.

It expedited matters that jurymen were accepted whether or not they were opposed to capital punishment. It was also taken for granted that all would have formed previous opinions; they were merely asked whether their opinions were so firmly fixed that no possible evidence heard in court could change them.

The press found one exclusion slightly baffling. A middle-aged farmer named George Winslow was called. He stated that he had no opinions and was willing to serve. As the clerk uttered the old formula: "Prisoner, look on the juror, juror look on the prisoner," Mr. Jennings darted forward and whispered in Lizzie's ear. Lizzie rose and spoke the word, "Challenge." Winslow is a good Fall River name; he may have had relatives.

While the papers did not report it, there seemed to be a split-second chance that not one but two city slickers might be accepted to make up the twelve. Mr. Willis of New Bedford was asked, "Have you read the newspaper report of the hearing at the district court?" Mr. Willis replied that he had been away on business and missed it. He was asked if he had ever been Knowlton's client; he denied it firmly. He was, however, challenged by the defense.

Mr. Knowlton challenged no jurors. The jury chosen, he requested that before the case opened they be taken to Fall River to view the house and grounds. The defense protested. Chief Justice Mason, however, here made one of the two or three rulings in favor of the prosecution, and the little company set out, along with the lawyers from both sides.

On the second day, Mr. Moody opened for the Commonwealth.

Lizzie's defenders have always missed a trick on William Moody. It has long been the custom to blacken the characters of the police who testified against Lizzie and of Knowlton who headed the case for the Government by pointing out their various advancements in life. Governor Robinson was the first to thus use the human heart's free-floating jealousy to cast doubt upon the evidence of Medley and Harrington, and to reinforce that of the amiable Officer Mullaly, who alone of the policemen testifying had missed out on the year's routine promotions.

Knowlton got to be Attorney-General, which is bad enough, but by this method of character-assassination young William Moody comes out as black as hell. He not only became Attorney-General of the *U.S.A.*, and thereafter Secretary of the Navy, but he ended his days on the bench of the Supreme Court.

Moody's style of address was tidy and unemotional.

He spoke of the known ill-feeling between Lizzie and her stepmother, and of her visit to Alice Russell with its prophecies of impending doom. He showed diagrams of the house and neighborhood, pointing out the unlikelihood that two murders so widely separated in time could have been committed by an intruder. He contrasted Lizzie's statements that she had rushed into the house on hearing a groan, a scraping, a "distressing sound" with her story to Mr. Knowlton of having entered casually, laid down her hat, and started upstairs to sit down.

He told of the dress-burning. He showed the hatchet-head and promised proof from experts in forensic medicine that its size exactly matched that of the wounds that had penetrated the skulls.

Lizzie heard him through with an empty face. To the reporters it indicated a detachment just this side of boredom. The whole courtroom was startled when, just as Moody sat down, she fainted.

She was unconscious for only a minute or two. Mr. Jubb and Mr. Jennings were at her side at once with cold water and smelling salts. Upon coming to, she sat upright again with the same look of bored detachment.

She sat so while Kieran, the engineer, repeated the testimony he had given in Fall River.

The newspapers observed after that day that the prosecution had scored a surprise by indicating that a bloody garment and a murder weapon had not, after all, been lacking.

⇶ 29 ⇷

On the third day, Morse testified to his visit at the time of the murders and to other visits, including the one in May. He admitted that he rarely saw much of Lizzie on these occasions. The purpose of his questioning was to give the general background.

In cross-questioning, Governor Robinson stressed the prodigal riches of the breakfast table, with its mutton soup, johnnycakes and other dainties. Uncle John agreed: "Plenty of it."

Lizzie smiled as her uncle tried to calculate her age and shook her head vigorously when he came out at thirty-three. ("Very much the woman," the Baltimore *Sun* observed with delight. And Uncle John had, in fact, missed it by a month.)

Twelve witnesses to Andrew's morning downstreet testified; Lizzie yawned. Their purpose was to time Andrew's absence and his return; Knowlton planned his cases with elegance. Next in order were the witnesses who had been at the house on the murder day.

The first of these, Bridget Sullivan, was called. Lizzie sat erect and watched the door for her entrance.

Bridget came in looking like a million dollars. She wore a stylish maroon-colored dress, a big matching hat with a big matching plume, and kid gloves.

It was the Government's purpose and its successful purpose to place Lizzie, by Bridget's testimony, in the house at the time of the murders. Yet while Bridget was on the stand Lizzie showed no anxiety, only a lively interest and at times even a camaraderie. As Bridget detailed the Borden diet of mutton and warmed-over fish she laughed, and Lizzie caught her eye and smiled with her.

Mr. Robinson was a far more dangerous man in cross-questioning than Mr. Jennings had been, but Bridget was no longer timid and confused. She took his attempts to trip her, to make her lay it on a bit too thick about the household sweetness and light, in calm good part.

(Wasn't it the man's job, now? And what could he be doing to her, with her knowing the thing that Lizzie and Emma were scared to death she'd let out?)

All power corrupts, absolute power corrupts absolutely. Lizzie evinced satisfaction throughout Bridget's testimony. Alas, I like her far less in those fine new clothes than I did when, shabby and shy, she kept quiet for no other reason than her fondness for Lizzie and a firm south-of-Ireland distaste for telling the authorities one word more than they needed to know. Besides, back then I think she had no doubts. A silence worth selling raises doubts, and a silence sold rots the heart.

I'm sorry, Bridget.

Her conscience, as you will learn, troubled her throughout her lifetime; but she tried to assuage it by assuring herself (accurately) that she did not speak one word at the trial that was not true.

She refused to agree, as she had at the inquest, that Lizzie was crying when she first found her. ("I couldn't have said that, for she wasn't.") She evaded questions about the meals taken apart, saying, "They always did eat in the *same dining room*." Robinson tried to force the word "together" back into her mouth; she had spoken it cheerfully in Fall River, but here she would have none of it. (His technique at this point was sharply criticized by several eminent contemporary jurists.) Of Lizzie's dress she would only say, "It wasn't a *calico* that the girl was in the habit of wearing mornings." (Again, a literal truth.)

The press felt that Bridget presented an amiable view of the Borden household. There was no quarreling *in her presence*, and that morning she heard Lizzie answer her mother "very civilly" as she passed her in the dining room. "I never saw or heard anything out of the way, and during my three years of service everything was pleasant *for me.*"

One grimly amusing touch in Robinson's cross-questioning was his attempt to bring out the facts of the daylight robbery. The prosecution objected: the matter was remote. However, Robinson managed to get the whole story before the jury by explaining the purpose of his questions: not family ill-feeling but fear of burglars kept the door between Lizzie's room and her parents' locked.

The implication was plain. A locked house had been entered, a locked room robbed, under the nose of three witnesses—clearly by the same uncanny hand that later killed Andrew and Abby.

It was, in fact, a brilliant play on Robinson's part. The floor-plan of the narrow little house, the close-packed neighborhood, were still fresh in the jurors' minds. Moody had mentioned the stonecutters at the rear, the next-door hired man working so close to the side gate, the host of witnesses on Second Street. Robinson erased all that with a quick flick of the wrist. Countering objection with that brief, apologetic, "Merely to show . . ." he told a story that went to the heart of things. Few have ever equaled George Robinson's gift for seeing and saving a central issue.

He knew what he had accomplished; he was feeling his oats when young Mrs. Kelly took the stand. (She had not been able to arrive, as planned, with the other witnesses to Andrew's morning walk.) He vastly enjoyed making her admit that her clock was an hour late, had now ceased to run altogether, and was "in other words, not much of a clock." But he let it stand that Andrew had not returned her greeting and that he carried something wrapped in white paper, size and shape unspecified, in his hand.

Apparently his fun with Mrs. Kelly hurt her and rankled; for one of her descendants told a researching acquaintance of mine that people came up from the railroad depot to set their watches by her miraculously accurate old clock.

From the same source came a fascinating story about the two men in the buggy. They were Victoria Lincoln's grandfather, "then a young man," and a youth he had brought to the house at that surprising hour as a likely beau for Lizzie; when Andrew slammed the door, they laughed and drove away. My grandfather, at the time a middle-aged man with a son who had entered the family business, was never the type to play Cupid's helper—not even when young, or at nine in the *evening;* I have his diaries.

I myself, you remember, long dined out on having lived next door to Lizzie, *not* at the end of the next block. Tales grow; I have learned that hearsay is better checked.

On the third day, evidence on the murder morning continued.

The first witness was Dr. Bowen, whose testimony is chiefly interesting for its pointed omissions: nothing about Abby's fears of poison, nothing about the missing note. He was there as a Government witness, but he gave the State little aid. They wanted him to describe Lizzie's dress. His word for it in Fall River had been "drab," by which he meant not that it was khaki-colored, but that it was not eye-catching; he still insisted, with obvious sincerity, that he was a poor hand at noticing such things.

But his presence was welcome to the defense. The jury had doubtless heard rumors about Lizzie's "conflicting statements." Melvin O. Adams cross-examined; Dr. Bowen, who had his reputation as a physician to protect, was unobligingly specific about dosages, but Adams made do nicely.

First he asked about the total medication that Lizzie was given "all the time up to the time of her arrest and while she was in the station house"—for a period, that is, of over three weeks—and followed hard upon the answer with a large general question: "Does not morphine *given in double doses* to allay mental distress and nervous excitement somewhat affect the memory and change and alter the view of things and give people hallucinations?"

Dr. Bowen said, "Yes."

Col. Adams said quickly, "I have no further questions," and sat down.

Wisely, Adams had not mentioned the "trifling variations" at the inquest to quicken latent memories and make talk in the jury room; but the jury now understood them in so far as any might still feel the need.

Mrs. Churchill took the stand. You know her story from our narrative. She was the only witness who thought that Lizzie had worn the Bedford cord that morning; she was the neighbor who dropped in, and it was the dress she would have expected to see since she had learned that it was not the other wrapper, the pink-and-white stripe. Mr. Moody in closing asked her to repeat again that she had heard of the missing note from Lizzie, not Bridget.

Miss Alice Russell was called.

Throughout the morning, Lizzie had seemed inattentive, staring off into space and playing with her fan. At the sound of Miss Russell's name she became tense. Her eyes never left Miss Russell's face while she testified, and her lips worked continuously. Miss Russell looked at her questioners, at the floor, at the ceiling, anywhere but at Lizzie. The difference between them was so marked that I have found no news story of the day that failed to mention it.

She told of all that happened from Lizzie's Wednesday evening call until she left the house on Monday, after the final departure of O. M. Hanscom. Cross-questioning shook no part of her story; it only brought out one unwanted bit of clarification. The Bedford cord had not been in the big pantry-closet where the cleaning-rags were kept, but in the little coal cupboard whose shelf held only heavy kitchen utensils.

It was the prosecution's one big day, for the other major witness was Assistant Marshal John Fleet, who after detailing his conversations with Lizzie told of finding the hatchet-head—thus neatly packaging the missing weapon and the bloodstained dress.

Robinson met the enemy head on.

There had been other hatchets in the box; there was an ash heap in the cellar. Fleet, over showers of objections, had managed to describe the difference between the dust and that white, adherent ash; Robinson labored to make the ashes fly and cover everything in the cellar. Fleet would only reiterate that the other contents of the box had been simply dusty, with a dust quite unlike the white ashes.

He was firm, he was convincing; his quiet poise and courtesy were dangerous. Robinson snatched up the claw-headed hatchet that had been found in the fruit cellar—rusty, not dusty, and not under discussion—and held it under Fleet's nose: "Tell me if you see any ashes on it. Tell me as a *man*, not as a police officer."

Knowlton rose and asked if that were a proper way to address a witness. Robinson recovered his normal finesse, the "fatherly gleam" often noted with approval by the press came back to his eye, and he admitted that it was not.

But he had not managed to undo the damage done by Fleet's quiet and exact testimony. The prosecution must have been satisfied that a doubt had risen as to whether a bloodstained garment had, after all existed; and that the myth that "the weapon was never found" was now done to death, once and for all.

The other witnesses of the day were unimportant, for instance, the man from the livery who first called the police. Officer Allen added a human touch, with his admission of having twice fled, and his memory of Andrew's delicate ankles.

The New York Times said: "There is much talk [in Fall River] about Assistant Marshal Fleet's story regarding the murder weapon. Mr. Fleet's description of the weapon is so minute and his reputation for veracity . . . is so great that belief is general that he found the weapon with which the murder was committed. Many of Miss Borden's friends feel greatly exercised over this testimony."

It was a Thursday, up to then Lizzie's unlucky day. The murders, her arrest, her conviction by Judge Blaisdell as "probably guilty" and the Grand Jury vote for a true bill had all fallen on a Thursday.

≫ 30 ≪

Robinson was a great trial lawyer. He knew better than to scatter his shot.

It was obvious that the case would be judged on three points: Was a bloodstained dress destroyed? Was the murder weapon found? (In the house apparently household property.) And was Lizzie the youngest daughter? (Lear's Cordelia the gentle Antigone?) Evidence of motive was insufficient, sole opportunity is always difficult to prove, and Lizzie's own word concerning sole opportunity was almost certain to be ruled inadmissible—but those three questions were emotionally loaded.

The answer to the third question was the defense's safe investment.

Alice Russell's testimony on the first question must wait until the last day of the trial for its undermining; her firmness and gentleness must fade from the minds of the jury. While she had to be asked repeatedly to raise her voice, there was no hesitation in what she said, and she had both a crisp mind and a keen eye for detail. To take care of her would take planning, and also careful coaching of Emma, obviously a bad actress.

But Fleet's head must roll, and promptly.

On Friday, Robinson was ready and waiting.

He spared himself any waste effort. He was casual, even playful, with Officer Harrington, who had found Lizzie "cool," saw Dr. Bowen burn a torn-up note, and observed the charred roll of documents in the stove. He had a little fun over Officer Harrington's detailed memory of the pink-and-white wrapper with its red ribbon belt (a daring color combination then usually rejected as "Portuguese"). When Officer Harrington mentioned the pretty shirred front and the "semi-train such as ladies wore that year" Robinson asked dryly if he had been in the dry-goods business before he joined the force. Harrington, unruffled, said that he had been a painter, and still noticed colors "to admire them."

Harrington also mentioned the thick dust in the loft, and the heat, which had still been overpowering after the hay door was opened for air by the officers who searched the place. Other than by bringing out the sinister fact that Harrington had that year been promoted to a captaincy, Robinson could not do much about that point.

But suddenly his luck changed. The prosecution returned to its evidence about the first finding of the hatchet-head. And Officer Mullaly saved the day.

Mullaly's memories lacked detail and got out of order, but he bumbled amiably along, correcting himself—"Wait, now, I've got that wrong"—until he came to the moment when Fleet took a look in the box and found the hatchet-head. There was a stick in the box, too. Officer Mullaly thought he remembered; he had handed it to Fleet, who had put it back in the box.

A stick! Oh, lucky Robinson, clearly the hatchet-handle! A blade could be washed clean of detectable blood; a wooden handle could not. And the prosecution claimed to have heard of no such stick!

Joyfully, he recalled Fleet. Handsomely, well within the rules of the legal game, all by the gentlest implication, Robinson made his point to the jury: Fleet, in his lust to frame Lizzie, had concealed that hatchet-handle, which all too easily could have been proved bloodless.

It was no trouble at all for a man with Robinson's gifts to throw the proper light on Fleet's firm statement that Officer Mullaly's memory was incorrect and no stick had been in the box. The honest underling had shown up the corrupt Assistant Marshal. The effect was completed by the revelation that when the year's promotions were given out, poor Mullaly, victim of his own integrity, had remained a patrolman.

It was a great moment for Robinson, but not for Lizzie, who lacked proper appreciation of the legal mind at work. While Fleet and Mullaly were being questioned her face showed deep boredom.

But with the calling of the next witness, it was noted with

puzzled interest that Lizzie's sallow skin turned first grayish and then "livid" and that her whole body went tense.

"Miss Annie White."

The court stenographer from Fall River! Would the inquest testimony be admitted?

It was ruled that counsel would be given a full day in which to prepare their arguments on this point. Two minor witnesses spoke, chiefly about clocks that had not been telling the right time on the murder day, and the court recessed.

With the noble exception of *The New York Times,* the Saturday headlines featured Officer Mullaly. The public rejoiced to learn of his probity in refusing to cover for the superior who had concealed the bloodless hatchet-handle.

Curiously, no newspapers attached any importance to the matter pending, the inclusion or exclusion of the inquest testimony. However, it was noted that Lizzie looked ill as she entered the court next morning, and in answer to a solicitous question from Robinson said that "she had not had a pleasant night."

She would have to live out yet another unpleasant night; the arguments on both sides needed careful preparation.

That day Medley told of his visit to the barn loft and his experiment with his palm-prints in the heavy dust. Robinson's cross-examination was not up to form; he dealt with irrelevancies, and tried to make Medley look a careless incompetent for not going into the barn loft and searching it then and there (thus destroying the very evidence he had wished to show Fleet). The attempt did not come off.

Robinson did better almost at once.

One by one, Seaver, Desmond, and Medley told of the reexamination and wrapping of the hatchet-head. Seaver, who had once, you may remember, been a carpenter, came out strong about that new break in the wood. But both Desmond and Medley clearly remembered having wrapped the head in paper. As we know—and as *The New York Times* honestly explained—both had done so, Captain Desmond unwrapping it again to give Seaver a look, and Medley rewrapping it for them as they talked it over. Desmond, who had found the w.c. so conveniently stocked with newspaper, remembered what he had used to wrap it in;

Medley, who had merely picked up the once-used wrapping and folded it again, remembered only that it had been some ordinary kind of paper lying to hand. After all, it had happened ten months before and had not been a major occurrence. But Robinson was in his element.

Nothing can confuse a jury better than being presented with an apparent either/or situation when two witnesses are in fact both telling the truth. Recalling Desmond and Medley separately, Robinson worked up a first-rate vaudeville skit by having them wrap the hatchet-head in a sheet of newspaper one after the other. Since one recalled for such a purpose would naturally assume that the defense wished to show that the hatchet-head had been carelessly wrapped and could not have retained, as claimed, its coating of ash, both wrapped with studious care and fine comic effect.

Robinson also got a laugh by countering Desmond's vivid memory of that particular instance of Andrew's famous thrift by asking, "You don't remember what the newspaper was?"

The whole show was a breather, a refresher for the jury. It scored nothing solid, unlike the previous day's smear of Fleet, unable to answer questions honestly like a man and not a police officer. But it was well timed. Yesterday's gravity combined with today's good laugh had restored the "missing weapon" to full status as an article of faith.

Lizzie paid no attention. Throughout that whole day while the question of the inquest testimony still hung in the balance she looked ill and remote.

For the rest of the day, witnesses testified to the unlikelihood that a stranger could have left the Bordens' house unobserved.

I think that the wait was also telling on Robinson; Dewey was in the driver's seat, but old Mason was nominally, at least, the Chief Justice. Robinson got a laugh over the fact that *two* of the laborers in "Crowe's yard," the stoneyard, were called Pat, but he was only able to shake one witness, Lucy Collet, who had come to "watch" Dr. Chagnon's telephone while he was away, and found herself locked out. She could not even hear the phone, though she learned later that it had rung at least once while she waited on the porch. She was a timid girl, easy to rattle, and the "fatherly gleam" was lacking as Robinson rattled her more and more.

"Oh, the phone rang but you could not hear it?"

He seldom bothered to make a minor witness look like a liar. No, I do not think that he was altogether calm as the day ended.

However, when a statement had been handed to the bench, signed by all parties, as to the circumstances under which the inquest was held, and the court adjourned for the day, Robinson called a press conference in the corridor with the fatherly gleam once more in working order.

They had seen the supposed murder weapon disposed of, he told the reporters. They would shortly also see it proved that the Borden girls "often burned up dresses."

It was this good news that made the next day's headlines. Robinson not only had a superb eye for the main issues; as his own press agent he was, throughout his career, one of the all-time greats, and in his handling of the Borden case he reached his pinnacle.

Apropos this odd habit that the Borden girls had of burning up their dresses: Alice Russell after testifying found herself deluged with mail from strangers. Compulsively, she read it all, the foul and the threatening, day after day; she found it hard to be denounced as a police spy, a Judas. I was always told that Mr. Swift also took it to heart and felt responsible for her unhappiness and new self-questionings; he had been firm about her speaking to Mr. Knowlton.

This is one of those countless bits I always laid to unreliable hearsay until I found it in newsprint. Alice Russell was widely loved, people talked, and reporters on the Fall River scene picked up the story and played it for its human-interest value. I am sure that she never knew that she was featured in the Baltimore *Sun* as the victim of all that nastiness; nor would she have liked to know it. Like her dear Emma, she was retiring.

On Monday morning, Mr. Moody spoke for the admission of the inquest testimony. He cited fourteen recent cases in which such testimony had been allowed, all closely parallel in their circumstances: cases in which persons not in custody and hence not formally warned of their rights had given preliminary testimony about a crime, and later had that testimony ruled admissible at their own subsequent trial for that crime. His point was good. If Lizzie had *admitted* her guilt under such circumstances, a court would have had understandable reason to exclude her evidence. However, what was being excluded was her *denial* of guilt, her own explanation of what had happened on the murder morning so far as she had knowledge of it. To exclude such evidence was a complete break with precedent.

(The question, as another jurist pointed out after the trial, was really whether Lizzie was to have it both ways: to be permitted to give testimony when a refusal to testify would have made her look guilty and later permitted to withhold that same testimony when her counsel decided that it was incriminating.) [1]

Robinson admitted unfamiliarity with many of the cases cited, but he criticized the accuracy of the parallels in some of them and the judgment of the court in others. Lizzie, he stressed, had been under suspicion and not warned of her rights.

The court withdrew for three-quarters of an hour. Then Justice Dewey made their statement.

The justices admitted that all fourteen of Mr. Moody's parallels were accurate; the same legal situation had held in them that existed here. However, Dewey continued, "The common law regards substance more than form." *Effectually, virtually,* Lizzie had been under arrest at the time of the inquest and not warned of her rights. Her testimony was excluded.

It was what Knowlton had foreseen for the last two months.

Robinson was in high form when Officer Hyde took the stand to describe the night-time emptying of the slop pail. When Hyde described Miss Russell's trembling at the door of the room where the blood-soaked garments lay, Robinson got a big laugh from the court with his parody of a convulsively shaking woman: "You mean, she shook like *this?*"

Hyde alone remained unamused. It was not so much as that,

[1] Judge Charles Gideon Davis.

he replied, but it was trembling that one could see plainly as she shrank back and stood there waiting.

Robinson continued gay: With a lamp in her hand? And she hadn't shaken the lamp chimney *right off?*

Reading the trial, one becomes oddly fond of Robinson, with his zest for the game. But at this passage, while I am sure that the jury were vastly appreciative, I must admit that I found his style enraging.

⇶ 31 ⇷

Lizzie was excused from the courtroom throughout that afternoon. It would have been a hard time for any daughter, guilty or innocent. Plaster casts of the skulls were brought in, their incisions marked in blue; the hatchet-head was represented by a piece of tin cut to exact size, and the wounds were discussed by Dr. Dolan, two state doctors, and three professors from Harvard; all six, men with long experience of criminal cases demanding a background in forensic medicine, five of them experts in the field.

(It is a favorite legend that Lizzie was unexpectedly confronted in the court with her parents' skulls and swooned.)

The Harvard surgeons demonstrated how, while the angled and glancing cuts could have been made by a weapon of indeterminate size, some of the deeper incisions had fallen square and could have been made only by a weapon precisely the size of the hatchet-head in question.

The chief Harvard professor of surgery stated that of these, even the deepest could have been made onehanded by a woman of no unusual strength "granted sufficient leverage," a qualifying phrase that turned out to mean "using a hatchet with a handle a foot long."

Robinson tried to force an admission that the bit of wood remaining inside the handle would have necessarily received bloodstains. The professor cheerfully agreed that this would have been so if the hatchet had been broken before it was washed, but not otherwise, since the fit of wood to metal was extremely smooth and snug.

All the physicians agreed that the murderer might have received little blood on his person, since its trajectory in both cases had been away from the direction in which the blows fell.

The blood-spot on the underskirt was also thoroughly discussed. The Harvard specialist on bloodstains freely admitted that menstrual blood cannot be distinguished from other blood, but he returned to stress the uncomfortable fact that it was a clear-edged spot, though tiny, six inches from the hem, which had indubitably come from *outside*, not inside the garment.

Robinson, hitting a little wild, demanded assurance that the professor could state it as a fact that it was *human* blood at all.

The professor—blessings on the breed—hesitated and cogitated before he replied. Then he made a grudging admission: "It could, just possibly, have been the blood of a seal, an opossum, or *one* species of guinea-pig."

Robinson had done better with the police than he did with the medical profession. He could not shake their main points: the murder weapon was the exact size of the hatchet-head; the blows were oddly weak and ill-aimed to have been struck by a man; the murderer need not have become drenched in gore; and the spot on the underskirt came from the outside.

The doctors had him at total disadvantage, or would have had in a period that did not feel automatic distrust for men of science—the "experts" with their "theories."

Since Lizzie was spared this ordeal, she spent a restful afternoon. On the day before the inquest testimony was excluded, the *Times* had said that Miss Borden looked ill. Thereafter, the papers began to comment on the fact that she was looking "wonderfully well."

The trial entered its tenth day.

Marshal Hilliard told of his call with the Mayor, when they had made their way through the crowds to the house with such difficulty. Mayor Coughlin in turn described their visit at greater length. It was unlikely that after ten months any member of the jury placed the day as that upon which the Providence *Journal* suggested that "a woman" might be the criminal. Yet there was a chance; Robinson was on the ball.

He intervened quickly as the Mayor reported Lizzie's extraordinary question: "Why, is there anybody in this house suspected?"

Q: Spoke right up to you promptly and earnestly, did she?
A: She made that statement.
Q: Will you *answer my question?*
The Chief Justice: He may answer.
A: She spoke up somewhat excitedly, I should say.

Sixteen superbly determined questions later, Robinson succeeded in eliciting this reply: "So far as I am able to determine by her actions, she was earnest."

Robinson made good the deficit: "That is what I said. *Prompt and earnest.*"

Mrs. Hannah Gifford, the Quaker lady who made cloaks and suits, told of Lizzie's outburst in the March before the murders, when she had indiscreetly spoken of Abby as "Mother."

Miss Anna Borden took the stand. Remembering her, I know how reluctantly she must have appeared, not only because of her innate taste and breeding, but also because of those floods of letters that poor Alice Russell now compulsively read. I was amused to learn from the transcript that she had to be requested "to lift her veil."

She knew Lizzie, and Lizzie's feelings about Abby. They had been acquainted for five years, ever since Lizzie had become "a Congregationalist moving in the best circles." She came prepared to say more than the prosecutor, in his summary, managed to get into the record; however, she said nothing. Her testimony was excluded as remote.

Mrs. Hannah Reagan, matron of the Fall River station house, was presented, and told the story you already know: Lizzie accused Emma of giving her away about something, Emma denied it, neither spoke to the other again throughout that morning, and Lizzie's friends pressured Mrs. Reagan to say that it had not been so.

Mr. Jennings now made his first appearance, to cross-examine. He was spared some initial embarrassment, since Mrs. Reagan (perhaps through the same kindness or the same timidity that had made her retract at the time), on being pressured, curtailed Emma's denial. Its form as originally given in the Providence *Journal* was, "No, Lizzie, I only told Mr. Jennings what I thought he ought to know for your defense." In court, as I mentioned earlier, Mrs. Reagan gave it simply as, "No, Emma, I did not."

Mr. Jennings did not attempt to cast doubt on the morning-long silence between the sisters, but he stressed that Emma had returned that same afternoon, after her dinner. Then, with some difficulty, he led Mrs. Reagan to recount an odd anecdote.

She could not understand at first what he meant by asking her to tell "something about an egg." "About an *egg?*" Then it came back, though she doubted Mr. Jennings' memory that it had taken place on the afternoon in question.

She had bet Lizzie a dollar that she could not break an egg with her bare hands without first cracking the shell. Lizzie lowered the stakes to a quarter, tried, and failed: "And she says, 'There,' she says, 'that is the first thing that I ever undertook to do that I never could.' "

What Mr. Jennings intended this story to show eludes me. Neither Lizzie's iron will nor her terms of easy friendliness with Mrs. Reagan were points to be stressed at the moment.

Mr. Jennings also evinced surprise when Mrs. Reagan reported that just as she left the room she said to Emma, "Have you told her all?"

Q: *I* said that?

A: Yes, sir, you did. I was standing right beside you.

He did not pursue the subject. His whole cross-questioning of Mrs. Reagan seemed oddly pointless, skirting the major issue; her discrediting was left to witnesses for the defense.

The next witness called was Eli Bence.

He had been, he began, employed as pharmacist at Smith's on the corner of South Main and Columbia for over fourteen years. . . .

It was as far as he got. Robinson was on his feet at once, objecting. Justice Dewey dismissed the witness and ordered the jury to retire. It was strikingly prompt action, since no grounds for objection had yet been given.

Mr. Moody said, "I perhaps ought to state first what the testimony is that we offer."

He read a brief summary of Mr. Bence's testimony as already given in Fall River and Taunton. He also stated that another druggist was waiting to testify. (This was the one whom he considered the best qualified to make an identification of the New Bedford druggists who had been asked for prussic acid.) Besides this, three men with special qualifications would comment on the matter.

At this point, which to the layman appears to be at long last, Mr. Robinson was asked for the grounds of his objection. He gave them in oratorical style and at remarkable length. While a full quote would take up a good many pages, they are fortunately easy to summarize.

In brief, the purchase was not actually effected, the sale of poison was not illegal, and the whole story was irrelevant.

"Does it have any tendency at all to show that the defendant killed these two people with an axe? I maintain that it does not."

Mr. Moody was clearly prepared for this moment.

He pointed out the fear of poison Mrs. Borden had shown on the morning of the attempted purchase. He quoted Wharton's work on evidence: "All facts which go either to sustain or impeach a hypothesis logically pertinent are relevant." Since the uses of prussic acid are so well known, could not this attempted purchase have indicated that the prisoner was in a *murderous state of mind?*

He cited nine recent cases that had used such collateral evidence: an assortment of weapons laid in, though only one was used.

Mr. Robinson replied that there had been no real evidence that Lizzie bore either of her parents any real ill-will. It was not as if she had said, "I intend to kill somebody by the end of the week." Why, even if she had, she might have meant to kill Bridget Sullivan (general laughter in the courtroom). Moreover, people bought prussic acid to poison cats. (A technical inaccuracy already pointed out: one bought Rough-on-Rats—which was chiefly arsenic—for inconvenient animals and relations.)

But above all, Robinson stressed, one should bear in mind the fact that there is a world of difference between an innocent act and a criminal act. "And the buying of prussic acid *is* an innocent act."

Robinson once again confessed himself unfamiliar with the cases Moody cited. It did not matter; though no great reader, he was creative.

The justices withdrew. On coming back, Mr. Justice Dewey gave out their ruling. Mr. Moody, in summarizing the testimony he wished to present, had mentioned a pharmacist not connected with the purchase, an analytical chemist, and a furrier whose notions about the uses of prussic acid were substantially those of Mr. Bence. They might speak tomorrow. If what they had to say "came up to proffer," the testimony of Mr. Bence would be judged relevant.

After that split-second drama in which Mr. Bence and the jury had been so promptly swept apart, the prosecution must have been not only dazzled by their sense of reprieve, but also wholly surprised. They may even have reminded themselves that the next day was a Thursday; for their experts, as the bench surely must realize, were quite qualified to show that there is no innocent use for "ten cents' worth of prussic acid."

And the case hung in the balance. It hung in the balance because a jury attends far more closely to evidence concerning a woman who was *known to be plotting murder on the day before murder was done* than to evidence concerning a young lady to whose detriment nothing is known except that she wore party dresses around the house, did not save cleaning-rags, and once said something cross about her stepmother to a seamstress.

Only Lizzie's inquest testimony could have *proved* that sole opportunity lay either with her, or with Bridget and her working as one—since, in spite of all her desperate meanderings, she had placed herself on the first floor all morning. Thus, since the front door was bolted after both murders, the murderer had to be someone inside. But all the evidence thus far had powerfully indicated her sole opportunity; and if Mr. Bence could speak, the jury could really be made to consider that evidence seriously for the first time. They would consider the murder weapon in a new light, and the evidence that it was household property hidden by one who knew the house well. If they knew that Lizzie, on the day before the murders, tried in vain to buy prussic acid, all the evidence, which had, up to now, been only a blur of ill-attended words, of words unheard through the deafness of preconception, could be brought back to them. It would not matter that clear and convincing *motive for murder* could not be demonstrated, if only the jury were convinced of her *intent to murder.*

It was crucial, and the bench had shown that they knew it. Now, by some miracle, they seemed to have relented. It began to look as if old Justice Mason's sense of legality, of responsibility, had at last prevailed.

The Thursday came. The pharmacist stated that except in minute amounts as a prescription drug, he knew of no innocent use for prussic acid; its lethal fumes ruled it out as an exterminating agent. So far as the analytical chemist knew, it had no commercial use whatsoever, even as an ingredient in rat poison. The furrier stated positively that prussic acid is never used for cleaning furs and that sealskin provides no nidus for insect eggs and is naturally immune to moths.

(A recent book in Lizzie's defense says that "it is no trade secret" that prussic acid was then used in commercial insecticides; if the author is right and the witnesses wrong, one still wonders why Lizzie did not buy a packaged product, rather than try so long to buy such an ingredient so hard to come by.)

Robinson challenged the furrier to state that prussic acid would *not* kill moths in sealskin, granted that there *were* moths in sealskin for once. The furrier admitted that it would kill almost anything that ingested it, or inhaled its fumes over any length of time.

There was then a half-hour whispering at the bench. The court stenographer and the press could hear none of it. Upon what grounds the justices reached their decision is unknown, but the poison testimony was excluded. The bench had heard expert evidence that prussic acid—bought in bulk, not prescrip-

tion doses—had no innocent use. They had also heard an admission, elicited by the defense, that while moths do not breed
in sealskin, they do not thrive on prussic acid, either. And for
reasons arrived at in guarded whisperings, they had decided that
this damaging admission outweighed the expert evidence.

This, in both senses, finished the case for the Commonwealth.
The prosecution rested.

At the end of the previous day the justices had led Knowlton
to expect at the least debate, not a cut-and-dried job. He had
telephoned Boston to ask John W. Cummings, a top-ranking
trial lawyer, to come and consult with him on the points likeliest
to be raised. He came promptly, and too late.[1]

He found Knowlton and Moody in their private room at the
courthouse. Knowlton was slumped in a chair, pale and heavily
depressed. Moody, still young and idealistic, was pacing the floor
in a rage.

The court, they both felt, was hopelessly biased; Justice
Dewey, Robinson's man, called all the tricks. And the farce just
ended—the overnight cat-and-mouse game of pretense that expert
evidence would be objectively heard and impartially weighed—
was the last straw.

Moody was urging furiously that the prosecution should then
and there withdraw from a trial that he saw as a mockery of
justice and throw upon the court the responsibility of freeing
the prisoner.

Knowlton would not agree. He had known beforehand what
he was up against, and he would finish it.

It may have been Lizzie's highest stroke of good fortune that
Hosea Knowlton was a conscientious, brave, and somewhat
dogged man. If he had acquiesced in young Moody's angry demands, it would have made talk; a mis-trial could possibly have
been claimed—and the Lizzie Borden mystery lost its hold on
generations to come.

The prosecution's case had been admirably planned, but the
best and tightest planning cannot overcome the fact that over-

[1] This and the following, Cummings' personal reminiscences to Pearson in 1933.

lapping testimonies that clarify each other when studied at leisure and in cold print are a meaningless jumble when heard out of order from successive witnesses in a hot courtroom.

What had the jury learned? That nobody agreed on what Lizzie wore the day of the murders; that an invitation her stepmother had received had been mislaid; that a hatchet-head was believed by those automatically suspect types policemen and "experts," to be the murder weapon. They also knew that Lizzie burned up one of her dresses. But they had been shown the dress she wore on the murder morning, as clean and unrumpled as any dress could be; Robinson, so delightfully shrewd, humble, honest, and unpretentious, had identified it for them. It was *wasteful* to wear clothes fit for a party around the house; it was wasteful to burn up paint-stained cotton dresses rather than save them for cleaning-rags. But they were there to try her for *murder,* not for her rich girl's extravagant ways.

They had heard much else, of course; but it was hard to follow and to interpret. A tight-thought summary could restate and organize the evidence they had half-heard; there *was* evidence, though now Mr. Bence was excluded, much of its weight, its meaning, was obscured. But a tight-thought summary demands keen attention; weary juries respond better to emotion, to a hypnotic style. Knowlton was no hypnotist.

The case was lost.

The New York Times did not overstate matters in their headline: LIZZIE BORDEN TRIUMPHS. . . . A WEEK OF DISASTER FOR THE PROSECUTION.

The disasters they enumerated were three, all mentioned as of equal importance. It was decided that the testimony given in Fall River by the defendant was not competent as evidence; Miss Anna Borden was not allowed to testify "about Lizzie's unhappiness about going home," and, "the testimony of several drug clerks was excluded." (No hint given as to what they wanted to testify about.)

⇉ 32 ⇇

The Baltimore *Sun* commented on Lizzie's appearance on the morning she entered the court to hear the decision on Mr. Bence: "Miss Borden is beginning to show the terrible strain."

A terrible strain it must have been. With her temperament, no matter how often Governor Robinson said, "It's going to be all right, little girl," she would have had to take it with a full handful of salt; Mr. Bence had made a powerful impression under his severe cross-questioning in Fall River.

But by the recess, how everything had changed! The evidence of the pharmacist, the chemist, and the furrier had not "come up to proffer." If a moth *were* in a sealskin, prussic acid would kill it. Throughout the recess, Lizzie was "overwhelmed with sympathy in the shape of flowers," and even ladies who had hitherto stayed shyly in the background crowded around her to press her hand.

In the afternoon, Mr. Jennings was permitted to open for the defense.

But he was a changed and muted Mr. Jennings. His words, far from breaking Lizzie down, scarcely seemed to engage her attention; she sat throughout half-smiling in her "characteristic attitude," the baton of her folded fan just touching her cheek.

Mr. Jennings did not mention tiny twining fingers; his mention of Lizzie's being the youngest daughter came out sounding like a dry statistic. His one mild essay into oratory was probably wasted on a jury unlikely to have been great readers; and even here one notes a zestless timidity in the wording. "Apparently," for example, is an unfortunately delimiting word for the task at hand.

"We shall show you that this young woman ... had apparently led an honorable, spotless life; she was a member of a church, she was interested in church matters, she was connected with various organizations for charitable work....

"Perhaps some of you have read the drama of Richelieu ... and you remember that dramatic scene, one of the most dramatic in all literature, where, when the king ... sends to drag the pure and virtuous ward of Richelieu from his arms, how the old Cardinal draws that circle about her, and no man dares to cross it.

"Just so, Mr. Foreman and gentlemen, the law of Massachusetts draws about every person ... the presumption of his or her innocence.... Until they show beyond a reasonable doubt that he or she is the guilty party they are not allowed to cross the line and take the life of the party who is accused."

Yes, it lacks punch. It is merely an impersonal reminder of a basic tenet of Anglo-American jurisprudence. And Justice Dewey was obviously no hanging judge; this had been made clear even at the start, when the jurors were chosen without regard to their feelings about capital punishment. Should the unthinkable worst come to worst, nobody was going to take the life of the accused.

In any event, Mr. Jennings merely dropped the literary reference to Bulwer-Lytton and went on quietly. He pointed out that if Lizzie had killed her stepmother, she would have gone out to establish an alibi rather than wait about to kill her father, with whom she was known to have no disagreement whatever.

He avoided mentioning the hatchet-head that had been so long discussed and authoritatively identified as being either the murder weapon or its exact duplicate. He merely observed that the stains on the claw-headed hatchet from the fruit cellar had not been made by blood, and led from this irrelevance to a nice non sequitur: "They have either got to produce the weapon which did the deed and ... connect it in some way directly with the prisoner, or they have got to account in some reasonable way for its disappearance."

He spoke of the fact that nobody had seen Andrew on his way downstreet. Why was it easier for him to escape notice than for someone walking quietly away?

(Actually, Mrs. Churchill had seen Andrew; but it is unimportant. A persistent quirk of the defense was the assumption that Lizzie could not have committed the murders without getting herself drenched in gore; while the mad maniac, hatchet in hand, would have been so tidy as to attract no attention.)

He promised proof that Lizzie had been out to the barn and that "this—well, if it were not for the tremendous importance of the case I should be tempted to call it *cakewalk* of Officer Medley in the barn existed in his imagination alone."

And finally he mentioned a subject that he must have found distasteful: Lizzie had burned a soiled and useless dress by broad day in the presence of witnesses.

That was all. He pulled no stops, he scaled no heights. In one calm sentence he asked the jury to find that Lizzie did not kill her stepmother or her loved and loving father, and he was done.

It was not the speech of a happy man. I cannot guess what unwilling thoughts he may have entertained on those fruitless journeys to interview Bridget at the New Bedford Jail; and as his friends knew well, he always suffered from scrupulosity and lacked that careless joy of battle that made George Robinson great. But the change is marked. A fire—if I may use so unfortunate a word—had gone out of his style since the previous August: "Are there any shoe buttons in the fire?"

Given both speeches to study without attribution, one would scarcely guess them to have been made by the same man.

The prosecution had taken the better part of seven days to present the witnesses for the Government; the defense took a day and a half. Evidence for the prosecution came chiefly from witnesses who had been on the scene directly after the crime and from medical experts. That of the defense was farther-ranging. None of it was challenged as irrelevant, as the testimony of Mr. Bence had been, though its relevance is sometimes hard to determine.

The first two witnesses were Dr. Chagnon's wife and her stepdaughter. At eleven on the night before the murders they had heard a noise like pounding on wood, which had gone on for several minutes. Mrs. Chagnon had at first thought that it was caused by dogs getting bones out of trash barrels. Cross-questioned, the witnesses admitted that they had not been curious enough to look out of the windows, were not sure of the direction from which the sound came, and that such sounds sometimes from the icehouse next door.

Mr. Grouard, a housepainter, deposed that he painted the house in May. At first the color "didn't suit Miss Lizzie," so he "fixed it to suit her"; it was "kind of a dark color, drab," with the doors and trim done in a darker brown.

(According to one of Lizzie's defenders, her father told the painter on this occasion, "Any color she selects will be fine with me." While these words would bear out my thesis that Andrew was anxious at the time to keep Lizzie calm and happy, I have found them in no source material; they would in any case be a misquotation: "fine with me" was not a locution of Andrew's class, time, and place.)

Mary A. Durfee heard a man quarreling with Mr. Borden nine months before the murders. Charles N. Gifford found a drunk asleep on Uriah Kirby's doorstep on Third Street the night before the murders. Uriah Kirby did not see the drunk, but deposed that Mr. Gifford actually did board in his house.

The seventh, eighth, and ninth witnesses are given strong character reinforcement in the Phillips *History of Fall River*.

Mark Chase, the livery proprietor who saw the buggy stand near the house for at least an hour, is called "prominent," which in Fall River terminology meant "both rich and a Yankee." He is also identified as "a former police official." Mr. Chase had indeed been a patrolman when young; he kept two rooms, one in the St. James Hotel, a small hostel, and one in the house next door to the Churchills'; and his family name is one of the oldest in the locality. I have no wish to denigrate him since, like Mr. Phillips, I consider his evidence trustworthy and important. I merely point out that Mr. Phillips' equating of "prominence"—in his sense of the word—with percipience and veracity is both superbly Fall River and typically short-sighted, since a more important witness for the defense was a Jewish ice-cream vendor—whom I am also happy to believe.

Dr. Handy, who was not only "prominent" but "very observing" told of the pale young man on the sidewalk; so did Mrs. Manley, whom Mr. Phillips identified as a former neighbor—the young man had stayed in the same place all the time that she and her friend Mrs. Hart were admiring "some pond lilies that a young fellow had in a wagon." (Mrs. Hart came to court the next day and agreed with her.)

Jerome Borden testified—apparently to refute Bridget and Officer Allen—that when he called on the day after the murders he pushed open the front door without having to knock or ring. (He *was* "prominent," with a controlling interest in most of the mills, though when asked his business he answered simply and modestly "Lumber.")

Next to be called was Hyman Lubinsky, the ice-cream vendor. He came to court without an interpreter, and he sadly needed one who could speak either Russian or Yiddish. His English had got to a state we all remember in mastering a foreign language: he could make himself understood, but he could not understand.

He had seen Lizzie coming back from the barn at the time she claimed. He had finished delivering up on the hill, and he was taking his cart back to the proprietor's stable. He knew that it was not Bridget whom he saw; he knew Bridget from previous back-door deliveries. It was a lady; a lady in a dark dress.

Unfortunately for Lubinsky, Mr. Knowlton had a head of steam to work off. That morning the prosecution had received its knockout blow; that afternoon he had heard ten witnesses whose testimony had been only an irritant, not a threat worth fighting. Lubinsky was, at least, to the point.

For the only time in the trial Knowlton was reported as tense, nervous, irascible. He paced the floor before the witness stand firing off one question after another, while again and again poor Lubinsky pleaded, "Please, I don't understand what you say. You go too fast."

Why had he been looking into yards? It is how you do in the business, looking for people, to buy; even sold out you still do it. How did he know the time? The boss would tell, it was the time to come back. But Lubinsky's English fell apart more and more under the onslaught; his replies were easier and easier to reduce to apparent nonsense. By the time Knowlton had finished wiping the floor with him nobody thought much of his story; even the defense considered it a tactical error to be ignored thereafter.

But the courtroom had enjoyed a good laugh at the low-comedy foreigner and were rested and alert when the defense produced Me and Brownie, whose disproof of Officer Medley's cakewalk would make the next day's headlines from coast to coast.

Me and Brownie, as the nation called them in echo of the frequently reiterated phrase of one of them, were Thomas Barlow and Everett Brown. They were in their earliest teens. By the time of the trial, one of them had got a job setting up the balls in a poolroom, but on the day of the murders both were as free as air. They happened by the Borden house just after the crime was discovered; Mr. Sawyer refused to let them into the house, so they went to the hayloft, where they searched through the hay for the murderer and then hung around the premises until five in the afternoon.

Cross-questioning brought out a story full of human interest.

On the way to the Borden house they were "playing go-down," a game consisting of taking turns at pushing each other off the sidewalk into the gutter. Unlike the other witnesses who visited the loft, they were sure of the time, because of their families' unusual dinner hour.

Q: Didn't you have your dinner pretty early that day?
A: Yes, sir.
Q: About half past ten?
A: Yes, sir.
Q: You did?
A: Yes, sir.
Q: Every day?
A: Yes, sir.
Q: That isn't so now?
A: No, sir.
Q: Changed now?
A: Yes, sir.

They turned over all the hay in the loft looking for the murderer, which would clearly have disturbed the dust that

261

Medley claimed to find undisturbed. They had found the barn door fastened outside "with a kind of a thing, pinlike."

Q: You thought that the man had fastened himself in on the outside, I suppose? . . . And you went up there because you thought you could see a man up there?

A: Yes, sir.

No, they were not afraid while they turned the hay over; they just wanted to look at that murderer. They walked around and stayed there "quite a while" because it was "nice and cool" there.

Q: Now, did I understand you to say it was cooler up in the barn loft than it was anywhere else?

A: Yes, sir.

Q: You recall, don't you, that the barn loft was a place where the roof was sloping, don't you? And hangs right down low on the sides? And isn't very high anyhow? And not a large room? What should you say made that so much cooler than the rest of the country?

A: I couldn't say. It *is* always warmer in the house, I should say, than outdoors.

Q: And you should think that the barn loft was cooler than any other place you found that day? You mean that, do you?

A: Yes, sir.

Q: Has anybody told you to say that?

A: No, sir.

Q: Have you talked with anybody about the case?

A: Nobody but Mr. Jennings.

As it turned out, this important evidence had been discovered only during the past week.

The New York Times, to their enduring credit, called Me and Brownie "inconclusive evidence." As with Mullaly's stick, they were the sole stand-out. Everyone else saw their importance: Me and Brownie knew the time, thus discrediting Medley; more important, they proved that the other witnesses had been as wrong as Lizzie about the loft's being so hot.

A confusing cross-examination had got Officer Harrington to admit that he did not know whether the window had been opened at the same time that the hay-door was, to make the loft bearable for the search-squad; by implication, it might have been open all along. It had not been enough, but now Me and Brownie had spoken; the loft in which Lizzie loitered while Andrew was killed had been temptingly cool.

(Mr. Phillips, who had discovered Me and Brownie, wrote proudly of that discovery many years later. I do not think that Mr. Jennings would have liked to remember them. In those sequestered copies of the inquest lay Lizzie's own statement that the window was closed and the loft *"very* hot." This was not the sort of job that the man I remember could have enjoyed.)

Me and Brownie were the only witnesses cited to refute Medley in the summary for the defense, the only witnesses whom Judge Dewey found worthy of mention on this point in his charge to the jury. They were firm, unshaken, and definite.

The final witness of the day was Joseph Lemay, present with an interpreter. It was he who twelve days after the murders had seen a bloodstained man on the edge of his property sitting with his head bowed over the hatchet in his hands and saying, "Poor Mrs. Borden," or, to be accurate, *"Ah, Mme. Borden, la malheureuse!"* On hearing Lemay's footsteps he sprang to his feet, waving the still bloody weapon, and vanished into a nearby scrub-growth of young trees.

Lemay was not allowed to tell his story. He had got no further than saying that the event took place at Steep Brook on August 16 when Knowlton stood up.

"Unless you want to depart from the rule which I have sedulously observed not to have any evidence from witnesses who . . ."

Mr. Robinson approached him quickly, voices fell into inaudibility, and both sides approached the bench, where a second conference in unrecorded whisperings was held. The witness left the stand, and the jury was excused until the next day. Mr. Jennings submitted a written statement to the justices like that which they had considered from Mr. Bence.

When the next day's session opened the court, with perfect impartiality, excluded Mr. Lemay's testimony, as it had Mr. Bence's.

⋙ 33 ⋘

The defense continued. The witnesses to Mrs. Reagan's having recanted in Fall River were heard; you know about them. The reporter whom Mr. Phillips described as the only reporter "with a semblance of fairness except for the genial Mr. Archer of the *Transcript* . . . my friend Manning" and Manning's buddy Caldwell also gave additional evidence to indicate that others had been in the loft before Medley. The large and genial Mr. Sawyer ("Well, I am an ornamental painter, fancy painter") agreed that this was possible. Mr. Sawyer rocked the courtroom with laughter as he described his fear that the lurking maniac might pounce on him from the stairs behind the screen-door; the timid giant delights the child in us all. However, all three were so vague about the time that the court had to rule out their evidence on this point.

Mr. Winward was called. Unfortunately, he could not remember that there had been a gold ring on Andrew's little finger when he laid him out so nicely on one side.

Mrs. Holmes was the most interesting of these eight witnesses, and her testimony covered wider ground.

To her credit, it should be said that she was less smooth and voluble than her husband in what she had to say about Mrs. Reagan. Though I have heard that initially she roped him into the business, a man of affairs has usually had practiced at explaining little things away, which a virtuous lady lacks.

Nor did she, somewhat surprisingly, lay any stress on Lizzie's churchly and charitable activities; she called them "the sort of thing all the young people do." Asked about Lizzie's Sunday school teaching, she said that she knew nothing about it because Lizzie was "in the Chinese department."

Amusingly, some reporters got a mental picture of Chinese men, not of the children whose lack of discipline (as the Sunday school superintendent had told the Providence *Journal*) caused Lizzie "disproportionate excitement." Hatchets were the favored weapon in the "tong wars"—inter-Chinese rumbles that were then making New York headlines—and a theory gained favor that the murders were done by one of Lizzie's converts. (The suggestion was not seen as casting discredit on Lizzie's teaching of Christianity.)

Mrs. Holmes's value lay chiefly in her self-assurance. She could say, "If I were spending the night *I* should want the slop pail emptied," with a manner that quite obliterated its attempted quiet emptying by night. In speaking of the afternoon after the murders, she mentioned locking herself in with Lizzie "to keep out all the men." Since nobody had entered Lizzie's room without courteously asking permission, Knowlton tried to save the jury from an erroneous impression.

He said, "I think the witness is overstepping."

Mrs. Holmes tossed her head. "I'm *supposed* to overstep. I'm not used to all this kind of thing."

This is one of the many human touches omitted from the published version of the trial. Yet it is not unimportant. Think of Anna Borden behind the heavy veil that she had to be asked to lift; of Emma's friend Alice, repeatedly asked to raise her voice. The minor characters give us a clearer view of Lizzie herself. A lawyer must slash through irrelevance to seize the main issue, but a detective who does so is lost.

Lizzie sat forward and watched her friend Marianna testify with the keen air of "having her wits about her" that the press had earlier noted with approval. Before she could step down, Lizzie beckoned to Mr. Jennings and whispered to him.

Mr. Jennings did not ask for further opportunity to question Marianna. He merely told the bench flatly that Lizzie wished to prove through the witness that she had kissed her dead father in his coffin. The testimony, having been thus directly requested by the prisoner, was not allowed.

Mr. Jennings was a man of delicate sensibility; I do not think that lack of courtroom skill made him so bungle the move. Lizzie was always tasteless, yet to my mind she had shown something more than her fundamental tastelessness. That request was not made by the young woman who kissed the body of the father she loved and killed, the young woman who had been wracked by convulsive sobbing ten months before when Mr. Jennings spoke with unguarded fervor of that love, that death.

At the trial, Lizzie had her wits about her. She shared smiles with the richly turned-out Bridget. Except for two trying mornings after two bad nights, she looked "wonderfully well." I think that the blank-eyed, jowly woman I remember had already been born, and that extra flesh and new pince-nez do not account for the startling difference in photographs of Lizzie taken just before and just after the year of the murders. And I think that the friends who dropped away from her so soon after the trial—her real friends, I mean, not those who had merely huddled together against the winds of opinion—dropped away because they found a stranger staring at them out of those large pale eyes.

Perhaps not. And, yes, one on trial for murder is not likely to overindulge herself in the more delicate feelings. Let it pass.

The next witness was Emma, presented by Mr. Jennings.

Her black was dowdy, and she looked much more than ten years older than Lizzie, and frightened, but she had a pretty voice, small but crisply articulated, carrying like the notes of a harpsichord. The reporters liked her.

Before she began, Mr. Jennings had the impressive figures of Lizzie's savings and several checking accounts read aloud. Thereafter he asked her about the ring that Andrew wore throughout his last fifteen years.

Then they came to the blue wrapper, the Bedford cord.

Emma produced an inventory of the dresses that had been in the closet at the time of the search. Mr. Moody asked when it had been made; Emma replied that she had made it from memory a week before. But when Mr. Jennings went on to ask her how many dresses there had been in the closet, she said, "I can't tell you without looking at this paper."

Mr. Jennings went on to ask about the search. "Do you know how minute or extended it was?"

"I heard you say . . ." She had forgotten her cue.

"You cannot tell what you heard *me* say. Did you hear Dr. Dolan or Marshal Hilliard?"

Past objections and with further prompting, she remembered her piece: "He (Dr. Dolan) told me that the search was as thorough as it could be made unless the paper were torn from the walls or the carpets taken up from the floor."

Next they came to the making of the dress in May. The defense plan was to show a little family sewing-bee, Abby, the girls, and the dressmaker all working together. Mr. Jennings' try at it was not successful; he got only one syllable, "Yes," when he asked if Lizzie helped the dressmaker. He encouraged further, "That was your habit, was it?" But Emma balked: "Yes, sir, *I* always do." Wisely, Mr. Jennings left that particular job to Robinson and the dressmaker and got on to the paint stains.

Emma did no better here. She awkwardly separated the house-painter's and the dressmaker's visits by two weeks, and could only bring herself to say that the dress was dirty and faded; no leading made her mention the stains of brown paint. Mr. Jennings had to bring it out at last by sharp questions like a cross-examination.

But by considerable leading and prompting she was brought to say that Lizzie had burned the dress at her own suggestion. Emma sincerely wanted to help; but she must also have had a painfully vivid memory of that evening under discussion, the evening when she went upstairs after the Mayor's call and asked Alice to exchange bedrooms with her.

The passage ends thus:

Q: Did you say anything to your sister about that dress in consequence of your not finding a nail to hang your dress on?

A: I did.

Q: What did you say? [Knowlton's protest that the question was incompetent was overruled.]

A: I said, "You have not destroyed that old dress yet, why don't you?"

Q: Is that all that was said?

A: All that I remember.

[Apparently it had been fuller and richer in rehearsal. Even so, Knowlton was growing restive at all the leading and coaching of the witness.]

Mr. Knowlton: I don't think, your honors, that answer should stand.

Q: What was the condition of the dress at the time?

A: It was very dirty, much soiled, and badly faded.

Knowlton had not rated even so much attention as to have his objection overruled. Mr. Jennings did not push his luck, though Emma had once more forgotten to mention the paint. He took her to the story of the dress-burning.

We shall note how carefully every detail in Miss Russell's story had been taken care of.

"I was washing dishes and I heard my sister's voice and I turned around and she was standing at the foot of the stove between the stove and the dining-room door. This dress was hanging on her arm, and she says, "I think I shall burn this old dress up." I said, "Why don't you," or "You had better," or, "I would if I were you," or something like that. I can't tell the exact words, but I meant, do it. And I turned back and continued washing the dishes and did not pay any more attention to her at the time."

She is washing dishes, turns to speak to her sister, and turns back to the sink; the sink, that is, has moved into the kitchen. And Lizzie is not in the cupboard corner, but on the far side of the stove, by the dining-room door. This took thought and visual imagination on Mr. Jennings' part, or Robinson's. Next, a question about the doors and windows—all wide open—makes it easy for anyone outside to see the stove.

Now:

Q: Were the officers all about at the time?

A: They were all about the yard.

The narrow strip of grass between the house and the Kelly cottage becomes a lawn, the lone officer on guard before the house keeping an eye on the crowd becomes a multitude at the open windows, which afford a clear view of the stove. And a jury who could note and carefully differentiate between two-weeks-old observations and their presentation after that long, hot, tiring confinement would be a most remarkable jury.

Now it was time for the long-promised proof of the habitual dress-burnings.

Q: What did you do with your rags or pieces of cloth that you had that morning, or what did your sister do? What was the custom?

Mr. Knowlton: Wait a moment. I pray your Honor's judgment.

Mr. Jennings: I will withdraw that question for the moment with your Honors' permission. (Q.) Did you or your sister keep a rag-bag?

Mr. Knowlton: Wait a minute.

A: We did not.

Mr. Knowlton: I pray your Honors' judgment.

The Chief Justice: Excluded.

Q: What was done with the pieces of cloth or pieces of old dresses that you had to dispose of?

Mr. Knowlton: Wait a moment. I pray your Honors' judgment.

Q: Or that your sister had to dispose of?

The Chief Justice: Excluded.

Q: What was the custom and habit of your sister in disposing of pieces of clothing or old dresses?

The Chief Justice: Excluded.

Mr. Jennings: We desire to save an exception to that, your Honor.

I enjoy that passage. While such leading questions were too much even for old Justice Mason, Mr. Jennings was always a man of fixed intent; once he made up his mind to a thing, he stuck with it.

But the next passage moves me with sympathy both for poor honest Emma and for him. Neither enjoyed lying; Emma had as little knack for it as Lizzie, and nobody could have known better than Mr. Jennings how thin a lie she now had to tell. Yet to underline the essential innocence of the dress-burning, it had to be told. Miss Russell had let the jury know how O. M. Hanscom questioned her about Lizzie's dresses. The task in hand was to make the jury think that the sisters had refused to be party to any deceit about that casual, habitual occurrence, that they had made Miss Russell go right back to O. M. Hanscom and deny her silly, needless fabrication.

It had to be done, as Mr. Jennings saw it, despite the inconvenient fact that the prosecution had brought it out that Alice had kept the dress-burning secret both in Fall River and at her first appearance before the Grand Jury four months later —which made it, to say the least, unlikely that the sisters had urged her to tell a suspicious detective about it right then and there.

But that was not all of Mr. Jennings' problem. He always credited the world with sharper wits and a longer memory than it has, as a tin bath full of forbidden memorabilia still bears witness to this day. Do you remember his stunning rhetorical question before Judge Blaisdell: "Are there any shoebuttons in the fire? Is there any smell of burnt clothing? No!" As anybody who knew Mr. Jennings could assure you, he would never have risked such a line if he himself had smelt burnt clothing. But, he had said it; and, *it had been in the papers.* A juryman could have read it.

Alas, something else had been in the papers, too. Mr. Jennings had believed Lizzie innocent, but he was too intelligent to blink at the overwhelming likelihood that the murders were an inside job. When the girls sent O. M. Hanscom packing, Mr. Jennings retained his services for some weeks in the hope of getting the dirt on Bridget. While the inquest was going on, O. M. Hanscom called several times at Mr. Jennings' office to report his progress. (Or, rather, his lack of it, for as the prosecution and the defense both discovered independently, Bridget's former employers all spoke warmly of her reliability, willingness, and pleasant disposition. She stayed long with each job and had never been dismissed.) But, as you remember, during the inquest news was scarce. The papers, noting Mr. Jennings' frequent calls from a Pinkerton's man, had seized on them gladly as something to write about and pad with conjecture.

It had been ten months before. Objectively, Mr. Jennings could have taken it for granted that those calls and his stirring question were both forgotten. A man of happier temperament would not have feared that a jury would remember the two news items, put them together, and perceive that Alice could scarcely have told O. M. Hanscom about the dress-burning. Hanscom, a detective interested in a missing dress, would certainly have found it a matter worth mentioning to his employer, who, if the burning were all *that* casual, would not have denied it in court with such bravura.

Mr. Jennings did not have a happy temperament, and he did not look at such things objectively.

With this lengthy but necessary preparation, we can now listen with more understanding to Emma herself—the really important character under consideration.

You may have noticed that in her version of the dress-burning, the inconvenient presence of Alice is ignored. Mr. Jennings' next question, introducing her new recitation, now mentions Miss Russell's name for the first time.

Q: Was anything said by Miss Russell in the presence of Miss Lizzie, in regard to this dress?

(Actually, the forthcoming answer should not be called a recitation, for unlike the dress-burning, which had so many fine points to be taken care of, it had obviously not seemed to need rehearsal. Almost anybody could have said simply, "Yes, she told us that she told Mr. Hanscom that all Lizzie's dresses were still in the house, and we told her to go right back and tell the truth." Emma could not; it took subsequent questioning even to make it clear to the jury what she had been trying to say.)

A: Miss Russell came to us in the dining room Monday and said that Mr. Hanscom asked her if all the dresses were there that were there on the day of the tragedy, and she told him "Yes," "and of course," she said, "it is a falsehood."

No, I am ahead of my story. She came and said she told Mr. Hanscom a falsehood and we asked her what . . . it was about, and then she said that Mr. Hanscom had asked her if all the dresses were there. . . . There was other conversation, but I don't know what it was. That frightened me so thoroughly that I cannot recall it.

I know that the carriage was waiting for her to go on some errand and when she came back we had some conversation and it was decided for her to go and tell Mr. Hanscom that she had told a falsehood and to tell him that we told her to do so. She went into the parlor and in a few minutes she returned and said she had told him.

Lizzie, in Emma's shoes, would have been equally dim, but she would not have suddenly mentioned the fear that swept over her on hearing of O. M. Hanscom's question, thus destroying the whole effect of casual habit that had just been built up with such labor. When I called Emma's lies like Lizzie's, I was thinking of her mention of the *parlor*.

For in that intractably actual parlor O. M. Hanscom had sat so that he might question the family separately, and the women had talked in the dining room, because it did not open into it as the sitting room did. So there he must sit while Alice goes off on some errand sufficiently distant to make it worth a shabby-genteel spinster's money to take a carriage. (I expect she did go off somewhere by carriage that morning.) He must sit there, waiting it out, until she comes back to find the sisters just where she had left them, not yet having had a word with him, simply standing there and waiting for her return, as if time had stopped. A parlor, a dining room—probably a carriage, too—overmastering physical actualities. Yes, Emma's inability to work out a good, sound lie in convincing visual images is startlingly like Lizzie's.

Mr. Jennings was satisfied, with a very little clarification. Only one bit of Miss Russell's story needed to be touched up for the jury.

Jennings prompted:

Q: Now at the time when Miss Russell said, "It was the worst thing you could have done?"

A: Oh, yes, sir. She said *that* Monday morning when she came into the dining room and she said that she had told Mr. Hanscom a falsehood, we asked what she told it for, and she said, "The burning of the dress is the worst thing Lizzie could have done," and my sister said, "Why didn't you tell me? Why did you let me do it?"

(Poor Emma, how well she must have remembered those words!)

Mr. Jennings also wanted to go over Mrs. Reagan's story; but he had to do it himself, in the form of questions, for Emma volunteered nothing, merely repeating docilely, "No, sir," "No, sir, I did not," "No, sir, you did not," "No, sir," as he pushed heavily on.

Yes, poor Mr. Jennings, poor Emma, working so hard to cover their natural deficiency of original sin; so loyal, and so stubborn.

He asked her to repeat once more that it was Miss Russell who confessed to O. M. Hanscom that she had told a falsehood. Miss Russell *herself*; that it was not Lizzie or Emma who gave Miss Russell's falsehood away. That was all. He sat down and left Emma to be cross-examined.

Knowlton took Jennings' place and asked Emma about her relatives. Emma spontaneous and unrehearsed was unwary. Her tongue ran on. After she had ticked off aunts, uncles, cousins, she continued: "My stepmother had a half-sister. She owned half her house and my stepmother the other half; my father bought the interest in this house and gave it to my stepmother. This was five or six years ago. I think he paid $1500 for it."

It had come out in an odd, compulsive rush, with no hints from Knowlton, no questions.

Q: Did that make some trouble in the family?

Robinson: Five or six years ago! I protest.

The Chief Justice: She may answer.

A: Yes.

Too late, she saw what she had done. When Knowlton asked —for the only time it would go on the record except for the hint in Mrs. Gifford's story—if this had made trouble between Lizzie and her stepmother, she tried, clumsily, to hedge: "I never said anything to her about it."

Knowlton was gentle.

Q: If you will observe the question, I did not ask you that. It is a very natural answer, I find no fault with it. Did it make any trouble between your stepmother and Lizzie and you?

A: Yes, sir.

But she had caught up with herself. She explained that her

father had given them the Ferry Street house and after that the relations between Lizzie and her stepmother were as cordial as ever. Lizzie had stopped calling her Mother before the murders, but it did not relate to the gift of the half-house.

Knowlton read to her from her own inquest statement: "That, however, did not heal that breach?" "No, sir." [1]

Emma could not remember having said it or having said further words he read to the effect that Lizzie's relations with her stepmother were not "cordial"; she would have to take it back, then, for they *were*.

Knowlton went on to bring out facts about the front door that was twice found bolted inside on the murder day, and the advertisements that were run for the missing note. He asked about O. M. Hanscom. Emma could not remember whether she and her sister had retained him for two or three days or for two or three weeks. (Which was true, in a way, since though he reported to Mr. Jennings they footed the bill.)

He then wasted some time on the raincoats that had been in the house.

He asked if she had known that one of their hatchets was broken, and she said that she had only found it out in November, when she was asked about it before the Grand Jury.

She admitted that Miss Russell was not an intimate friend of Lizzie's but she hastily stressed that there was no lack of harmony between them. (Throughout, Emma rarely knew what to deny or affirm.) Knowlton then questioned her at length about the disparate versions of the dress-burning, and she denied that she had said, "Lizzie, what are you going to do?" Firmly: "I didn't say it because *I didn't say it*."

Finally, she admitted that Lizzie had worn the Bedford cord after it got paint on it—mornings, that is. She added, "Very *early* mornings."

Knowlton let her go. One feels, reading his questions that he liked her.

Of Emma's testimony, Joseph H. Choate, himself a famous trial lawyer and our one-time ambassador to the Court of St.

---

[1] Only Lizzie's portion of the inquest was ruled inadmissible.

James's, wrote to his wife: "I suppose you read the reports of the Lizzie Borden case. Her defense yesterday and today has come out very strong, especially her sister Emma's evidence, and she must, of course, be acquitted."

Robinson had been wise to attack Fleet quickly but to wait until Alice Russell's evidence should go dim in the minds of the jury and the readers of newspapers.

Directly after Emma left the stand, he presented Mary Raymond, the dressmaker, whose memories were more useful than Emma's. The paint got on the dress almost at once; the whole family joined together in the sewing, Abby as part of the pleasant little group. The blouse that Alice remembered as pulled loose was a new style, intended to hang out loose in the front. She even remembered that Lizzie had strolled in on them, torn up a dress in their presence and announced that she was about to burn it up. Indeed, as I pored over her wealth of memories, I did not wonder that Lizzie's latter-day supporters have passed over them so lightly.

Yet, like Emma, once the well-rehearsed bit was over her tongue ran on, and she told of Detective Shaw's call for a long talk in private with Miss Lizzie: "I don't know what they talked about."

Mary Brigham was called back to strengthen her previous evidence against Mrs. Reagan. Dr. Bowen's wife took the stand and remembered the bengaline; alas, she also remembered Lizzie's white hands lying in her lap. Yes, they looked "nice and clean"; no, not at all as if she had been looking for scrap metal in a dusty loft.

She was trapped into those admissions, and I am sorry for her; for her husband's sake she wanted to do her part in getting Lizzie acquitted, and he needed whatever protection she could give him from those sharp tongues that I well remember. Even my kindly mother would later refer to him as "that old Bowen."

Miss Annie White was recalled to read a line from Bridget's inquest testimony.

" 'She hollered, Come down, and she was crying.' "

And, last witness of all, Officer Mullaly was recalled, this time by the prosecution. Mullaly bore nobody ill-will; his memory was at the service of all. And he remembered well that the ice-cream man told him it was half past ten, not eleven, when he saw the lady come back from the barn.

That was the whole defense. In these chapters, plus the quotations incorporated into the body of the story, I have given you the works. The rockets and starshells had burst and faded; there now remained only the set pieces to complete the trial of Lizzie Andrew Borden.

⇥ 34 ⇤

Lizzie was disappointed by Governor Robinson's summary. She had expected the peal of a mighty organ, a miraculous shower of forensic roses, not uninspired ploddings that made her—a Borden who had made the Grand Tour—sound downright ordinary. Listening, she was disillusioned; later, when he billed her for twenty-five thousand dollars, she was volubly shocked.

The New York Times, on the other hand, was impressed by Robinson's job, "naked of oratory, an impartial weighing of the evidence." And a jury of aging farmers ate it up.

He began: "We are challenged to find somebody whose life is a tissue of crime, whose past is a prophecy.... A maniac or a fiend, we say ... one of those abnormal productions that Deity creates or suffers, a lunatic or a fiend."

The jury should bear it in mind that any policeman, "saturated with the thoughts and experiences he has had with bad people," reacts only too readily to pressure to "get the murderer in the lock-up."

Yet, how striking had been Lizzie's calm throughout! "If the little sparrow does not fall to the ground unnoticed, then indeed in God's great Providence this woman has not been alone in this courtroom."

It was not the jury's duty to unravel the mystery, only to

ask themselves, "Is this woman guilty?" They must leave out of consideration any rumors that they might have heard before the trial began.

"You have not heard some discussion that we have had at the bar, because in order that there should be no prejudice you have been asked to step aside." But the things that had been discussed had nothing to do with the case; nothing of importance had been held from them, and they must consider only what they had actually heard in that courtroom: "I do not care what you have read."

The prosecution "claimed" that Andrew had come home "with an old lock in his hand" *after* his wife had died; "that is *probably* correct—at any rate no issue is made of it."

The crime could have been committed "for sheer deviltry"; yet the prosecution tried to dig up a motive for Lizzie. "Nobody saw or heard or experienced anything that connects her with the tragedies. . . . There was no blood upon her, and blood speaks out, though it is voiceless. Think of it, think of it for an instant!"

He mentioned both paper-burnings. Dr. Bowen had burned up an old letter about his own family matters, something of no account. And, "the Government possessed itself of the idea that *the handle was rolled up by the defendant in a piece of paper* and put in there to burn, and it had all burned up except the envelope of paper. Did you ever see such a funny fire in the world?"

(The Government did *not*; Knowlton had shrewd doubts, though he could not voice them in court. He clung to the "missing will." But surely, this turning to good account of the suggested burning of the supposed will is one of the most brilliant strokes of legal misdirection ever accomplished.)

There is also charm in his handling of the matter of sole opportunity:

She was in her house in the forenoon? "Well, that may look to you like a very wrong place for her to be in, but it was her home. I suspect you have a kind of an impression that it would be a little better for her than it would be for her to be out traveling the streets. I don't know where I would want *my* daughter to be, than to say that she was at home ... as a dutiful member of the household."

Robinson's next stroke, which took him about fifteen hundred words, was subsequently deplored in the *American Law Review*, but it was skillfully done. Mrs. Churchill, having heard of the missing note from Lizzie, later asked Bridget about it, too; her original testimony ran together Bridget's recap of Lizzie's story and her own comment on it rather confusingly. Cross-questioning had sorted this out, but a weary week and a half earlier; Robinson, by reading Mrs. Churchill's original testimony and adding his own comment, made it appear that *while* Mrs. Borden was dusting, she told Bridget about the note, and hurried out without telling Lizzie.

(As you remember, Lizzie herself placed Bridget already outside while her mother was still dusting and chatting about her intention to spend the morning making pillowcases.)

Now, how long was Lizzie in the stable loft?

"It takes Assistant Marshal Fleet here to tell us about the thirty minutes—*thirty* minutes! You see him. You see the set of that mustache and the firmness of those lips and the distinction he wrought here in the courtroom telling that story. And there he was, up in this young woman's room in the afternoon ... plying her with all sorts of questions in a pretty direct and peremptory way. . . .

"What would *you* do to a man—I don't care whether he had got blue on him—that got into your house and was talking to your wife and daughter that way?"

(Note the sweeping erasure from the scene of Alice, Dr. Bowen, Mr. Buck, and Mrs. Holmes.)

Of course Lizzie had been out under the pear trees, as she claimed; the prosecution themselves had *proved* it. Hadn't they found partially digested pears in her parents' stomachs? And it was August; Lizzie had been ironing in the heat. "Do you not see families out in the yard ... sitting under the trees, especially when they have a right to a little leisure?"

Yes, Lizzie in that well-earned rest from her ironing had spent most of her time under the trees. Fleet's story? "Recollect, he is the same man that said that Dr. Bowen was holding the door—holding the fort—think of it! . . . Now, this man Fleet was on the scent for a job . . . he had a *theory*."

Lizzie's reasons for being in the barn were not always given just the same? "*Honest* people are not particular about punctuation and prepositions all the time." Probably she only thought she heard those noises as she came back. Why, she thought she heard Mrs. Borden come in. She'd *thought* she heard something, and what did that mean?

They would try to show that she was without feeling because she laughed, upstairs, or because she stayed by the door. Did they ask her to "go and wring her heart over remains that were mutilated almost past recognition?" They would say that she showed no fear. Hadn't she said to Bridget, "You must go and get *somebody*, for I can't be alone in the house?"

(A wise misquotation; the jury had seen the fragile Alice for whose protection she preferred to wait alone rather than stay flanked by a sturdy servant.)

Next to be demolished was the notion that Lizzie was discontented with her home. Inconveniently, the jury had seen it; the New Bedford worldling might even have noted that it had no bath.

"Well, gentlemen, I hope that you all live in a better way than the Borden family. Do you have pictures and pianos and every comfort and luxury? . . . Do you have carpets on every one of your floors, stairs and all? Well, I congratulate you if you do. There are lots of comforts in country homes . . . but I remember back in my boyhood we did not have running water in every room." (Definitely not in the parlor.)

He dwelt upon that lavish heat wave breakfast, with its soup, mutton, bananas, cookies, johnny cakes: "Better than the fixed-up notions that we get on the hotel table." Yet despite it, the defense "would say that Lizzie was starved to death, so pinched she could not live!"

He brushed away the inconsequence that Lizzie, a woman of thirty-two, no longer called her stepmother Mother, and that she had said something impulsive to Mrs. Gifford in a moment of annoyance. "...I have some doubts whether all of *you* are saints; that is to say, whether you never speak hurriedly or impatiently."

He cited Bridget on the pleasant atmosphere of the house and Mrs. Raymond on her memory of the happy family all sewing together, "a regular dressmaking party.... Was that a murderous group?"

He spoke of Lizzie's ring that Andrew wore, "the ring that was the bond of union between the father and the daughter. No man should ever be heard to say that she murdered the man who so loved her."

Yes, a peaceful, loving home. And the prosecution would try to make it appear that those locks that were simply an extra precaution to baffle burglars were a sign of family ill-feeling.

Next Robinson posed again Mr. Jennings' question: if Lizzie was guilty, why did she not go out and establish an alibi? He answered his own question with a reason with which I fully concur: because she was too sick to walk.

He returned to his weighing of the evidence.

She emptied her slop pail. There had been people looking at the bodies and then washing their hands in her room all day; the jury had heard Mrs. Holmes say that she would want the slop pail emptied. (They had, however, heard of nobody who washed up in Lizzie's room.)

Now came seventeen hundred and twenty-one words on the burning of the dress. Robinson is always long-winded—my condensations are drastic—but he was never more wordy than here. He had to be, for the Government had two strong points: the hatchet-head, and the fact that after a search for a bloodstained dress Lizzie destroyed a dress supposedly stained with brown paint.

Wisely, he opened low. The fact that the Bordens, so provident in the matter of toilet paper, did not save cleaning-rags was striking enough to raise questions, questions better obliterated by a follow-up picture of the sisters in their wide-open kitchen surrounded by a cloud of witnesses as they casually engaged in their old habit of burning up dresses.

"Then they say that she burned a dress. Well, the general

thought ... is that if someone burns up something in connection with some important transaction, he does it to get it out of the way for the purpose of avoiding observation. In the olden days ... rags were sold to the papermakers because they were worth something to them, but nowadays you almost have to pay a man to take them away ... and a common way of getting rid of old things is to put them into the fire, to save being pestered and annoyed by tramps."

Having made this point, he was in full swing. The sunlit, innocent morning dazzled all around, and that customary, sensible act showed for what it was. What woman wants to be pestered and annoyed by those spying tramps, who know, even before they knock, if a house contains that dangerous lure, a ragbag? Robinson was great as he told how it really happened, with the police looking in at all those open doors and windows.

The next matter to be considered called for another technique. Mrs. Reagan's story, which had occasioned Lizzie's friends such anxiety, demanded not long storytelling but curt mention sandwiched between more arresting thoughts.

"I would not wonder if they are not going to claim that this woman denuded herself and did not have any dress on at all when she committed either murder. The heart waits to learn what theories they will get up about this woman without evidence. First create your monster ... and you have created a character. But start with a woman, with a woman's love and a daughter's impulses, and your imaginings are foreign and base.

"Then they say that she murdered these two people because Mrs. Reagan—I almost forbear to mention her name—came up here and told you that the sisters had a quarrel and that Lizzie said to Emma, 'You have given me away.' Gentlemen, if there is anyone given away in this case, it is Mrs. Hannah Reagan, and nobody gave her away but herself....

"Lizzie did not try to get Bridget out of the house. If she had undertaken to do these deeds, think you not that she would have sent Bridget downstreet ... to go for marketing ... or one thing or another? But instead of that, everything goes on as usual, and Bridget was about her work. And she spoke to her about the cheap sale at Sargent's, and there is no doubt about *that* being true because they could readily find it out in Fall River whether there was any cheap sale at Sargent's at the time."

This virtuoso passage deserves a moment's pause of appreciation.

First, the horrid suggestion that one with a woman's impulses and woman's love would not only murder, but also do it bare naked. (The prosecution, rest assured, had dropped no such lewd hint.)

Next, Mrs. Reagan, whose name he almost forbears to mention.

And at once, without drawing breath, proof positive that Lizzie mentioned a dress-goods sale, since the prosecution otherwise would have denied that such a sale was held. (A fascinating double-play, since the prosecution—as I think, misguidedly—had hoped to have this interpreted as Lizzie's attempt to get Bridget out of the house so that she might get on with the second murder. The prosecution, of course, was not permitted to mention Lizzie's *denial* of this conversation.)

At long last Robinson came head-on to destroy the Government's strongest point: the murder weapon, household property, concealed where only a member of the household would have concealed it.

To us, outside and informed, George Robinson sometimes reads like a clown. He was no clown, but a superbly clearheaded man who saw the main issues from the first day and kept to them: the beloved youngest daughter was immaculate, no bloody garment was destroyed, and the murder weapon was never found.

To change the surreptitious burning of the dress to an open, casual act only called for the manipulation of a witness's evidence. But circumstantial evidence is hard evidence. An artifact can only tell one story. A bullet can be matched to the gun that fired it; a hatchet-head, newly snapped off and clumsily made to counterfeit dustiness, can be matched by detectives and surgeons with the incisions it has made in a skull.

A murder weapon *had* been found and identified by experts

282

in forensic medicine; to obliterate the facts in the minds of the jury called for a clear head, supreme nerve, and a total perfection of the magician's patter.

Robinson began by displaying all the axes and hatchets that had been proved innocent in the first week of August. As if it were a new conclusion, he told the jury that he had learned *"this very day"* about the rust-stains and cow's blood. He dwelt upon the point with emotion, and suggested that if Lizzie had been tried in *September,* this mistake could have hanged her.

Then, laughing, he held up the hatchet-head. There had been *no* suspected blood on this—which proved, of course, that it was used for the murders. (Much laughter in the court.)

Only then, with an audience warmed up and participating, he began his great piece of legerdemain. The hand is never quicker than the eye; the patter does the trick. Elsewhere, Robinson lulled the jury with pages of irrelevance. Not here. No word in this chatty, friendly passage is useless. Consider the first four words, which dispose of the testimony of several policemen, a ranking detective, and a Harvard professor of chemistry, who all described the coating of coal-ash into which the hatchet had been dipped while moist.

"One of the policemen tells us it had been *dropped* in the ashes. Well, it is down cellar, it had been lying in the ash heap. Mr. Borden who never threw anything away, who even carried an old lock home and was going to put it in his barn sometime had probably put it there to save it, and it happened to be in the ashes and was tossed up there in the box and had fine dust upon it and they say it had coarser dust upon it.

"This is an Underhill Hatchet . . . one of the kind that you and I remember when we were young. There have been thousands of them in use all around our New England towns. When you get your magnifying glass and examine it, you will see the words upon the blade: *Underhill Edge Tool Co. You* can tell just as well as I, and you will not stop long discussing these *theories* about dirt and coarseness of ashes on that old hatchet down in the cellar. You will not stop there."

The passage goes on much longer, for it is a theme with

variations, but the rabbit is already out of the hat. Whether George Robinson had ever heard of the Underhill Edge Tool Co. before he received his inspiration hardly matters, though it was a long-established firm. Whether any jurors in boyhood had ever taken a magnifying glass to read the name incised on daddy's hatchet matters yet less. Robinson was famous for his warm, confiding smile; he could create the nostalgic memory, true or false.

Nor did the passage need to be spelled out. It was stronger for being left as he left it, an implication made by a shrewd man to twelve shrewd cronies: that hatchet-head dating back to their boyhoods was old—too old, in fact, to have any cutting edge.

He did not mention its having been newly broken from its handle; and its size and the corresponding size of the wounds it had inflicted had already been taken care of, also by implication, with that mention of the initial mistake about the rust and cow's blood: "So much for the theory of *experts!*"

The murder weapon had vanished. Robinson relaxed; he wandered. That young man seen hanging around the front of the house that morning could easily have got out and in; they only had a *policeman's* word for it that the front door was bolted.[1] And Lizzie's hair! It is almost impossible to get blood out of hair except by special treatment; even *experts* admitted that. This was *very* significant.

Clearly, Robinson was tired. The jury must occasionally have scratched their scalps without needing "special treatment," and they knew that Lizzie's head of reddish-brown curly hair had not been sent to a laboratory for analysis.

Fortunately, it was time for the final wind-up. This was first rate, for Lizzie had given him one point upon which he could fight fair, and he used it well—and at length—as he cited her refusals to implicate others.

At the end, he asked them once more to look at her.

"To find her guilty, you must believe her a fiend. Does she look it? Take care of her, as you have, and give us promptly

[1] Bridget's word is discounted; he trusts her only when she contradicts Lizzie.

your verdict of "not guilty" that she may go home and be Lizzie Andrew Borden in that bloodstained and wrecked home where she has spent her life for so many years."

And Lizzie was annoyed at his bill for twenty-five thousand dollars!

↠ 35 ↞

Hosea Knowlton lacked Robinson's showmanship; worse, he lacked his ear, that delicate sixth sense that taught Robinson, for example, never to say *downtown*, like a city slicker, but *downstreet*, properly, like real people. Despite its convictions, *The New York Times* admired Knowlton's grave summary; but with a jury of middle-aged and elderly farmers, it did not click.

"Upon one common ground, in this case all humane men should stand together. . . . I do not disguise my appreciation of the fact that it is a most heartrending case.

"My distinguished friend says, 'Who could have done it?' The answer would have been, nobody could have done it, if you had read the account of these cold and heartless facts in any tale of fiction. . . .

"It was a terrible crime. It was an impossible crime. But, it was committed. . . .

"We are trying a crime that would have been deemed impossible, except for the fact that it *was;* and we are charging . . . a woman who would have been believed incapable of it but for the evidence which it is my duty, my painful duty, to call to your attention."

He reminded them that murders have been done by church members; that youth—to that jury Lizzie must have looked very young—does not mean innocence. Not long ago a boy, Jesse Pomeroy, had been convicted of a sickening series of sadistic murders and received a life sentence. And, four years back, Sarah Jane Robinson of Somerville had killed seven members of her family to get a small inheritance: "Women are no better and no worse than we."

He suggested, somewhat dryly, that Andrew and Abby had also deserved a little sympathy. He pointed out that not only the scorned police had witnessed for the prosecution, but also Lizzie's friends and a long employed servant, and that we depend upon the police to protect us from crime and expect police detectives to think.

He tried to sell the idea that scientists from Harvard do not merit automatic distrust, and to show how many of our daily judgments are based on *sufficient* circumstantial evidence, many facts all pointing to one conclusion.

The first news reports had it that someone entered the house, killed the old man, chased the old woman upstairs, and killed her there. The medical reports had changed that. "It is the key of the case. . . . It was malice against *Mrs.* Borden that inspired the assassin."

Who had entered that house, chosen an innocent old lady for his first victim, and then lain in wait an hour and a half to kill Andrew? Nobody but Lizzie was known to have any ill feeling toward Abby. A man could have smashed her head in with one blow; the jury had heard about the blows that killed her, struck by one "strong only in the desire to kill."

The house was locked inside and out, even to the closet at the head of the stairs. The barn was locked each night. The front door, that day, was double-locked and bolted. When Bridget went out, Lizzie was downstairs in that railroad-flat layout where a murderer would have had to pass her coming in. Who could have entered before Abby was killed?

Lizzie might not have seen Abby's body, but she had ears as well as eyes: "And do you believe that those blows could have been struck . . . that she had fallen without a jar . . . nearer than I am to you, sir . . . and Lizzie know nothing of it?"

But her father came home, "a stern and just man who knew all the bitterness that was between them." So she made up a story about a note that had called Abby away, to hold off the questioning and the search. There had surely been no note, or the advertising, the reward for information leading to its sender or the messenger would have brought some result.

(We need not wonder that he thought so, or that all who have studied the case carefully and honestly have agreed with him.)

The court rested for the day. The jury, having listened for so many hours to Robinson, great showman though he was, must have been glad of a chance to stretch their legs and light a cigar.

Knowlton opened the next day by pointing out how few murders have what a sane, well-balanced person would consider sufficient motive. Murders *happen:* "The wickedness was all before the fourth day of August. The ingratitude, the hate, the stabbing of the mind... had gone on for many, many months. ... And we cannot tell what new fuel was added to that fire of discontent.... All we know is that there was a jealousy...."

Emma had shown them that in court, as she told about the Whitehead house and said that they felt that Abby was not interested in them. It was not likely that Lizzie planned to kill her father: "But Lizzie Andrew Borden, the daughter of Andrew Jackson Borden, never came down those stairs. It was a murderess... and she was coming downstairs to meet Nemesis."

He organized and traced out all the evidence that we have studied. He came to her alibi: "The jury are asked to believe as reasonable men that she spent the whole time that Bridget was upstairs in the loft of the barn, a place hot beyond description, with the broiling sun of that August day directly over the roof."

(Knowlton was thinking of Lizzie's words, not Robinson's; the jury had been shown Lizzie out under the pear trees, cooling off after her ironing.)

She wanted iron to fix a screen, lead for sinkers. But what screen had needed fixing, where was her fishline? The defense could produce neither.

And what about that call on Alice Russell? "My distinguished friend talks about the frequency of presentiments. They are frequent in the storybooks, Mr. Foreman."

Shock could have masked her grief. But fear? The courtroom had laughed at Mr. Sawyer, a big man with many people around him, so frightened at standing near that entryway. Lizzie stood there alone. To be sure, she was brave; she went alone into the shadowy laundry room where her parents' clothes lay, "for some purpose that has I know not what connection with this crime."

He spoke of the dress-burning, presenting the jury once more with that blind-alley problem of the dress: silk *or* cotton.

He came to Mrs. Reagan, whose story he was "not quite willing to dismiss in so supercilious and satirical a manner as (his) distinguished friend." Lizzie's excited friends had vouched for its significance as they "came round in troops to harass Mrs. Reagan into taking it back." And she had done so. "But that was out of the kindness of her heart, not the malice of it."

Yet, "Miss Emma who knew what took place, Miss Lizzie who knew what took place, never came to Mrs. Reagan and said, 'You have told a lie.' They were the ones who ought to have denied it. *They* were the ones who ought to have asked her to take it back."

He had put his finger on the weakness of the defense, here.

But it was a minor matter, and the next was central. With a truly stunning organization of the evidence, Knowlton presented the prosecution's strongest point—the presence in the house of the murder weapon.

A hatchet-head newly broken off from its handle; a hatchet-head that could have been washed free of detectable blood, though its handle could not; a hatchet-head concealed in a high-placed box, which no stranger to the house would have found, and coated with white coal ash from the nearby ash-heap to look less conspicuously clean in that box of dusty tools; a hatchet-head which according to the surgeons could not have been a shade longer, shorter, thicker, or thinner to have made a certain few of the many incisions in the skulls.

This evidence was so superbly presented that it is amazing to read it and realize that Robinson's counter-evidence—the name of the Underwood Edge Tool Co., clearly legible through a magnifying glass—has continued so to outweigh it through the years that even those who believe Lizzie guilty will tell you that the weapon was never found; or, sometimes, that the weapon was found when the barn was torn down, or behind a partition when the house was remodeled.

The human race has a remarkable ability to select and interpret facts according to its emotional needs.

Knowlton had covered the prosecution's case. He ran over the facts once again quickly. A woman killed by weak, unskillful blows; a woman who had no enemy but her daughter. Killed in a house guarded by locks, bolts, barbed wire; killed in the early morning, when it passed credibility that it could have been done without Lizzie's knowledge.

"Her father had not always told all that he knew. He had forbidden telling of that burglary of Mrs. Borden's things ... but he would not have so suppressed or concealed this tragedy, and she knew it....

"She had all she wanted, and she did not call Maggie until she got ready, until she got through....

"We find a woman in a house where there is a hatchet which answers every requirement of the case, where no outside assassin could have concealed it.... We find a dress which was concealed from the officers until it was learned that the search was to be resumed and safety was no longer assured."

Facts, like chips floating on the stream of our thought, showing the direction in which the river flows. And, beyond them, all the elements of any ordinary crime: hatred, malice, falsehood, absurd and impossible alibis, contradictory stories which are not even attempted to be verified, destruction of evidence ...

"What is the defense, Mr. Foreman? Nothing, nothing. Some dust thrown on the story of Mrs. Reagan—which is not of the essence of the case. Some questions of time put upon the acts of Mr. Medley—which is not of the essence of the case. Some absurd and trifling stories of drunken men the night before, and dogs in the yard, the night before ... of a pale and irresolute man walking up the street in broad daylight. Nothing, nothing.

"Let mercy be taken care of by those to whom you have entrusted the quality of mercy. It is not strained in the Commonwealth of Massachusetts.... We are responsible only for the justice, the courage, the fidelity with which we can find and answer the truth."

It was on for dinnertime, and the jury must have been glad that he was through. Robinson knew how to keep you listening, he talked sense and he was right down to earth; not like Knowlton, with all his five-dollar words.

⇥ 36 ⇤

If the reporters had expected Lizzie to swoon again, as she did after Moody opened for the prosecution, they were disappointed. She was calm; after the recess she was still calm. She seemed only deeply abstracted.

She ignored the hovering ladies with their floral offerings and the warm glances of Mr. Buck and her assembled counsel. She sat down and fixed indifferent eyes upon the bench—on old Justice Mason with his muttonchop whiskers, Blodgett, the elegant, with his hooded eyes half-closed above their bagging lids, and little Dewey, busy with his palm-leaf fan, his pointed smile now somewhat set.

Knowlton's factual, emotional approach had disturbed Lizzie's supporters; so had the way in which he made it plain to the jury that there was no danger of the death penalty. He had made some effect; it was likely that the jury would debate long. But it was almost over.

Justice Dewey laid down his fan and spoke: "Lizzie Andrew Borden, although you have been fully heard by counsel it is your privilege to add any word which you desire to say in person to the jury. You now have that opportunity."

The prisoner rose and repeated the formula that left the strategy of the defense unchanged: "I am innocent. I leave it to my counsel to speak for me."

Justice Dewey then delivered the charge to the jury. Its description, "a plea for the innocent," was apt. While it repeatedly cast doubt on the prosecution, it voiced no doubts as to any part of the defense. Robinson had no cause to regret that he had raised Dewey to the bench.

The charge was little over a third as long as the summaries had been; but they had been remarkably lengthy. At the outset, Justice Dewey described the limitations of his office: he might not express opinion on the credibility of any witness, but only indicate what degree of weight should attach to any whole class of testimony.

As he warmed to his own words, his interpretation of these limits became increasingly liberal—reportedly to the surprise and displeasure of Blodgett and the Chief Justice, to whom he had outlined his plan of address the night before.

Was Lizzie Borden, he asked, under a real and operating motive to kill her parents? Andrew Borden had left a large estate; but the Government also claimed that she felt ill-will nearly, if not quite, amounting to hatred for her stepmother, for which claim they depended largely upon her conversation with Mrs. Gifford. But Mrs. Gifford had quoted the language of a young woman, "not a philosopher or jurist. What is the habit of young women in their use of language? ... Consider whether they do not often use words which go far beyond their real meaning. ... What you wish is a true conception of the state of mind of the defendant ... not *years ago*, but later, and nearer the time of the crime."

Years ago? He himself had dated it, at the start of his leisurely passage, as slightly under five months before the crime; nor did he mention Emma's sworn inquest testimony, which the jury had heard, about the "breach" that five years could not heal despite that prompt gift of "more than equivalent" property.

Instead, Justice Dewey recast Bridget's testimony, smoothing out her new-found, labored insistence on literal truth; stressed Mrs. Raymond's picture of the cozy sewing-bee at which poor Emma had balked; and quoted Emma's testimony, "Yes, sir," that they all "went" to the same church.

No witness, he pointed out, saw Lizzie commit the murders. Sometimes inference from circumstantial evidence is direct and certain, sometimes it is not. "This is illustrated by the case on trial here."

Facts, he explained, are essential or helpful. The hatchet-head is only *helpful*—the Government does not claim that another weapon *could* not have been used for the murders. (This was quite true, since another weapon of identical size with that which was broken and concealed at the time of the murders could have been used to commit them; though it would have been a striking coincidence.)

Next, Dewey made a suggestion about the missing note that has had recurrent popularity: it was part of a "plan or scheme" to get Mrs. Borden out of the house before the assassin killed Andrew; when the "plan or scheme" failed, the assassin took it away, "in a reasonable and natural wish to remove that as one possible link in tracing himself." (Dewey offered no suggestion as to why a murderer was untroubled by having two husky young women on the scene, only by the fat-crippled old lady; nor have any who subsequently embraced this idea.)

Dewey then questioned the medical evidence. He assured the jury that they need not be overinfluenced by doctors who believed that the murderer need not necessarily have received much blood on his prson. He also—going even Robinson one better—cast doubt on the time-lapse between the deaths as shown by analysis of the stomach-contents, and put a strong question for the jury to consider: "It is reasonable or *credible* that she could have killed Mrs. Borden at or about the time claimed by the Government, and then, with the purpose in mind to kill her father at a later hour, have gone about her household affairs with no change of manner to excite attention?"

Few, indeed, could have got through those few minutes of ironing in Bridget's presence—the only part of the morning in which Lizzie was observed by a survivor, though she herself denied even that. The question, "Is it likely?" is perhaps in order to a jury that had been denied knowledge of the inquest testimony. The question, "Is it *credible?*" is a horse of another color: it is a virtual instruction to the jury to find for *not guilty*. (Judge Charles Gideon Davis, a respected elder statesman of Massachusetts jurisprudence, subsequently wrote of this with severe disapproval.)

Next, Justice Dewey pointed out how little importance should be attached to Lizzie's conflicting statements. He then returned to belittling what he called "the words of some gentlemen of medical and scientific knowledge who are termed 'experts.'" Once more he warned the jury that the separation of the two deaths must be "to some extent a matter of opinion" and repeated Robinson's assurance that when they were given the skulls and the hatchet-head they would be able to judge "as well as any 'expert.'"

The Government, he said, had asked him to put a further question to the jury: if Lizzie was innocent, must she not have been an accessory before the fact? But he added his warning about such a decision: "She must have encouraged it."

He then explained Lizzie's decision not to testify. He suggested the very words in which she might have put her position: "I have told the officers all I know. . . . Whatever is mysterious to others is mysterious to me." (This implication that a prisoner takes the stand in the role of detective, not simply to convince a jury of his own guilt or innocence, is surprising, even from Justice Dewey.)

Properly, and as any judge should, he explained that if the evidence merely made the jury suspect guilt "or even a strong probability of it," that it was still their duty to vote *not guilty*.

He pointed out how cooperative Lizzie had been with the police. He asked whether Lizzie's call on Alice Russell, with its girlish confiding of premonitions, did not indicate innocence, not guilt. He did not speak of the dress-burning, and mentioned the dress only in passing, thus: "Take this matter of the dress . . . can you gentlemen extract from that testimony such a description . . . as would enable you to identify the dress?" (I delete no *meanings*, only garlands of repetitive verbiage.) "Then take, again, the matter of Mrs. Reagan's testimony. It has been suggested that there has been no denial of that testimony. . . ."

Mr. Knowlton: "Not from me, sir. I admit it."

Mr. Justice Dewey: "Admit what?"

Mr. Knowlton: "That she did deny it."

Mr. Justice Dewey: "Mrs. Reagan?"

Mr. Justice Dewey must have dozed through some part of Mrs. Reagan's testimony and Mr. Knowlton's summary, for getting back in stride, he said: "It is not suggested that she *does* not deny it" (which, of course, she no longer did), and continued, "But I say that the parties who represented the defendant in the matter and who were seeking to get a certificate from Mrs. Reagan were proceeding without having received any authority to get the certificate and without having received any assurances from anybody that the statement was false and one that ought to be denied." (One of the better non-sentences, like that clarified above by occasional use of ellipses.)

"You have heard the statement of Miss Emma about it here ["No, sir"] and it would be for you to judge as reasonable men whether such men as *Mr. Holmes* and the *clergymen* [the only clergymen involved would not testify] started off . . . without first having taken steps to satisfy themselves that it was a report that ought to be contradicted." (It is hard to see what steps they could have taken, since Lizzie and Emma were too involved to count as objective counter-evidence.)

So prepared, Justice Dewey sent them out to deliberate.

They must be unanimous, he told them; they must ignore the reports and rumors by which the press had "ministered to the excitement." He closed nobly:

"And entering upon your deliberations with no pride of opinion, with impartial and thoughtful minds, seeking only for truth, you will lift this case above the range of passion and excited feeling, into the clear atmosphere of reason and law. If you shall be able to do this, we can hope that, in some high sense, this trial may be adopted into the order of Providence and may express in its results somewhat of that justice with which God governs the world."

Justice Dewey had taken scarcely an hour and a half to make the dark places plain. The jury retired. The exhibits were sent in for their examination; the bedspread so strikingly unbespattered; the doorjamb that had received only one splash, at the height of a woman's waistline; the spotless bengaline; the underskirt, with its one drop of blood that had come from outside

the garment; the skulls; the weapons that had been proved innocent; the hatchet-head—and as promised, a magnifying glass
with which they might all read the words *Underwood Edge Tool
Co.*

The jury returned in one hour, to the dot. Their names were
called and counted off by the crier.

The clerk said, "Lizzie Andrew Borden, stand up."

In the words of *The New York Times:* "Her face became livid,
her lips were compressed as she tottered to her feet and looked
at the jury in accordance with the instruction of the clerk."

"Gentlemen of the jury, have you agreed upon your verdict?"

"We have."

"Lizzie Andrew Borden, hold up your right hand. Mr. Foreman, look upon the prisoner; prisoner, look upon the foreman.
What say you, Mr. Foreman—"

The foreman could not wait for the finish of the ancient formula. He broke in: "Not guilty!"

The trial transcript runs, "There was an outburst of applause
which was at once checked by the court. The prisoner dropped
into her seat."

A cheer went up "that might have been heard half a mile
away." There was a lengthy, joyous, unchecked pandemonium.
Spectators stood on their seats cheering, waving hats and handkerchiefs. It was old Sheriff Wright of Taunton who held the
gavel, but he did not try to use it. He was weeping, blind and
deaf to the excitement of the crowd.

Miss Borden's head went down upon the rail before her. She,
too, wept.

Jennings' voice broke as he said, "Thank God, Oh, thank
God."

He held out his hand to Melvin O. Adams. Adams, the Baltimore *Sun* reports, "seemed incapable of speech." George Robinson "gleamed on the jury with kindly interest in his fatherly
eyes as they filed out, and stood up as Knowlton and Moody
came to shake his hand."

The jury on whom his fatherly eyes gleamed were all of his
age or older, but in that moment I am sure that he saw them
as his boys.

It was over. Lizzie was vindicated. As the Baltimore *Sun* spelled out the happy ending: "When the spectators were gone, Miss Borden was taken to the rooms of the justices, with only the eyes of friends upon her, and the caresses of devoted admirers."

The New York Times' editorial condemnation of those who had let Lizzie bear an ordeal so meaningless and brutal was in the full stream of public opinion. The Providence *Journal* permitted itself to say that the verdict might not be wholly acceptable to some people, but it was alone in expressing even so much dissatisfaction.

The great mass of the reading public found in their morning papers only an echo of their own joy that a jury had been so quick to "express ... somewhat of that justice with which God governs the world."

BOOK SIX

Lisbeth of Maplecroft: An Epilogue

⇒ 37 ⇐

IT was over.

One Boston newspaper received a premature flash reporting that the jury took two votes, on the first of which one juror had voted guilty. This error was promptly corrected in the bar of the nearest hotel; for as soon as the twelve had shaken Lizzie's hand they made a concerted dash for freedom, beer, and spirits, after two weeks of captive abstention.

There it was learned that the vote was immediate and unanimous. The exhibits were ignored; nobody so much as took up the magnifying glass to assure himself of the actual presence of the magic words *Underwood Edge Tool Co.* However, to avoid giving any false impression that their minds had been made up in advance, the jury decided upon a full hour's wait, and sat it out.

In the room of the justices, Lizzie held an informal reception for the press. Her tears upon learning of her acquittal had been a brief, sunshiny shower. She was radiant as she received the congratulations of the reporters.

She had an especially warm handshake for the influential columnist Joe Howard, who had come to court every day with pomp, surrounded by an impressive staff of underlings. He had given her a splendid press throughout, and his column, which appeared in New York and Boston, dwelt gratefully the next day upon that appreciative singling-out of her favor.

Governor Robinson stood by Lizzie's side, their tender father-and-daughter relationship as yet unmarred by his bill for twenty-five thousand dollars. Knowlton and Moody had quickly congratulated him and retired. Nor did the justices take their place in the receiving line; there were only Lizzie's three lawyers, Mr. Buck, Mrs. Holmes, Emma, and Uncle John.

Mr. Buck was still in tears. Mr. Jennings, after his first broken-voiced outcry, was reported to be "the most calm" of the group.

Uncle John had not dropped in to see Lizzie at Taunton Jail, where visitors were always welcome; nor, so far as I can learn, did they ever meet again. It would be nice to know what he thought and felt during that diminished family reunion. As Mr. Phillips put it, more than half a century later, Andrew "thought highly" of him; he had, in fact, been the closest approach to a friend that Andrew ever had.

Lizzie, at least, was on the top of the wave. Her smiles became brilliant when she saw the waiting throngs outside the courthouse. After she had been helped into her carriage, she did not let it drive on until a long, long procession of men and women had filed past her, hungry to shake her hand. Small children were lifted up for the privilege, and babies, for her to kiss.[1]

It was, I suppose, such a bodying of the dream as comes to few of us between cradle and grave.

Mrs. Holmes had invited Emma as well as Lizzie to spend the night at her house after a party of celebration. I am told that the party was wonderfully gay. "The girls" had collected newspapers from far and near, full of sketches of Lizzie that they all found hilariously bad likenesses. Lizzie herself laughed heartily over them.

That afternoon and evening were Lizzie's unblemished triumph; and for me, they epitomize her mystery. I know something of her limitations and of her small-town ambitions—which before and after that brief glory were always unfulfilled; I know something of her temperament, lost in fantasy and at the same time strangely deficient in imagination, blind to the real world of people and still so terribly anxious for its acceptance, its admiration—so self-defeatingly anxious. Those who knew her best and spoke of these limitations, ambitions, mechanisms of self-defeat have often seemed to me to be describing themselves—and my own early girlhood—when they spoke of her. She was Fall River: a term of wide application; in this sense you might say that Emma Bovary, too, was Fall River. I know this much of her, and it is not enough.

She hated her stepmother with long, concentrated, dedicated

1 See Providence *Journal* for details.

hate. She loved money to spend as much as her father loved money to keep. She wrote the dullest letters that ever spilled from the pen of woman in a copybook hand as empty of life as the words it set down. Mr. Jennings racked her with awful weeping in the Second District Court of Fall River. And on the day of her acquittal, she triumphed and laughed.

I have unraveled only minor mysteries. The central mystery still stands. Lizzie is like her own eyes, so hugely open, so transparently pale, and so utterly uncommunicative.

The next day, Lizzie went back to Second Street with Emma. There were no crowds. A few reporters watched the scene from a sympathetic distance.

June in that part of the world is becoming to even the shabbiest streets, and Second Street was at least still leafy and shaded back then. The big brass doorplate bore the name Andrew J. Borden engraved on it in flowing script; it was buffed to a nice shine. The carriage drew up, the women got out, hesitated for a moment, and then rang their bell.

The housekeeper whom Emma had hired during Lizzie's absence opened the door, the women went in, and the reporters went away.

The Providence *Journal* said that the sofa on which Andrew had died was still at the police station; they would not have that unhappy reminder, at least. It added that many had changed their minds after hearing the verdict; it was, after all, being well received.

A day or two later, Lizzie went to Taunton, to thank Sheriff Wright and his wife in person for their many kindnesses. The gesture was very Lizzie.

She also made a neat packet of her press-clippings and relevant photographs, including photographs of the bodies, and sent them, with a polite note, to young Mr. William Moody "as a memento of an interesting occasion." As I have said, one cannot fit her into a tidy framework.

Her friends knew that nobody would want to stay in a house with such unhappy associations. The Remingtons lent her a summer cottage down near Newport while she found and furnished a new home.

She bought a house in a good neighborhood, just a block away from Mr. Almy and Mr. Milne, whose papers had not found Mr. Bence newsworthy and who went bail for Uncle John. It is a largish house, but not as houses went in that period and that neighborhood; the *haute bourgeoisie* of Fall River set their own strict standards of what is correct, standards that owed nothing to the larger world. Too much would have been as unacceptable as too little; Lizzie knew it.

What pretentious effect the house had came from its being modern—McKinley-Queen Anne, with a non-functional clapboarded turret at one side and one of those glass-windowed front porches, so stylish at the time, that look like a back entry absentmindedly displaced. It sat in a nice, roomy, shady yard.

Lizzie's sole error, which caused much unkind amusement, was in giving the house a name, Maplecroft, which she had engraved on a front step like a gravemarker; the naming of houses was not acceptable Fall River practice. She also asked to be addressed thereafter as Lisbeth and had herself so listed in the telephone book, though she never legalized the change.

There is an odd amoral streak in your southern New England Yankee. Many who in time could have taken the murder in stride—a thing that probably happened, but all water under the bridge now—could not stomach that bit: Lisbeth of Maplecroft. Yet, it is also very Lizzie, and it sums up all that makes the end of her story hard to handle. A murder should not end in anticlimax. If we cannot have *exeunt to a dead march,* then we want the prison, or the mental hospital, with mind and spirit either rotting away with proper drama, or else healing, quickening to contrition, to expiation. Lisbeth of Maplecroft was anticlimax personified.

And Maplecroft did not serve its happily anticipated function. Lizzie had not been widely liked before the murders, and they brought her only the briefest social success. Though Mrs. Hezekiah Brayton had led a group in prayer for her, she did not thereafter entertain for her or show any desire to become more intimate.

The congregation at Central also showed reticence at Lizzie's return. Lizzie's churchgoing first fell off, and then ceased.

Her friends expected her to clear up many questions once the trial was over. She never did, though in time she became more positive and outspoken in her suspicions of Hiram C. Harrington. She mourned when he died, saying that now her one chance of being really cleared was gone.

⇒ 38 ⇐

Yet the awareness that she was not really cleared grew slowly. At first friends were amazed by her resilience. In a little article called *Legends of Lizzie*, Edmund Pearson once published a story that I believe because we both had it from the same source: old friends of Emma's, who at the time they first told it were still stout believers in Lizzie's innocence.

It was about a year after the murders; Lizzie and Emma had come to spend the day at their country place. A devil was in the conversation, those tactful friends were sure, for one innocent reference to hatchets after another kept threatening to crop up and having to be delicately skirted: rope in the hangman's house.

Now at one end of the grounds was an old woodshed, very dilapidated, which spoiled the view of the bay. Lizzie's hostess, looking at it, said to her sister, "The very next time Mike comes we must remember to have him knock that thing down for firewood."

Lizzie sprang up, all health and energy.

"Why wait for Mike?" she cried. "Give me the axe!"

In time, the children began to sing. For some years, on the anniversary of the murders the *Globe* ran articles that suggested that "the murderer or murderess" might still be at large in the town. These were eventually stopped—as I believe at the suggestion of Monsignor Cassidy, a religious activist full of good works.

Later writers have attributed Lizzie's loss of popularity to the *Globe*'s articles and the children's song. And this may have been so, "under the hill"; Professor Richard Thompson, who once lived near me "up on the hill" recently wrote me that when his nursemaid took him out to walk she went blocks out of her way to avoid passing Maplecroft.

But old Fall River, that village-within-a-city which was called "the people you know," was another matter. Your provincial Yankee is bone-stubborn and a glutton for lost causes. Whether the pattern is genetic or cultural doesn't matter; it is real, and persecution is the meat it thrives on. George Robinson appealed to its deep core when he asked that a tragic girl might "go back and be Lizzie A. Borden in that bloodstained and wrecked home where she had spent so many years." Lisbeth of Maplecroft had no such appeal.

Further, everyone vividly remembered Andrew's notorious pennypinching; the plushy bourgeois style of Maplecroft and the indiscreet speed with which it was acquired quite definitely raised certain second thoughts.

The town was further irked when Lizzie bought up *The Fall River Tragedy* and nobody had a chance to read it. Everyone wanted to. As I told you at the start of our story, I had to wait for the pleasure forty years before I found the first copy that I had ever seen, in the Library of Congress. Also, a handful of intellectuals read the critique of the case that Dean Wigmore of Northwestern, the author of a standard work on evidence, ran in *The American Law Review;* and many more read and discussed the views of Judge Charles Gideon Davis published in the Boston *Daily Advertiser*—the *Transcript's* then morning equivalent, impeccably Republican and sound. Judge Davis was senior to those judges who had sat on the trial, his reputation carried weight in our part of the world, and he was telling in his point-for-point exposition of the thin deal that the prosecution had received.

Yet Lizzie was so essentially uninteresting that I think the pendulum might have swung back in her favor—after all, she *was* a Borden—if it had not been for the unfortunate Tilden-Thurber episode.

Those who believe Lizzie guilty generally pass over this matter unhappily, as a letdown, not in the grand manner. Her defenders never knew what to do with it until a fraud was perpetrated in the 1950's with a forged confession, sold as having been extorted from Lizzie at the time of the affair. This made it possible to tie fraud to misdemeanor and disallow both, by the same kind of thinking that had once confirmed the public belief in Lizzie's innocence by means of the sins of McHenry and his creative friend Trickey.

However the thing happened, like the daylight robbery, and like many other odd non-criminal episodes, which I do not report, since stories multiply, and while I am sure that far from all of them are false, I am equally sure that some are sheer moonshine—as incorrect, if not as patently absurd, as that favorite out-group yarn about her shooting the horse that threw her. I shall say only that until her middle years she did odd things; and this is a known example.

Lizzie dressed really well, but though I never saw the interior of Maplecroft I have been assured that it distressingly fulfilled its architectural promise. Lizzie also loved to give presents. A caller admired a new acquisition in Maplecroft, a pair of paintings on porcelain called *Love's Dream* and *Love's Awakening*. Lizzie gave her one—indiscreetly, for she must at least have known that there was something odd about finding them in her shopping bag on the way back from Providence.

The paintings came from Tilden-Thurber, an excellent old Providence jeweler's where most of us kept an account. The small shop of our one fine jeweler, Ellis Gifford, specialized in well-set precious stones; we usually went over to Tilden's to buy wedding presents.

The name Tilden-Thurber was on the backs of the paintings. Lizzie's friend dropped and broke her gift and took it to Providence to be repaired. The clerk requested her to wait and came back with the manager, who asked when she had bought it. She told him—name-dropper—that it was a present from Lizzie Borden.

Lizzie was a regular customer, but the plaques had been as expensive as they were ugly. Tilden's was an old firm run by nice people, but they did not want to encourage habits they might find expensive. They had a warrant made out in Lizzie's name, instructing the police detective that he was only to serve it if Miss Borden was not willing to come to Providence to discuss things.

Lizzie showed initial excitement and indignation; the detective reported that same red-purple mottling of the skin and the contrasting light of the pale eyes so often noted earlier in the papers. However, she agreed to go with him. She went alone. (Mr. Jennings, I believe, had ceased to be her lawyer before this episode, though this cannot be documented unless the Jennings papers are at some time made public, in full. His daughter, who now controls them, has, up to this time of writing, preferred not to turn them over to the Fall River Historical Society.)

Lizzie met with the detective, Mr. Tilden, Mr. Thurber, the employee who eventually perpetrated the fraud of which I have spoken, and Mr. Stephen Metcalf. (Oddly enough, Mr. Metcalf was another family acquaintance of ours; a summer-place, not a Fall River, friend.)

Since a warrant had been made out and Lizzie's name was news, the leak from the police department was unavoidable, but it was given mercifully small play. Lizzie, I think, had Mr. Metcalf's influence to thank for this; he was a controlling power on the Providence *Journal*.

Unfortunately, the first day's headlines were out: LIZZIE AGAIN. They did not escape notice in Fall River, though the second day brought word that no charges were being pressed. The store accepted payment for the plates and dropped the matter.

But petty theft is not only easier to believe in than murder; it is somehow less socially acceptable. The Borgias had family pride; they did not pick pockets. Old rumors, vaguely consonant with this episode, which had largely been discounted up to that time as a shade *too* peculiar, became more widely believed.

That was in 1897. It was the sorriest instance of those "signs of lack of balance in later years" to which Mr. Phillips referred in defending her—so outdatedly—fifty years later.

To the small remaining handful of Lizzie's friends it was worse than shocking; it was embarrassing.

Lizzie and Emma found themselves increasingly alone.

⇒ 39 ⇐

They kept a housekeeper, a cook, a second-maid, and a coachman. It was Lizzie's house and Lizzie's staff; Emma had little to do to take up her mind. She still wore mourning; indeed, she wore it for the rest of her life. And in the matter of churchgoing, she reversed Lizzie's pattern; while before the murders she had not been a churchgoer, she now began to go every Sunday. She became increasingly friendly with Mr. Jubb's sister; the loss of Alice Russell had left a gap in her life, and she needed someone, someone not deeply part of her former world, to fill it.

Lizzie took trips: to Washington, to New York, and, with increasing frequency, to Boston.

Her overnight trips to Boston had a fixed pattern. A favorite hack-driver—later, a taxi-driver—met her at the station and remained at her disposal throughout the stay. They drove from Back Bay station to the old Bellevue, near the State House; the staff all recognized Lisbeth A. Borden, but they courteously pretended to know her only from her past visits. She would spend the day in shopping and visiting the Art Museum; in the evening, invariably, she went to the theater. She loved the theater, and she was particularly obsessed with the gifts and beauty of Nance O'Neil, the star of a Boston stock company who specialized in tragic roles with which Lizzie identified.

It was still the heyday of the big summer hotel. Those huge, shingled firetraps with their verandahs and croquet lawns were the prime courting-place of the young and a popular, effortless vacation place of their elders. Well-to-do families often summered in them, leaving the servants at home to care for the house. Visiting such resorts was another of Lizzie's great pleasures, and it was at one of them that she finally met her idolized Nance.

Nance, it turned out, also had pressing real-life problems, chiefly financial. At one time, her manager brought suit against her; Lizzie not only tided her over with gifts, but followed her her into court throughout the proceedings. It was a situation ready-made for her own particular emotional needs: the glamorous actress to whom she could look up, the needy friend upon whom she could look down.

Perhaps Nance liked Lizzie; perhaps she only knew a good thing when she saw it. However it was, the whole business made Emma intensely unhappy. She disliked the publicity attendant upon Lizzie's courtroom appearances, and she suffered when Lizzie began to entertain Nance at the French Street house, Maplecroft. Emma did not like people in show business, and she had definite ideas about certain lifetime proprieties to be observed by those who had once featured in a murder trial.

The murders were twelve years behind them when Lizzie one night threw a tremendous party for Nance and her whole company. There were caterers, hired palm-trees, an orchestra—for once, Maplecroft fulfilled its intended function as Lizzie must have imagined it when she bought it, still full of faith in caresses that would never diminish and "floral offerings" that would not fade.

The house blazed with lights from top to bottom and blared with music.

That night, Emma left. She stayed with Mr. Jubb's sister until she could arrange to go to Fairhaven. Thereafter, she lived in Providence.

Shortly thereafter, Lizzie hired a house up in Tyngsboro so that she and Nance's company could enjoy a week-long houseparty; to judge by the accounts of those who had been in the neighborhood, it was not a notably quiet and sober time.

I have often read that Lizzie's big Maplecroft party for Nance, which drove Emma from home, was the last nail in Lizzie's coffin so far as Fall River society was concerned; and I think that it was so. However, the suggestion that Fall River was shocked because Lizzie had entertained an actress—which is the way outsiders always put it—is simply absurd. We were provincial, yes, but not farmers, villagers, American Gothic; my bachelor uncle entertained incessantly for theater people, and his invitations were much sought after.

Nance finished Lizzie off on three quite different counts.

There were a handful of dirty-minded old puritans in Fall River who saw Lizzie's association with Nance as a blatantly flaunted homosexual affair; they were the ones who whispered, and a few ancient survivors still do. I think that they were wrong—in any overt sense, at least. Young, Lizzie had crushes on school teachers that she talked about freely; her closer friendships had always been slightly overcharged and demanding; she was sentimental, and sexually immature. But I doubt that she was capable of any kind of love affair. I see the Nance business only as another instance of the same nature that led Lizzie to bury her pets in the local pet cemetery around a central monument that bore the tender inscription *Sleeping Awhile*—in other words, as the sort of sentimentality to which my mother used to refer mildly as "sort of sickening."

On the other side of the coin from the dirty-minded puritans there were the cynics, who saw Lizzie being taken for a sucker by a second-rate actress on her way out. They laughed and shrugged less than kindly and turned aside.

But the most widespread and the strongest disapproval came from those whom you might call the clean-minded puritans. Like Emma, they felt that a woman who had stood in Lizzie's shoes—whether or not those shoes had ever been stained with blood—should thereafter lead a retired life. She had been acquitted largely on the grounds of being the picture of piety and domesticity—as the Boston *Journal* had called her, "a woman of pure and noble life." As this group saw it, Lizzie was not playing fair. They felt so yet more strongly when the accounts of the Tyngsboro houseparty reached town; after all, the W.C.T.U. had been one of the trumps with which Lizzie made grand slam.

I don't know when the Nance affair finally blew up. Since Lizzie was not only sentimental but shrewd, she had been long overdue for her disillusionment. But meanwhile she had lost what little Fall River support she still had.

In April of 1913 a Boston newspaper wrote an article about Lizzie's life in Fall River, an Ishmael, cut in public and mentioned with distaste. It was not overwritten; I was her neighbor then, I can remember. Yet almost daily, we saw her. She had

been one of the first in town to buy an automobile; every afternoon, unless there was a downpour, she "went out for a ride over
the river" in the well-known big black limousine that looked
like a stray from a funeral procession, sitting alone and staring
straight before her.

I have said that a murder should not end in anticlimax; but
perhaps the mechanical emptiness of her last years is not, after
all, a totally unsatisfactory end to her story.

At least my mother thought so, when Grandfather had brought
in Miss Helen Leighton from Boston to be our librarian and she
became Lizzie's friend and ours. Miss Helen took a good deal of
unpleasant ribbing about her faith in Lizzie's innocence. She
liked to talk about her at our house when she came to tea, and
Mother would pour her another cup and say, "Oh, of course; oh,
I see just what you mean."

(Lizzie, by then, had passed the menopause. There were no
more "peculiar spells" to confuse a new friend.)

Lizzie never talked to her of the tragedy, but Miss Leighton
found it touching that in those last years Lizzie often rounded
off some little maxim or old-timey phrase with the words, "as
Father always used to say."

It was plain, Miss Leighton felt, that they had been close, and
that she had never ceased to miss him.

On those afternoons, when Miss Leighton had left us, Mother
would stare at nothing, working her flattish, fine-cut lips and
speaking to herself quietly. "Poor thing, poor thing, living alone
in that big ugly house ... what a hell. Thank God that she has
someone to believe what she wishes that she could believe."

I suppose that I really began to think about Lizzie as a person
then, to realize that the hate she had nursed up to that hot morning's breaking-point was—and God help us all—comprehensibly
human; that Lizzie was not quite as alien to the rest of us as we
liked to believe.

But, as I have already confessed to you, Mother was a Bostonian, an outsider.

And Lizzie was helplessly, ineradicably an insider. Longingly
and often she spoke to Helen Leighton of how lovely it was to
take a little trip to Boston, to New York, to Washington, to be

in a place where nobody recognized her, where she was only one more face in the crowd. And yet she never once considered leaving the city that had formed her and cast her out. Throughout her life she still clung, as she had in high school, to the wistful perimeter of the small world that never gave her full acceptance— yet still flung its protective, familial cloak about the story that was its own private disgrace.

⇶ 40 ⇷

Once the trial was over, Mr. Jennings always cut off any mention of it in his presence with a firm but courteous statement that he preferred not to hear it discussed. He died in 1922, a tragically oversensitive man who had our sympathy and our respect.

Bridget left town as soon as the trial was over. Our own various Bridgets and Bridies and Delias (who all claimed to know somebody who knew her cousins out on Division Street) promptly spread the word all over town that she had come into money, gone back to Ireland, and bought a farm. The assumption that she had been paid for telling less than she knew about the tension in the Borden house soon assumed the status of common knowledge. "As everyone knows," we used to say when discussing the case, "the girls saw to it that Bridget was paid off."

However, the more responsible and careful students of the crime, such as Edmund Pearson, always laughed at this notion. In the first place she had been a Government witness, brought in to show that Lizzie had been alone in the house at the time of Abby's death—scarcely a service to be paid for by the defense. And in the second place, such slight changes as she had made from her testimony in Fall River, freely given and under circumstances that pretty well precluded the idea of any pay-off *there*, at least, were not of further help to the defense. She had hedged, unwilling to add the word "together" to her statement that the girls and their parents "always did eat in the same dining room";

311

she would no longer disagree with the other witnesses and say that Lizzie had been crying.

For a long time, I was of two minds about this, unable to disregard Pearson's logic and unwilling to relinquish my old Fall River myth.

Eventually, I began to study the case closely, including the inquest, and to understand why Lizzie was so eager to indicate that Bridget had not watched her eat breakfast or spoken with her after Andrew's return from downstreet. I had no further doubts as to why Bridget's clothes were so fine and her manner so confident at the trial; but I wondered about her later life.

Then I read a book that set her forth as the true criminal and stated that she had died in Butte, Montana.[1] Its author told of having been permitted to examine the sequestered documents and Mr. Jennings' pocket memorandum book for the period. The lead seemed worth running down; and it was.

The story I now give you comes from Miss Mollie O'Meara, for thirty-five years head of the Butte Public Library and now retired. She is a charming and intelligent woman with whom I enjoyed talking, and I believe her to be wholly truthful; but I must remind you that her story is essentially incapable of being checked, since she had it from Minnie Green, now dead, who had it from Bridget, who died some years before Minnie.

Minnie had been Bridget's girlhood friend. When they first came to America together, Minnie was drawn to Montana, where a wave of Irish immigrants was being attracted to the copper mines. Bridget, less venturesome, stuck by the seaboard; but they kept in touch.

Yet they did not keep altogether in touch, for Bridget wrote Minnie nothing about her part in the Borden trial, only that she had come into a little money and was going home to buy a farm, which she proceeded to do. After some time in Ireland she wrote to tell Minnie that she had learned that lonely farming was not for her. After America, it was no life at all, and with all the young men crossing the ocean, Ireland was no place to find a husband. She had decided to come out to Montana.

[1] Edward D. Radin, *Lizzie Borden: The Untold Story* (New York, Simon and Schuster, 1963).

This she did. In Butte she met and married a young smelter, had numerous children, died in her mid-eighties, and lies buried in Mount Olivet Cemetery, in nearby Anaconda.

She kept her bargain of silence for a long time. She was quite old before she spoke of Lizzie Borden. She was gravely ill with pneumonia when she felt a desire to confide in Minnie. They were old friends, their later years had brought them close into each other's confidence, and, as Minnie told Miss O'Meara, it disturbed Bridget, lying there sick, to think that she had not been wholly candid about how she came by that windfall.

She asked Minnie to come over from Butte to see her, since she believed that she might not recover and she wanted a last sight of her dearest friend. And suddenly, her long reticence broke down and she began to talk.

She had always liked Lizzie, she told Minnie; she had always felt herself on the girl's side in the dimly understood troubles in that house. So she helped her out in the trial. And still she had not said one single word there was not true, not a word. Lizzie was thankful to her, and Lizzie's lawyer made her promise to stay in Ireland and never come back.

Well, so he'd let her change her mind, but not in any way that could do harm. Montana is a long way from Fall River, and she even took a different steamship line, one to New York, not Boston, and she came straight out to Montana by the first train, just like he wanted.

Bridget was very ill, the talking had tired her, and Minnie could get no more details that day. When she came back, Bridget had turned the corner toward recovery. She would only say that she was sorry she'd let out even so much, since she'd promised the lawyer never to say a word when she took the money, and she'd always liked Lizzie, too.

She asked Minnie not to talk about it.

Minnie did not, until after Bridget died. Miss O'Meara finally heard the story when Minnie, an old woman, turned up at the library to ask if they had any books about murders there, not the made-up kind but murders that really happened.

If some old Irishwoman from my part of the world had told

some purported first-hand tale about the latter end of Bridget I should not have taken it seriously; where I come from, the Borden case is still in our bones, and an old woman might have improved on an old memory until she believed it herself—or, at least found it worth sharing.

But Butte is far from Fall River, and Minnie, who waited until Bridget died to tell what she knew, only told it then to explain why she wanted to find out something more about the affair. Minnie showed herself to Miss O'Meara as fond of Bridget and not at all disapproving—only curious; for Bridget had wanted to drop the subject and she had respected her wish, since a promise is, after all, a promise.

I find Minnie's little story convincingly meager and undecorated. I believe it. I am glad that at least one character in the Borden saga married and lived happily ever after—and glad that she had some twinges of conscience, too; that power did not corrupt her utterly.

⇒ 41 ⇐

In 1923, Emma still lived in Providence.

Fall River's fifty-year-old life as a prosperous mill-town was nearly over. The big textile crash was just around the corner. Emma was far enough away to face up to it, as most of Fall River could not. So far as she could, she pulled out and reinvested. She wanted to sell her share in the Andrew J. Borden Building, the big downtown granite monument to Andrew's acumen as a real-estate man, which he had constructed shortly before his death. She knew that its value would be lost in the inevitable slump.

The bare idea struck Lizzie as sacrilege, and she started litigation. It got their names in the papers again, and a reporter sought Emma out. This frightened her into deeper hiding; she dropped her idea of selling the Borden Building and disappeared into New Hampshire, where she spent the rest of her life, only coming out of hiding twice a year, to take her fur coat to be cleaned and stored in Boston and to pick it up again.

But before she left, she gave a singular interview.

Often, before I read it, I had wondered what those eleven years had been like that the sisters spent together in Maplecroft. Now, in some part at least, I think I know.

Her lips, Emma said, must remain forever sealed about "the happenings in the French Street house" that eventually caused her to pack up and flee to Miss Jubb. She stayed until "conditions became absolutely unbearable."

She must have found those conditions unbearable in many ways. Like Lizzie, she was not free from jealousy, and she had thought of Lizzie as her child from the year she had been twelve and Lizzie two; the love that kept little Lizzie from accepting the new mother had doubtless taken a bad whipping from Lizzie's brief passion for Nance.

And Emma was not cut out for the great world; the least hint of what she would have called "loose living" would have distressed her cruelly. Moreover, she herself had firm ideas about the proper conduct of life after a murder trial, and lived up to them always, dwelling in seclusion and wearing mourning.

But the key to those eleven years they spent together lies in another part of the interview.

Yes, she said; it was strange that nobody else had been brought to trial, but as for Lizzie's having been guilty, "No, and again, no." And she gave her sole, undecorated reason.

"Here is the strongest thing that has convinced me of Lizzie's innocence. The authorities never found the axe, or the implement, or whatever it was that figured in the killing. If Lizzie had done that deed, she could never have hidden the instrument of death so that the police would never find it."

Poor Emma. The hatchet-head bore the words *Underwood Edge Tool Co.*, and in her role of one with perfect trust, it was all that Emma could produce: word, after often repeated word, the myth of the missing weapon.

"Time and again she avowed her innocence to me, and I believe her."

Time and again; twelve years of it, from the Saturday after the murders when the Mayor and Hilliard called, up to the day Emma left her.

Lizzie did not "avow her innocence" to Miss Helen Leighton time and again, or even once. She did not need to. Miss Leighton's untroubled faith showed in her eyes.

Lizzie lived on, in an increasing need for anonymity and with the same inability to leave Fall River for some place where she was unknown. Fall River she was, and Fall River she remained.

In 1926 she went into the hospital for an operation. She asked to be entered as Mary Smith Borden. While she was there under this strikingly unconvincing alias, the nurses and interns pretended, out of kindness, not to recognize her. She did not recover her health, and she died during the following year.

She had planned ahead for it.

A handful of those most likely to attend were invited to the house for funeral service, and almost all of them came—not all, one hopes, out of sheer curiosity. They found no coffin. Instead they heard a brief announcement that the funeral had been held the night before. After brief, unattended services at the undertaker's, her black-draped coffin had been carried by night to Oak Grove, where it was laid in the grave by black-clad men, Negroes chosen so that not even the pale gleam of a face or a hand might betray the secrecy.

A local contralto, Mrs. Turner, then sang, "My Ain Countree"; and the startled mourners went home.

In her lonely New Hampshire hiding place, Emma read the account in the papers. On the day of Lizzie's death, she had fallen to the floor, breaking her hip. She herself died just ten days later.

She roused herself on her deathbed to tell the doctor and the nurse that she wanted to be put in her grave by colored men, like her sister Lizzie. Her last request was respected.

At her death, Emma was worth $450,000, almost all of which was left to charity; Lizzie left only half as much. The disparity is generally accounted for by her greater expenditures; actually, it was chiefly due to her undying respect for her father's business judgment and her lifelong fidelity to the Fall River that had rejected her. She would not, like Emma, pull out and reinvest when Fall River's fifty-year boom in cotton cloth finally broke and began to fade away.

The Bordens lie buried together.

Oak Grove should be called Elm Grove; the trees stand like tall green fountains over the graves. It is quiet there, at the high east end of town; a green, good, gentle, old burying-place.

The family monument stands at the center of the Borden lot. The name of Lizzie Andrew Borden is not on it. Even in death she preferred to be Lisbeth of Maplecroft: Lisbeth *Andrews* Borden, with a final *s* to give the dignified sound of a family name.

Emma lies near her, and little Alice, the sister who did not live to grow up.

There, too, lie Andrew's wives, Sarah Morse and Abby. Andrew rests between them. If his bones still hold together, he lies on his side as if he had just dropped off in a nap.

And loose on one finger, with its calcified, old man's joints, there dangles a small gold ring.

VICTORIA LINCOLN

Victoria Lincoln was born in Fall River, Massachusetts. She graduated from Radcliffe, and later married Victor Lowe, a distinguished professor who taught both in the U.S. and in England.

Miss Lincoln's best known novel was *February Hill* (1934). George Abbot brought it to the stage as "Primrose Path", and it was filmed in 1940.

A PRIVATE DISGRACE received an Edgar as the best non-fiction crime book of 1967 from the Mystery Writers of America.

In 1981 Miss Lincoln died in her home in Baltimore. She was 76.